ROYAL H

STUDIES IN HISTORY

New Series

# LAW AND KINSHIP IN
# THIRTEENTH-CENTURY ENGLAND

# LAW AND KINSHIP IN THIRTEENTH-CENTURY ENGLAND

*Sam Worby*

THE ROYAL HISTORICAL SOCIETY
THE BOYDELL PRESS

First published 2010
Paperback edition 2015

A Royal Historical Society publication
Published by The Boydell Press
an imprint of Boydell & Brewer Ltd
PO Box 9, Woodbridge, Suffolk IP12 3DF, UK
and of Boydell & Brewer Inc.
668 Mt Hope Avenue, Rochester, NY 14620–2731, USA
website: www.boydellandbrewer.com

ISBN 978 0 86193 305 1 hardback
ISBN 978 0 86193 338 9 paperback

ISSN 0269–2244

A CIP catalogue record for this book is available
from the British Library

The publisher has no responsibility for the continued existence or accuracy of
URLs for external or third-party internet websites referred to in this book,
and does not guarantee that any content on such websites is,
or will remain, accurate or appropriate

This publication is printed on acid-free paper

# Contents

# List of illustrations

# List of tables

# Acknowledgements

This book almost did not get written. For the fact that it did I would like to credit and thank my advisory editor Professor Stephen Church who encouraged me to persist. I would also like to thank Christine Linehan and the Royal Historical Society for supporting this project.

I would like to thank the numerous libraries and institutions that enabled me to do this research, particularly the British Library, the Bodleian Library, Oxford, Cambridge University Library, the Institute of Historical Research, Worcester Cathedral Library, Winchester Cathedral Library, the Library of University College London and the Arts and Humanities Research Council.

For comments on this book, and ongoing support, I give particular thanks to Professor David d'Avray who has been generous, challenging and indefatigable. I would like to thank Dr Eyal Poleg and Charlotte Fear for reading chapters and asking the right questions. For comments on earlier work I also would like to thank Sir John Baker, Professor David Carpenter and Professor Charles Donahue, Jr whose forthright and constructive comments helped me immensely. I would also like to thank Professor Wendy Davies whose comments on my research always proved insightful. Special thanks also to Professor Andrew Lewis for his guidance over the years and Dr Paul Brand for his advice and for discussions that always made me think more clearly.

I would like to thank Simon Peachey and Anna Allen for their support while I have juggled work and this book, my patient family and friends. With love, I would like to thank and dedicate this book to Andy Houston, who has once again read more medieval history than he ever bargained for and was very good about it too.

In what follows all faults, omissions and errors are my own.

Sam Worby
July 2009

# Abbreviations

| | |
|---|---|
| BL | British Library |
| Bodl. Lib. | Bodleian Library, Oxford |
| *Bracton* | Bracton, *De legibus et consuetudinibus Angliæ*, ed. G. E. Woodbine, trans. (with revisions and notes) S. E. Thorne, Cambridge, Ma–London 1968–77 |
| *Britton* | *Britton: the French text carefully revised with an English translation, introduction and notes*, ed. F. M. Nichols, Oxford 1865 |
| CUL | Cambridge University Library |
| *Digest* | *The Digest of Justinian*, Latin text ed. T. Mommsen with P. Krueger; English trans. ed. A. Watson, Philadelphia 1985 |
| *Glanvill* | *The treatise on the laws and customs of the realm of England commonly called Glanvill*, ed., intro., notes and trans. G. D. G. Hall; guide to further reading M. T. Clanchy, Oxford 1993 |
| *Institutes* | *The Institutes of Justinian: text, translation and commentary*, ed. J. A. C. Thomas, Amsterdam–Oxford 1975 |
| Isidore, *Etymologies* | Isidore of Seville, 'Etymologiarum libri XX', *PL* lxxxii.73–728 |
| *LQR* | *Law Quarterly Review* |
| *PL* | *Patrologia cursus completus, series latina*, ed. J. P. Migne, Paris 1844–1904 |
| WCL | Worcester Cathedral Library |
| X | 'Decretales Gregorii P. IX', in *Corpus iuris canonici: editio Lipsiensis secunda post Aemilii Ludouici Richteri*, ed. A. Friedberg, Leipzig 1879–81 |

Gratian, 'Decretum', in *Corpus iuris canonici: editio Lipsiensis secunda post Aemilii Ludouici Richteri*, ed. A. Friedberg, Leipzig 1879–81, is cited in the conventional canon law manner; it is not named, but the sections are referred to as, for example, C.1 q.1 c.1 for causa 1, quaestio 1, canon 1.

# Introduction

In late medieval England, in order to marry, or inherit, people had to fit their own experiences of family through formal legal frameworks, which thus had a social force beyond the purely taxonomic and intellectual. In thirteenth- and fourteenth-century England the canon law was the foremost kinship system as a general framework for classifying the family. Even the common law, which had its own kinship system centred on inheritance, was touched by canon law ideas.

Charles Donahue Jr's magisterial comparative study of marriage in England, France and Belgium has confirmed a remarkable pattern of family interaction for England. His thorough and statistical analysis of the surviving records of cases before the archbishop of York's consistory court in the fourteenth and fifteenth centuries, and Ely consistory court between 1374 and 1381, incidentally seems to confirm that there was no clan or corporate kinship system operating in the areas covered, and, by inference, in England more widely (given the consistency of results between the two evidence sets). There were, he shows, even relatively low levels of parental involvement in marriage choice. Given the importance of marriage as a social institution and the potential consequences flowing from choice of partner – in property, alliance and social standing for example – it seems remarkable that an average of only 37 per cent of York cases showed evidence of parental involvement.[1] While there was evidence for arranged marriages in the records of both courts, many couples appear to have acted independently.[2] Whether this is qualified as 'astonishingly' or 'unusually' individualistic, the fact remains that many couples operated with relative freedom within the scope of the canon law marriage rules.[3]

This individualistic pattern confirms a picture of family interaction for England found elsewhere, through evidence of marriage patterns, but also more broadly.[4] From the Anglo-Norman nobility to later medieval peasants, the picture is of a limited family (although this book will not in fact

---

[1]  C. Donahue, Jr, *Law, marriage, and society in the later Middle Ages: arguments about marriage in five courts*, Cambridge 2007, 750 (*Texts and commentary* [http://www.cambridge.org/uk/catalogue/catalogue.asp?isbn=9780521877282], n. 524).

[2]  Ibid. 102, 216, 297.

[3]  Michael Sheehan had found this 'astonishingly individualistic', Charles Donahue, 'unusually': ibid. 297, 609.

[4]  See, for example, M. M. Sheehan, 'The formation and stability of marriage in fourteenth-century England: evidence of an Ely register', in J. K. Farge (ed.), *Marriage, family, and law in medieval Europe: collected studies*, Toronto 1996, 38–76. See also A. MacFarlane, *Marriage and love in England: modes of reproduction, 1300–1840*, Oxford 1986, esp. ch. iii,

focus on peasant kinship, but rather on kinship insofar as it was a general structure, transcending class and status). The extended kindred did not live together; the typical co-resident family appears to have been nuclear.[5] There is evidence of kin interaction, particularly suggestive of closeness between siblings.[6] There is a broad consensus about the narrowness of the operative kin group in England. It was rarely much larger than the immediate family, mostly the co-resident nuclear family, with some obligations and traceable contact extending out to cousins, and some closeness to siblings and occasionally to uncles and aunts. This pattern is unusual in comparison to other areas of Europe. It is suggestive to note that Franco-Belgian courts showed evidence for a higher level of family involvement in marriage arrangements.[7] It is also striking to contrast the pattern of relatively informal clans able to act together in some European countries, such as Italy.[8]

Formal legal kinship structures were among several potential overlapping layers of ideas about kinship. They had particular force because they applied at vital milestones in people's lives, such as marriage and inheritance. If thirteenth-century men and women wanted to marry legitimately they had to shape their actions to the kinship structures of the Church, or, at least, to have been aware of those kinship structures – to have narrated their kinship in a manner that fitted with the law, or tried to avoid it. To claim an ancestor's land and enforce their inheritance at common law via a writ of right, or a writ of cosinage, they had to narrate their family history and structure their kin in a way that fitted that system. The two great legal systems operating in England at the time were central to people's understanding of and practice in relation to kinship. This book will focus mainly on the thirteenth and fourteenth centuries. It will show that canon law kinship was in some senses dominant as a general way of thinking about kinship. Along the way it will also attempt to explore the gap between legal kinship in books and in practice, and between formal and official conceptions of kinship and people's

---

and *The origins of English individualism: the family, property and social transition*, Oxford 1978, for example at pp.197–8.

[5] On Anglo-Norman co-residency patterns see J. S. Moore, 'The Anglo-Norman family: size and structure', *Anglo-Norman Studies* xiv (1991), 153–96 at p. 193. On peasant patterns see B. A. Hanawalt, *The ties that bound: peasant families in medieval England*, Oxford 1986, and R. M. Smith, 'Kin and neighbours in a thirteenth-century Suffolk community', *Journal of Family History* iv (1979), 219–56.

[6] Z. Razi, 'Intrafamilial ties and relationships in the medieval village: a quantitative approach employing manor court rolls', in Z. Ravi and R. Smith (eds), *Medieval society and the manor court*, Oxford 1996, 369–91; C. Howell, *Land, family and inheritance in transition: Kibworth Harcourt, 1280–1700*, Cambridge 1983, 217–20, 234; J. C. Holt, 'Feudal society and the family in early medieval England, IV: the heiress and the alien', in his *Colonial England, 1066–1215*, London 1997, 245–69 at p. 259.

[7] Donahue, *Law, marriage, and society*, 513, 608–13.

[8] J. Heers, *Le Clan familial au moyen âge: étude sur les structures politiques et sociales des milieus urbanes*, Paris 1974. For bibliography on continental kinship see G. Melville and M. Staub (eds), *Enzyklopädie des Mittelalters*, Darmstadt 2008, ii. 408.

everyday experiences and their potentially less well defined ideas about relatedness.

Kinship connections were theoretically, practically and poetically important. In literature, for example, they often formed a background web of interconnectedness.[9] Yet they were also contingent in practice and could be used or referred to in such various circumstances that it can be difficult to apply the concept of kinship as a form of connection between people consistently. Formal legal kinship, however, offers structure. Anthropologists from Louis Dumont to Pierre Bourdieu have stressed the importance of official images and norms concerning kinship, of idealised patterns and structures, in shaping the way people understand family.[10] This is not to suggest that people always obeyed or followed such official, ideal patterns, rather that these ideal official norms visibly influenced the way in which people acted, or how they narrated their actions. The special force of law (for example in providing public recognition of licit marriages, and providing a mechanism of enforcement for the conventions behind inheritance patterns) made these legal images and norms potentially powerful.

Formal kinship systems also influenced the way people perceived the ordering of society. It has been argued that 'rational behaviour involves classification, and the activity of classification is a human universal',[11] and that taxonomy or classification is 'a basic need and imposition of mind upon an otherwise jumbled richness of nature'.[12] This applies equally well to the history of kinship systems. The structures and edifices of medieval kinship systems limited and ordered the jumbled richness of natural families. Or, at least, they offered a scheme to fit the immediate need or question, and a background narrative of connectedness. While these questions of taxonomy had immediate practical effect on people's lives, they also had less tangible effects on their thoughts and ideas. Therefore understanding these structures leads to an understanding of what and how people would have known about kinship and why this mattered, as well as exploring the historical trends and developments in this area relevant to England.

Kinship is many-layered. This book will descend through layers from the formal and written to the practised. The first two chapters explain the most formal (thus the simplest and most ideal) expressions of legal kinship, in the books of the canon and common laws. The fourth chapter explains how these rules were complicated by practice and litigants' attempts to use and

---

[9] For example in Malory, *Works*, ed. E. Vinaver, 2nd edn, Oxford 1971.

[10] L. Dumont, *Introduction to two theories of social anthropology: descent groups and marriage alliance*, ed. and trans. R. Parkin, Oxford 2006, 88, 93; P. Bourdieu, *Outline of a theory of practice*, trans. R. Nice, Cambridge 1977, 35, and *The logic of practice*, trans. R. Nice, Cambridge 1992, 172.

[11] M. Douglas, *Purity and danger*, New York 2002, p. xvii.

[12] S. J. Gould and R. Wolff Purcell, *Crossing over: where art and science meet*, New York 2000, 14.

manipulate them in the respective courts. The final chapter suggests that an informal pattern of practical kinship knowledge existed beneath the laws. The book centres on formal kinship because the two legal kinship systems explored were shared ways of understanding kinship and encapsulated the only widespread, structured conceptions of the extended family in late medieval England. Thus, an exploration of the dynamics of formal kinship is interwoven with the explanation of how kinship law operated. The third chapter demonstrates the dominance of canon law as a general way of thinking about kinship in literate and legal circles, a pattern shown to have operated more widely by the court-based evidence in the fourth chapter. The final chapter looks beyond the law and explains both the dominance of the canon law and why there was room for it in thirteenth- and fourteenth-century England.

## Kinship

Before exploring legal kinship systems in detail some preliminaries are necessary. The first of these is to make clear how the concept of a kinship system should be understood in this book. A casual modern understanding of kinship recognises it as a biological fact, based on procreation, a category very much informed by modern western assumptions and scientific knowledge. To this 'fact' is attributed 'social significance'.[13] It has a public element and is governed by both norms (expectations and models of how people should behave and even feel), and laws (rules about how people should or should not behave). Deeper thought about kinship might lead the casual thinker to recognise it as a formal category, encompassing in-laws and adoptees, based on analogies to blood relationships. Kinship can mean other things too (a sense of fellow feeling for example), that will not be dealt with here, since they go beyond the bounds of legal kinship.

Anthropologists have explored the question of what constitutes a kinship system in detail, although kinship studies have waxed and waned in fashion. Something called kinship is a widespread notion. It is commonly tied to descent; it is difficult to imagine a kinship system which would not include this. It is, however, possible to focus on bonds other than descent, for example to analyse and characterise kinship systems as based on 'relations of exchange between units', and focused on bonds created by marriage as successfully done by Claude Levi-Strauss.[14] It is also possible to seek characteristics of kinship systems. This book will take the latter approach as better suited to the legal cultures examined, and, at the risk of being too specific to those legal cultures, will suggest the specific institutions and features that can be said to characterise a kinship system.

---

[13] L. Holy, *Anthropological perspectives on kinship*, London 1996, 1.
[14] Dumont, *Introduction to two theories*, 71.

For purposes of convenience, a kinship system can be recognised as a way of thinking about and narrating bonds between people in terms of a recognised biological connection or analogy with biological connection. The term 'recognised' is used here because, for example, not all children are biologically related to both of their 'parents', a fact acknowledged by English medieval commentators. The author of the common law text *Bracton* was aware that, in the case of children born of adultery in circumstances where the husband could have fathered the child, 'common opinion sometimes is preferred to truth'.[15] So long as the marriage was legitimate and the husband could have been the father (and did not disavow the child) the child would have been the father's legitimate heir. Thus there could be a difference between legal and biological parenthood. Other characteristics of a kinship system include an in/out boundary and a method of ordering. These are the 'systematic' elements that imply that the kinship system is more than a casual and fleeting series of groupings. Kin terminology can reflect this ordering; internal reasoning can be used to justify it. Ordering also implies a focus, meaning a person to whom others relate or not. This need not be a monolithic or mythical ancestor; in fact every person will, in one sense, be the focus of their own 'kindred'. To make such a classificatory system worthy of attention (certainly of the amount of attention devoted to it in this book) it should also have a social force or purpose, meaning that it should be operative rather than purely ornamental or structural. A kinship system in this sense will not be a taxonomy elaborated only for its own sake. A kinship system may not contain all of these elements. It is possible to conceive of one without, for example an in/out boundary, but it is more difficult to conceive of such a system as having an effective social force. This checklist risks circularity, biased as it is towards the type of kinship system found in the legal cultures examined in this book, yet it offers a useful shorthand by means of which common underlying elements can be recognised. Thus, for the purposes of this study, a kinship system is a way of classifying people, rooted in biological relatedness, either directly or by analogy. To be more than an 'idle ingenuity' it should also have a social force or purpose.[16] As this definition makes clear, the discussion of kinship systems in this book is principally about structures and many practical matters will not be covered in detail. An approach to kinship that focuses on structures also directs attention to the interaction between structures and patterns of behaviour.

---

[15] Bracton, *De legibus et consuetudinibus Angliæ*, ed. G. E. Woodbine, trans. (with revisions and notes) S. E. Thorne, Cambridge, MA–London 1968–77, ii. 186. All references to *Bracton* will be to this edition.

[16] On 'idle ingenuities' see F. Pollock and F. W. Maitland, *The history of English law before the time of Edward I*, 2nd edn, with new introduction and select bibliography by S. F. C. Milsom, Cambridge 1968, ii. 389.

## Terminology

Kinship studies can be weighted with a significant baggage of specialist terms. This book will try to avoid technicalities, but some are insurmountable and should be explained. Consanguinity, affinity and *parentela*, will be the technical phrases most frequently met. Thus, consanguinity (*consanguinitas*) is used in the canon law sense to mean blood kinship; affinity (*affinitas*) is used to mean kinship created through marriage or sex (the fact that the canon law could regard kinship as created through a casual sexual encounter may seem peculiar. The underlying rationality, such as it was, will be discussed further in chapter 1); and *parentela* is used in the common law sense to mean a person's descendants.[17] The general term kinship can be a translation for a host of concepts in medieval Latin: thus one translator uses it for *parentela*,[18] *cognatio*,[19] *a sanguine*[20] and for *affinitas*.[21]

A particularly dangerous term in any exploration of medieval kinship is the word cousin since it could be used both specifically and vaguely to encompass a general sense of relatedness, and since there were occasions when the definition of who was a cousin was under dispute. An example of this is a canon law case where a man was reported to have called his granddaughter and potential grandson-in-law both 'cosin'.[22] Cousin could be used as a word for almost any kinsman, but could also be a term of art. The term cousin will therefore be avoided where possible in this book and otherwise defined. Instead, consanguine, affine or, generally, kinsman, will be preferred.

As well as general terms, each legal system had its own terminology of kinship.[23] The canon and civil laws had a rich collection of possible specific Latin kin names (*see* figure 1). Within this four-degree tree there are sixteen specific kin names on the vertical axis and twenty for collaterals, giving a total of thirty-six. A tree picturing the canon law kinship system prior to 1215 would have contained a total of sixty: an additional twelve named ascendants and descendants and a further twelve named collaterals. Half of each total were names for male relatives and half were for females. They built upon a repetitive pattern, for example *avus* for grandfather, *proavus* for great-grandfather, *abavus* for great-great-grandfather and so on. Other relatives were named through combinations, thus *filius propatrui* for the son of the great-grandfather's brother. Together it amounts to a formidable mass of

---

17 Ibid. ii. 296.
18 *Bracton*, ii. 195, 352, 353, 407; iii. 384.
19 Ibid. ii. 200.
20 Ibid. ii. 303.
21 Ibid. ii. 423.
22 Donahue, *Law, marriage and society*, 189, 729 (*Texts and commentary*, n. 387).
23 On Latin terms for kinship or kindred more generally see A. Guerreau-Jalabert, 'La Désignation des relations et des groupes de parenté en Latin médiéval', *Archivium Latinitatis Medii Aevi* xlvi–xlvii (1988), 65–108.

terminology. It is unlikely that this was often employed outside an academic context.

At common law a relatively narrow range of terms designating specific kin occurred in both the Latin records and Anglo-French reports. However, the situation was made more complicated by the two languages involved (even more so as English was likely to be used by litigants outside formal settings). In the ascending line the terms tended to be *pater* / *pere* (father), *mater* / *mere* (mother), *avus* / *aiel* or *ael* (grandfather), *avia* / *aiele* (grandmother), *proavus* / *besaiel* (great-grandfather), *proavia* / *besaiele* (great-grandmother), *abavus* / *tresaiel* (great-great-grandfather) and *abavia* / *tresaiele* (great-great-grand-mother). In the Anglo-French there are rare examples of *quartael* (great-great-great-grandfather)[24] and *quint ael* (great-great-great-great-great-grandfather).[25] In the descending line the terms are *filius* / *fiz* (son), *filia* / *fille* (daughter), *nepos* / *neveu* (grandson or nephew) and *neptis* / *nece* (granddaughter or niece). In the collateral lines they are *frater* / *frere* (brother), *soror* / *soere* (sister), *avunculus* / *uncle* (for either uncle), *amita* / *aunte* or *amite* (for either aunt) and *consanguineus* (as a general term for kinsman or male cousin) or *consanguinea* (as a general term for kinswomen or female cousin) / *cosin* (general term for kinsman or cousin). It should be said that these lists are not exhaustive. However, a provisional, impressionistic conclusion may be drawn, viz, that common lawyers, clerks or reporters were more comfortable using specific terms for direct ancestors rather than for collateral relatives, a conclusion that reflects the importance of the direct line to English kinship.

Generally, this book uses the term specific to the context, either grand-father, *aiel* (from an Anglo-French source) or *avus* (from a Latin one), and supplies a translation where necessary. It is now time to move on to examine the detail of first canon law, then common law kinship.

---

[24] *Year books of the reign of King Edward the first: michaelmas term, year XXXIII and years XXXIV and XXXV*, ed. and trans. A. J. Horwood, London 1879, 125.
[25] *Year books of the reign of King Edward the third: year XVI (second part)*, ed. and trans. L. O. Pike, London 1900, 571.

# 1

# Canon Law Kinship Structures

The canon law kinship system was one part of a set of rules about who could validly marry whom. They thus potentially affected the majority of the adult population in late medieval England. The kinship rules can be regarded as a variety of incest prohibition, although not one that is easily reconciled with either modern or anthropological definitions of incest. Indeed, in the high and later medieval period, it is extremely unlikely that the full extent of the kinship prohibitions were regarded as 'taboo' in this manner. The rules were not seen as 'moral absolutes barring the way to pollution'.[1] Because the term 'incestus' was used in sources from this period it is also used in this book, always bearing in mind the fact that this sense of incest (particularly for the more distant degrees) implies at core only that a man or woman could not validly marry a kinsman.[2]

The canon law is the law of the Church, enforced through a system of professional courts. In the Middle Ages it applied across Europe wherever a subject in its jurisdiction was affected, and it covered a jurisdiction ranging beyond clerics and into the realms of marriage law. Marriage came under the auspices of the canon law because a properly formed marriage was a sacrament. To be sacramental a marriage had to be between people capable of marrying. It could be formed by present consent (I take thee), or by future consent (I promise to take thee) followed by sexual intercourse.[3] Once properly formed such a marriage was, in theory, indissoluble, although the canon law of marriage did encompass 'divorce' of a sort. This was not a divorce in the modern sense. If a marriage was not validly formed there was the possibility of a *divortium a vinculo*, divorce from the bond, effectively an annulment. If the marriage had been validly formed, but was followed by, for example, adultery or some sorts of violence, there was the possibility of *divortium a mensa et thoro*, divorce from bread and board, effectively a judicial separation without leave to remarry.[4] Thus the canon law of marriage covered who could marry, whether a marriage was valid, or whether a marriage could be

---

[1]  D. L. d'Avray, *Medieval marriage: symbolism and society*, Oxford 2005, 114 n. 114.
[2]  For example Gratian, 'Decretum', in *Corpus iuris canonici: editio Lipsiensis secunda post Aemilii Ludouici Richteri*, ed. A. Friedberg, Leipzig 1879–81, C.35 q.2, 3 c.5, 7, 8, 9 (all references to *Gratian* will be to this edition), or *Lower ecclesiastical jurisdiction in late-medieval England: the courts of the dean and chapter of Lincoln, 1336–1349, and the deanery of Wisbech, 1458–1484*, ed. L. R. Poos, Oxford 2001, 11.
[3]  This is dealt with more fully in Donahue, *Law, marriage, and society*, 16–17.
[4]  Ibid. 33.

dissolved, and whether legal separation was called for. It held that a number of impediments could nullify a marriage (diriment impediments). A contemporary mnemonic put it thus:

> Error [of person], condition [i.e. servitude], vow, blood-relationship, crime,
> Different religion, force, [clerical] order, bondage, [public] honesty,
> If you should be affines, if perchance you will be unable to copulate,
> These prevent marriages being formed; they retract marriages already joined.[5]

In a more complete and analytical order the impediments are:[6]

1. Insanity; impotence/frigidity; nonage (for example, marriages formed by parties below the age of puberty); force or fear; error of person; error of status (for example. unknowingly marrying someone of servile condition); and conditional consent, all of which prevented true consent.
2. Disparity of cult (for example marriage to a non-Christian); orders (priests and deacons could not marry); and solemn vows, all of which were religious impediments.
3. Adultery followed by a conspiracy in the death of a former spouse; adultery followed by a pledge of faith while the spouse was still alive, both of which were criminal impediments.
4. Consanguinity; affinity; spiritual affinity; and public honesty (having previously contracted to marry a relative of a person the party subsequently intended to marry), all of which were kinship impediments.

It is a useful to see the canon law kinship system in the context of other impediments to marriage and to acknowledge that none of these were simple rules. As there could be uncertainty around kinship, so there could around, for example, impotence.[7] And it should be noted that the existence of an alleged prior contract was a by far more important ground than kinship for dissolving and enforcing marriages.[8]

In essence there were three types of kinship at canon law: consanguinity (blood kinship), affinity (kinship through marriage) and spiritual affinity (kinship through baptism), plus public honesty, which was not so much a type of kinship as an extension of the affinity rules, although, of course, these structures simplify the reality.

---

[5] 'Error, conditio, votum, cognatio, crimen, / Cultus disparitas, vis, ordo, ligamen, honestas, / Si sis affinis, si forte coire nequibis / Haec socianda vetant connubia, juncta retractant.': Tancred, *Summa de matrimonio*, ed. A. Wunderlich, Göttingen 1841, 17. For a longer, more poetic version see Donahue, *Law, marriage, and society*, 18–19.

[6] Donahue, *Law, marriage and society*, 19–31.

[7] C. Rider, *Magic and impotence in the Middle Ages*, Oxford 2006, ch. vii.

[8] R. H. Helmholz, *Marriage litigation in medieval England*, Cambridge 1974, ch. ii; Donahue, *Law, marriage, and society*, 70–1, 228.

## The basics

It is useful to start with one of a genre of introductory treatises on canon law kinship that were common in the thirteenth and fourteenth centuries. The most popular treatise was a brief introduction that began *Quia tractare intendimus* and was probably written by the eminent canonist Raymón of Penyafort in about 1235 (*see* appendix 1).[9]

Such treatises were explicitly linked to images that encapsulated canon law kinship. Canon law consanguinity (blood kinship), was depicted in the *arbor consanguinitatis*, an arrow shaped image made up of cells containing named kinsmen with whom marriage was prohibited (figure 1 is an example). Raymón included in his treatise two points that explained its popularity among canonists. First, the tree was invented because of the usefulness of visual images. He quoted Horace to support this: 'Less vividly is the mind stirred by what finds entrance through the ears than by what is brought before the trusty eyes.'[10] Second, the tree was authenticated by the canons that were some of the key sources of authority for canon law kinship. It was therefore accepted in the canon law.[11]

Raymón's treatise followed a simple plan. It explained the basic technical concepts of canon law kinship: what consanguinity was, why it was so named, what a line was and what a degree was.[12] It also explained the practical skills of canon law kinship: how the tree was formed and how to reckon in degrees. Scattered within and at the end of the treatise were notable points and questions around canon law kinship.

The treatise explained that consanguinity was 'a bond of different people descending from the same *stipes*, joined by propagation through the flesh'. The *stipes* was 'that person from who others descended' and the term consanguinity 'is so-called from "con" and "sanguis" as if having common blood or proceeding from one blood'.[13] These definitions were trying to encapsulate a sense of connection based on common descent and blood relationship. A point to add, which the canonist Johannes Andreae included in his short treatise on the subject although Raymón did not, was that consanguinity arose whether or not a child was legitimate.[14] Raymón explained

---

9   This was identified by S. Kuttner, 'The Barcelona edition of St. Raymond's first treatise on canon law', *Seminar* viii (1950), 52–67 at pp. 54–6. On popularity see H. Schadt, *Die Darstellungen der arbores consanguinitatis und der arbores affinitatis: Bildschemata in juristischen Handscriften*, Tübingen 1982, 206–8.

10   Appendix 1.8, from Horace, 'Ars poetica', in *Satires, epistles and ars poetica*, with an English translation, by H. Ruston Fairclough, London 1966, 180–1.

11   C.35 q.5 c.2 and c.6, as in appendix 1.9.

12   Appendix 1.1.

13   Appendix 1.2.

14   'Et quoad prohibitionem coniugii non distinguo, an tales consanguinei sunt producti ex uxorio coitu, vel ex fornicario': Johannes Andreae, 'Declaratio arboris consanguinitatis', and 'Declaratio arboris affinitatis', *Corpus iuris canonici*, i. 1427–36 at p. 1428 ss. 6.

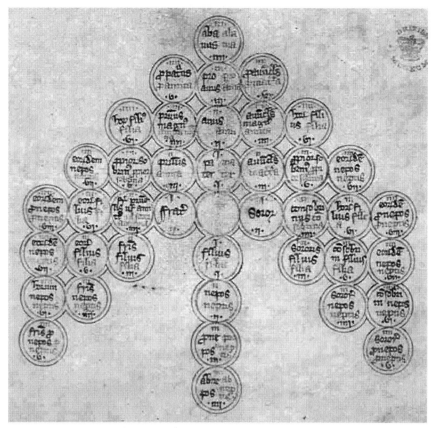

Figure 1. A four-degree *arbor consanguinitatis* (tree of consanguinity). This canon law image depicted which blood-kinsmen 'ego', the central character, could not legitimately marry. Reproduced from BL, MS Add. 41258, fo. 37v, a *Bracton* manuscript dating to c. 1300, where it was included alongside a treatise on canon law kinship, by permission of the British Library.

that a person's kindred was sorted into lines. A line was 'an ordered set of people joined by consanguinity, descending from the same *stipes*, containing different degrees, and distinguished from unity with the *stipes* according to numbers'. The ascending line contained ascendants: parents, grandparents, etc. The descending line contained descendants: children, grandchildren, etc. The collateral lines contained the remainder: those 'from whom we do not descend, and who do not descend from us'.[15] Within the lines people were ordered by degrees. A degree was 'a kind of relationship or distance of people' by which 'it is known by how many generations two people are different between themselves', meaning that it was a way of quantifying the distance between two people and of ordering kinsmen according to relative nearness.[16] Following the Fourth Lateran Council in 1215 no one could marry someone related to them in the fourth degree, that is sharing a common great-great-grandparent (before that, the exclusion zone was larger).

Raymón explained how the tree was shaped. He devoted most attention to the empty central cell. This was 'ego', the person whose kindred was under examination, thus the one to whom all the others shown on the tree related. This cell was empty because 'the names of ascendants, descendants, and collaterals (understood excepting those who are determined by the genitive) are chosen in respect of the *truncus*, as is apparent in the figure of the tree. Whence the *truncus* himself ought to have different names in respect of different people and thus [he] is not able to be called by one name nor by all names'.[17] Raymón tended to call ego the 'truncus', suiting the image of a tree. Other canonists also used the names Joachim, *Protheus* (after the shape-shifting minor sea god) and even Petrucius (used by Andreae, after his beadle).[18] Above ego in the tree were placed cells representing four generations of ancestors up to the great-great-grandparents; below, four generations of descendants; and at the sides four generations of collaterals, beginning with the lines descending from ego's brother and sister. Each kinsman was named for their relationship with ego, using the extensive learned terminology. The tree was organised with males and paternal kinsmen on the right and females and maternal kinsmen on the left. The degrees of consanguinity were written in each cell (as in figure 1) with the canon law degrees in the top part of the cell in red and the civil law degrees in the bottom in black, which was a conventional positioning intended to show the excellence of canon law knowledge.[19]

The tree was a schematic representation of one person's kindred. It did not reflect a real family, as should be obvious from the fact that it contained only one pair of grandparents (*avus, avia*), when in fact each person has two

[15] Appendix 1.3.
[16] Appendix 1.5.
[17] Appendix 1.10.
[18] Andreae, 'Declaratio arboris consanguinitatis', 1428 ss. 9.
[19] Appendix 1.26.

pairs, and so on.[20] The *avus* represented both ego's mother's father and ego's father's father; and could mean either, depending on which line was being traced. Lines too were not fixed entities. All collateral lines were descending lines when reckoned from the common ancestor. But between two descendants of the common ancestor a person in each might reckon the other to be in a collateral line to themselves.[21]

There were two methods of calculating degrees, one relating to canon law, the other to civil law kinship. Raymón dealt first with the calculation of degrees in the direct lines (ascending and descending). In these lines the canon and civil (Roman) law computations agreed and the rule was that 'person added to person by propagation of flesh adds a degree'.[22] For collateral degrees Raymón separated his discussion into canon and civil law calculations. The canon law measured the distance of relationship between two people by counting the generations from each party in question to a common ancestor. If the two parties were distant from the common ancestor at unequal lengths the longer line was preferred for deciding whether they could marry. The civil law method was to measure the distance between two people by counting the acts of generation between them, that is to count up one line to the common ancestor and then to count back down the other line. If an image was not available, it was possible to reckon kinship using the hand, by putting the two people who wanted to marry on the tips of each finger and counting each degree, using the joints to mark generations.[23]

The purpose of these calculations was to determine whether a couple could marry. Raymón wrote that prior to 1215 and the prohibition on kinsmen up to the fourth degree, prohibition had extended to the seventh degree, although in fact the evidence suggests that some had favoured six degrees as a limit.[24] After the decision of the Fourth Lateran Council in 1215, however, a person in the third degree to a common ancestor could marry one in the fifth.[25]

Canonists such as Raymón were not only conscious that the tree was a conceptualising tool; they also recognised that their kinship rules did not always fit with their understanding of natural family. Raymón posed but did not answer the question of whether degrees were artificial because the *propatruus* (paternal great-great-uncle) and his great-grandson were both the same degree to ego (*see* figure 1), while the *propatruus* was a much closer kinsman of ego than his great-grandson.[26] He also recounted that some

---

[20] Appendix 1.12.
[21] Appendix 1.4.
[22] Appendix 1.44.
[23] Appendix 1.38.
[24] Appendix 1.49. In C.35, c.2, 3 c.21 the limit was put at six degrees. Gratian explained this by noting that they used a different manner of counting that put the children in the second degree and therefore amounted to seven.
[25] Appendix 1.48.
[26] Appendix 1.41–3.

would have preferred the *propatruus* to be in the fifth degree (for example to use the civil law method of counting), while some would have preferred him to be in the third, suggesting a generational sense of kinship (the *propatruus* was in the same generation as ego's great-grandfather, who was in the third degree).[27] Like Raymón, the canonist Andreae also showed discomfort with the logic of the canon law kinship system. He discussed whether marriage between ascendants and descendants was prohibited beyond the fourth degree (a doubt shared by other canonists). The legal authorities were contradictory, but Andreae's sense was that such a relationship was prohibited, even although a strict interpretation of the rules would suggest that it was not.[28] Here is an example of academic game playing, a fault of which canonists writing on the subject of kinship have been eloquently accused;[29] such a relationship would be in fact highly unlikely given the potential ages of people involved.

Affinity tended to receive less space in these treatises than consanguinity. None the less, Raymón's discussion followed the same underlying pattern: he explained the concepts, the practical skills involved in counting in types,[30] and degrees of affinity, how the tree was drawn, and questions and notable things. Affinity, he wrote, was 'a proximity of people outside all blood-kinship, coming from fleshy joining'.[31] It came from sexual intercourse or marriage.[32] It was also, Andreae noted, a 'perpetual impediment and endures the death of the person who mediated the joining'.[33] After 1215 marriage was prohibited to the kin of a spouse or sexual partner up to the fourth degree. Degrees of affinity were the same as degrees of consanguinity, thus an affine was distant by as many degrees as the mediating consanguine was to the ego with whom he or she had married or had sex.

---

[27] Appendix 1.44–7.

[28] 'Quaero: an inter ascendentes et descendentes prohibitio copulae excedat quartum gradum? Et dicit Goff. in sum. de consang. et affin. ss Item quantum, quod non, per decr. Non debet, eod. tit., quae generaliter loquitur. Alii communiter contradicentes inter ascendentes et descendents perpetuam esse prohibitionem dicunt, et quod de quarto gradu dicitur, in collateralibus locum habet; ad hoc 35. quaest. 3. Progeniem. et duobus capitulis sequent., in quibus dicitur, quod olim non solum usque ad secundum gradum, sed etiam, in quantum notitia erat parentelae, extendabatur prohibitio. Ex quo ergo certum est alterum descendentem, et alterum ascendentem, perdurat prohibitio, ad idem Instit. de nupt. .ss.1. ff. de ritu nupt. l. Nuptiae, et hoc verum puto': Andreae, 'Declaratio arboris consanguinitatis',1429 ss. 12.

[29] Pollock and Maitland, *History of English law*, ii. 389.

[30] Canonists had previously discussed other 'types' of affinity with the subsequent spouses or sexual partners of affines. That these were practically applied is difficult to believe, although some sources refered to them as if they were. For more on types of affinity see appendix 1.59, 65–9 below.

[31] Appendix 1.50.

[32] Ibid.

[33] 'Scias autem, quod affinitas est perpetuum impedimentum, quod durat etiam mortua persona, qua mediante contrahitur': Andreae, 'Declaratio arboris affinitatis', 1433 ss. 2.

Figure 2. A four-degree *arbor affinitatis* (tree of affinity). This canon law image illustrated which affines (kinsmen by marriage or sexual relations) a person could not legitimately marry. Reproduced from Bibliothèque nationale, Paris, MS, Latin 4000, fo. 186v, a canon law manuscript, by permission of the Bibliothèque nationale de France.

16

The *arbor affinitatis* (*see* figure 2) was a less simple image than the *arbor consanguinitatis*. Raymón's explanation reflects this. He explained that the tree began with a spine of four central cells labelled with the degrees (with the first degree at the top, then descending down). Beside this was drawn a line of male descendants on the right, beginning with the brother, and a line of female descendants on the left, beginning with the sister. Beside each of these a further line of four cells was drawn containing the wives or husbands of the brother and sister and their descendants. This represented those with whom marriage was forbidden due to affinity. Raymón also explained several decorative and some useful commonplaces that were part of the tree. One was that the wife and husband of the brother and sister were called 'formerly widow/widower'; this was done in reference to the two additional cells added at the outer edges of the tree (the 'ears') which were to reflect the other types of affinity upon which the prohibition had since been lifted.[34] Another common point was that an image of a brother and sister was sometimes drawn above the tree (*see* figure 2), and that lines arched over the figure, showing that affinity arose between the brother and the sister's husband, and between the sister and the brother's wife. This was confusing (in the absence of same-sex marriage), however. The illustration was meant to convey the degree of relationship and the fact that that affinity was between a person and the kin of someone they had married or with whom they had had sexual relations irrespective of gender, rather than with the specific people shown. The kin of both parties were not affines to each other.[35]

There were other types of kinship that formed an impediment to marriage and were potential causes of scandal, although they were not so common or prominent. Briefly, the impediment of public honesty barred marriages between a person and the kin of someone to whom they had been betrothed, i.e. if they had exchanged a promise to marry in the future. Raymón mentioned this as a comparison to affinity in his treatise.[36] Certain relationships created through baptism were also understood as spiritual affinity. The clear rules were that a godparent could not marry a godchild, and a person could not marry the godparent of their own child. Whether a godchild could marry the child of their godparent was more controversial, but appears to have sometimes been regarded as an impediment by some authorities. It is not necessary to rehearse the detail here. Spiritual kinship was less common than consanguinity or affinity. There was a tree of spiritual affinity, but it was not commonly reproduced.[37]

---

[34] Appendix 1.55.
[35] Appendix 1.71.
[36] Appendix 1.73–4.
[37] An example (fire damaged) is in BL, MS Royal Appendix 85, fo. 36v.

## The rationale

The canon law kinship system was based on legal authority. Formally, this stemmed from papal decisions, known as decretals. Decretal collections also included records of letters, church councils and some forgeries. By the eleventh century there were fifty-three decretals on consanguinity; eventually twenty-four of these were included in what became one of the authoritative decretal collections, Gratian's *Decretum*.[38] The exigencies of papal decisions, however, were not the whole foundation of canon law kinship.

One of the roots of canon law kinship was Jewish law, as transmitted through the Bible, although canonists were also aware that several biblical exemplars, such as Adam or Noah's sons, had not followed their rules.[39] Leviticus xviii.6 had said that 'None of you shall approach to any that is near of kin to him, to uncover *their* nakedness.'[40] Here was the incest prohibition at the heart of the canon law kinship system. Canon lawyers tended to rely upon this general prohibition on kinsmen as a foundation for their rules, although some did discuss specific prohibitions from Leviticus.[41] Among those who did was the author of an unusual short kinship treatise (here called *Sciendum est*) that followed the history of incest laws from the creation onwards. It discussed how Adam was allowed to have intercourse with a woman in the first degree, his '*quasi* daughter', since Eve was made out of him. It mentioned how, with the increase in people, the prohibition was extended to the first and second types of consanguinity and affinity. It then listed the prohibitions in Leviticus xviii, assigning to each of them a degree. These cover (updating somewhat) a person's father, mother, mother-in-law, sister, half-sister or step-sister, granddaughter, aunt on either side, father's brother and his wife, daughter-in-law, sister-in-law, and a woman and her daughter or grandchild or sister. The treatise also quoted the *Sentences* of Peter Lombard and Augustine's *City of God*, explaining the extension of the prohibition on marriage to kinsmen to the seventh degree which, according to those sources, took place to promote social harmony. Then it noted the change to a four-degree limit introduced by the Fourth Lateran Council.[42] This echoed a historical progression discussed by canonists as eminent as Gratian,[43] or Andreae, who noted that the prohibitions in Leviticus had applied to only 'twelve people' while the 'positive' canon law had prohibited such marriages up to the seventh degree (before 1215). His conclusion was

---

[38]  J. A. Brundage, *Law, sex, and Christian society in medieval Europe*, Chicago–London 1987, 195, 602–3.
[39]  For example Andreae, 'Declaratio arboris affinitatis', 1436 ss. 10.
[40]  *The Bible: authorized King James version with apocrypha*, intro. and notes R. Carroll and S. Prickett, Oxford 1997.
[41]  G. H. Joyce, *Christian marriage: an historical and doctrinal study*, 2nd edn, London 1948, 526–8.
[42]  Appendix 2.
[43]  C.35 q.1.

that the prohibition on marriage to kinsmen 'partly came from divine law and partly from positive law'. Kinsmen who were outside the prohibition in Leviticus but within four degrees (after 1215) 'were able to join by divine law but not positive law'.[44] The essential point to recognise from these distinctions is that there was an awareness of the biblical prohibitions as one of the foundations of the canon law kinship system, but also that the system in the thirteenth and fourteenth centuries went beyond those foundations.

This wider kinship system with its internal structure of lines and degrees also had roots in the civil law kinship system. The civil law manner of reckoning kinship had determined Roman intestate inheritance. Briefly, for intestate succession, for a man, there were three categories of heirs. *Sui heredes* (children, grandchildren, etc) would be called to the inheritance first, although this was complicated by rules about adoptees and emancipation, and other matters. If they failed, then agnates, meaning 'cognates linked through the male line', were called. If agnates failed, cognates, meaning blood-kinsmen generally, were called.[45] People in the same degree would share *per capita*.[46] The distance between two people according to civil law degrees was reckoned by counting each generation up to the common ancestor, then each generation back out. Under this system agnates could extend up to the tenth degree.[47] Cognates could extend to the sixth or the seventh.[48] These kinship rules were explained in Roman legal texts, such as the sixth-century compilations of Justinian, particularly his introductory *Institutes*, and the more detailed and comprehensive *Digest*.[49]

These ideas about kinship came to the canon law by a circuitous route. Some were current in society. The detail of the civil law kinship system was preserved and circulated in Isidore of Seville's *Etymologies*, written in the early seventh century. This encyclopaedic work attempted to preserve Roman learning, and, in a sense, to organise and categorise the world with this knowledge. The *Etymologies* included definitions of the key terms (for kinship generally and for kinsmen in particular) and an account of kinship schemata.[50] By the ninth century the manuscript tradition of the *Etymologies*

---

44 'In Leuitico uero prohibitae fuerunt fere duodecim personae ... Demum ius posituum canonicum prohibuit consanguineos et affines primi generis coniungi in septimo gradu et citeriori, quae prohibitio postea usque ad quartum gradum est restricta ... quod prohibitio partim procedit ex iure diuino, et partim ex positiuo. Unde in secundo gradu aequalis lineae collaterales contrahere possunt iure diuino, sed non positiuo': Andreae, 'Declaratio arboris affinitatis', 1436 ss. 10.
45 *The Institutes of Justinian: text, translation and commentary*, ed. J. A. C. Thomas, Amsterdam–Oxford 1975, 3.1–6. All references to the *Institutes* will be to this edition.
46 Ibid. p. 178.
47 Ibid. 3.2.1.
48 Ibid. 3.6.6.
49 *The Digest of Justinian*, Latin text ed. T. Mommsen with P. Krueger; English trans. ed. A. Watson, Philadelphia 1985, 38.10. All references to the *Digest* will be to this edition.
50 Isidore of Seville, 'Etymologiarum libri XX', PL lxxxii.73–728 at 9.5–6.

also included images that illuminated kinship. Such had been promised in the *Institutes*, although it is not clear if they were ever supplied.[51] In contrast, numerous early examples of *arbores* appeared in manuscripts of Isidore's *Etymologies*, and this was one of the key ways whereby kinship schemata were transmitted in the early Middle Ages. The typical *arbor consanguinitatis* (*see* figure 1) stood at the end of a long development.[52] A comparison of the kinship terminology used in the *Institutes*, Isidore's *Etymologies* and the canon law system as per *Decretum* C.35 q.5 c.6 shows the consistency and influence of this schematic material.[53]

Terminology was not, however, the whole of the kinship system and there were vital changes in the manner of calculating kinship during the early Middle Ages. Initially the limits put on kinship could be quite varied but they eventually coalesced around the seven-degree limit, apparently borrowed from the civil law but transferred to the canon law way of counting, thus doubling the exclusion zone.[54] The serious study of the civil law was redis-covered in the early twelfth-century. Even before that, there was a certain amount of interest and some confusion, because some people wanted to count using civil law degrees while others, including the influential Peter Damian, preferred the more extensive method of counting that became familiar as the canon law method.[55] The common theory goes that this change from counting in civil law degrees entailed a shift to the Germanic manner of counting, which measured each generation as a degree. The evidence for this 'germanic' manner of counting is sketchy in the early period, although there are references in law codes that suggest that kin was counted in joints or generations.[56] Indeed, the early decretals on canon law kinship do not neces-sarily show a consistent pattern of counting in the 'Roman' manner, and give the impression of reflecting varying local practices.[57] Some well-known early canons had counted in generations rather than degrees.[58] The impor-

---

[51] 'Sed cum magis veritas oculata fide quam per aures animis hominum infigitur, ideo necessarium duximus, post narrationem graduum etiam eos praesenti libro inscribi. Quatenus possint et auribus et inspectione adulescentes perfectissimam graduum doctrinam adipisci': *Institutes* 3.6.9. However, none survives in the 'most authoritative' manuscripts: ibid. p. 180, n. 4.

[52] Schadt, *Arbores*, 368–83; more generally his ch. B, pts 1–4.

[53] S. Worby, 'Kinship in thirteenth-century England: the canon law in the common law', unpubl. PhD diss. London 2005, 255–60.

[54] Joyce, *Christian marriage*, 513–21.

[55] *Die Briefe Des Petrus Damiani*, ed. K. Reindel (Monumenta Germaniae Historica, 1983–93), i. NR 19 at pp. 179–99.

[56] In 'De reipus' kinship was said to extend 'usque ad sextum genuculum': A. C. Murray, *Germanic kinship structure: studies in law and society in antiquity and the early Middle Ages*, Toronto 1983, 165.

[57] For an exploration of the diversity of early canons, though he reaches the conclusion that the method of counting generally followed the Roman pattern, see Joyce, *Christian marriage*, 512–20.

[58] For example C.35 q.2, 3, c.1, 3, 16, 17.

tant point, however, is that the formal decision to accept counting degrees as generations potentially extended the system until people who shared a common great-great-great-great-great-grandfather could not marry, not to mention the wide potential application of the affinity rules if the second and third types of affinity (covering people with whom straightforward affines had had sexual relations or married) were applied, as some experts wished. There seems to have been a significant amount of confusion over the law in the various decretal collections of the eleventh century that was gradually resolved (thus the fifty-three canons on kinship that were pruned down to twenty-four in Gratian). The method of counting using civil law degrees for canon law kinship calculations was finally dismissed by Pope Alexander II and the pattern of counting canon law degrees in the 'germanic' manner was affirmed.[59]

By the thirteenth century this history was no longer so directly relevant. In 1215 canon law kinship changed, and the impetus was no longer to extend and argue over its extent. Prior to the changes in 1215 there had already been a consciousness that the outer reaches of the kinship structures were human and not divine law (in the sense discussed by Andreae in 1303). The principle was established that the prohibition of marriage in the more remote degrees was a matter of human rather than divine law. Alexander III who recognised this, was the first extensively to employ dispensations in the third and fourth degrees of consanguinity.[60] Donahue thus pinpoints the decretals of Pope Alexander III on consanguinity as the point at which the tendency to extend the application of the kinship system turned into a tendency to restrict.[61] And it was a change that correlated with the courts beginning to apply the rules more strictly, leading people to question their harshness. Alexander III's rulings upheld marriages in the more remote degrees or if they had endured unchallenged for a long time. As a consequence, by the start of the thirteenth century, the canon law kinship system in relation to marriage was complicated and case specific.[62] This would have made it more difficult to enforce and operate. Men and women might find their souls endangered within the context of a doubtful marriage. Change came with the decision of the Fourth Lateran Council in 1215. Because of 'urgent necessity' the scope of the incest prohibition restrictions was reduced. The rules as they stood were said to 'often lead to difficulty and sometimes endanger souls'. Henceforth marriage was to be allowed outside the fourth degree of consanguinity, and the first type of affinity. Beyond this limit the rules had caused 'grave harm'. They were 'human decrees' and so could be 'changed according

---

[59] C.35 q.5 c.2.
[60] Donahue, *Law, marriage, and society*, 28.
[61] Ibid. 27.
[62] Ibid. 27–30.

to changing circumstances'.[63] Whether the rhetoric is credible or not, the decision had, at a stroke, simplified the canon law of kinship. No matter the duration of the marriage, it was not valid within four degrees or the first type of affinity. And it still remained possible to purchase dispensations for the third and fourth degrees.

A prohibition on marriage to anyone who was related by a common great-great-grandparent seems wide, let alone one that potentially extended to the great-great-great-great-great-grandparent, not to mention one that forbade relatives of affines to those degrees also. So wide a reach was the reason why a scholar as astute as Frederick Maitland could suppose that almost every marriage could potentially be dissolved by the use of these rules.[64] These are the outer extremes of a canon law kinship system so wide that he could call them 'a maze of flighty fancies and misapplied logic'.[65] He said on the canon law of marriage that 'Behind these intricate rules there is no deep policy, there is no strong religious feeling; they are the idle ingenuities of men who are amusing themselves by inventing a game of skill which is to be played with neatly drawn tables of affinity and doggerel hexameters.'[66] Certainly this is a system that may appear peculiarly wide and artificial. Yet it is possible to call to mind other societies that set wide boundaries on kinship such as the Nuer, as well as others that sought the opposite, to encourage or mandate marriage to several types of close cousins.[67] Comparatively, the canon law system was no more peculiar than many others.

When examining the reasons for the extent of the kinship prohibition it is impossible to avoid the thought-provoking work of Jack Goody who compared the social structures of the European northern Mediterranean with those of other areas and times including ancient Rome, the Arab southern Mediterranean and sub-Saharan Africa. His contention was that the width of the consanguinity prohibition strikingly differentiated European social structures, leading to an unusual weakness of family ties. His explanation for it was that the Church extended kinship prohibitions (among other strategies) to restrict the number of heirs or limit the survival of the family line and thus increase its wealth.[68] Whether he supposed that they intended to do this by reducing the number of heirs, or lessening the cohesiveness of groups that would otherwise keep property within their collective ownership is not entirely clear, nor is it particularly historically plausible. There are several

---

[63] X 4.14.8; translation from Donahue, *Law, marriage, and society*, 676 (*Texts and commentary*, n. 38).

[64] Pollock and Maitland, *History of English law*, ii. 385–9.

[65] Ibid. ii. 389.

[66] Ibid.

[67] E. E. Evans-Pritchard, *Kinship and marriage among the Nuer*, Oxford 1951, ch. i, and pp. 152, 158. For examples of cross-cousin marriage see Dumont, *Introduction to two theories*, 70–81.

[68] J. Goody, *The development of the family and marriage in Europe*, Cambridge 1983, ch. iii.

logical and historical flaws in Goody's argument.[69] It is also not a necessary explanation. It seems simpler to credit the explanation advanced by Augustine, and later Peter Damian, and repeated by Gratian and Johannes Andreae. The prohibitions were set widely to encourage exogamous marriage because this was believed to increase the bonds between families and thus promote social harmony:

> For the law of matrimony is put together ... for the following reason: that the bond of mutual charity among men might be ineluctably maintained, viz., that so far as the order of inheritance (*successionis*) is extended, the love of and care for our neighbour (*vicarious amor proximi*) is supplied from the very necessity of blood relationship (*ipsa germanitatis necessitudine*). However, when [kinship] terms are no longer found and the clan (*gens cognationis*) now ceases to be, the law of matrimony steps in forthwith.[70]

This explanation is rather believable in the context of the, not-necessarily-peaceful, informal clans that may have existed in Italy in Peter Damian's time.[71]

As for the specific limit, originally six or seven degrees, the readiest explanation is the civil law exemplar, and probably also the influence of Isidore. Peter Damian explicitly linked his views on marriage to the extent of inheritance. Although elsewhere he was against reckoning kinship in civil law degrees, he was clearly aware that the systems could be complementary. Thus, the role of contingency in explaining the extent of canon law kinship should not be underestimated. An organising principle for kinship was conveniently at hand, although the Roman system was not adopted without change.

The four-degree kinship prohibition is less simply explained. It is a lesser, but still substantial, extent. The change brought the benefit of removing confusion, clearly arising from the removal of the potential second and third types of affinity. It brought the extent of kinship closer to living memory, and so should have made the strict application of the rules easier since four generations were presumably easier to prove than six or seven. The fourth degree was not an inherent boundary, however. Alexander III had given dispensations within the third and fourth degrees, so this change was not structured to bring the limit of the system into line with the extent thought divine, or, at least, non-scandalous.[72] The specific choice of the fourth degree seems

---

[69] For discussion of Goody's work see D. L. d'Avray 'Peter Damian, consanguinity and church property', in L. Smith and B. Ward (eds), *Intellectual life in the Middle Ages: essays presented to Margaret Gibson*, London 1992, 71–80 at pp. 74–7, and Donahue, *Law, marriage, and society*, 563–4.

[70] d'Avray, *Peter Damian*, 73.

[71] Ibid. 80, and 'Lay kinship solidarity and papal law', in P. Stafford, J. Nelson and J. Martindale (eds), *Law, laity and solidarities: essays in honour of Susan Reynolds*, Manchester 2001, 188–99.

[72] Donahue, *Law, marriage, and society*, 28.

to rest on the fact that several earlier canons countenanced the possibility of a marriage being able to stand in the fourth or fifth degree, although this tradition was not wholly consistent.[73] The explanation given by the Fourth Lateran Council is less satisfying: 'The number four agrees well with the prohibition concerning bodily union about which the Apostle says, that the husband does not rule over his body, but the wife does; and the wife does not rule over her body, but the husband does; for there are four humours in the body, which is composed of the four elements.'[74] To regard this as little more than an appeal to magical numbers, or a justification for the sake of it, is perhaps being unfair. A clear extent was necessary for legal certainty. Canon law history had offered one with some equivalence. A lessening of the extent of the incest prohibition was probably welcome, but a relatively wide extent encouraged exogamy and thus the good of increased social harmony. This was human law and a balance had to be struck.

## The infrastructure supporting canon law kinship

The canon law kinship system was not merely an abstract set of rules and a few decisions. It was a system in practice that touched, over the course of generations, millions of souls. It was an international legal system, promulgated in local laws. The prohibitions on marriage to kinsmen were included in the statutes of various English dioceses for which records survive. The rules tended to be mentioned either as a prohibition of marriage to consanguines, affines or kinsmen through baptism; as a notice of the changes introduced by the Fourth Lateran Council; or as part of a longer list of impediments to marriage.[75]

Rules and laws were, of course, not enough to ensure that the system operated in practice. The canon law had an effective mechanism to make sure that properly formed marriages did not contravene the rules, which, given the implementation structures available at the time, was very elegantly designed. The Fourth Lateran Council decreed that

> we altogether forbid clandestine marriages and we forbid any priest to presume to be present at such a marriage ... we decree that when marriages are to be contracted they shall be publicly announced by the priests in the churches, with an adequate term fixed beforehand within which whoever wishes and is able to may adduce a lawful impediment. The priests themselves shall also investigate whether any impediment stands in the way [of the proposed marriage]. When there appears to be a credible reason against

[73] C.35 q.2 & 3, c.3, 12, 20; C.35 q.8 c.1; cf. C.35 q.2 & 3, c.21; C.35 q.8 c.2.
[74] X 4.14.8; translation from Donahue, *Law, marriage, and society*, 676 (*Texts and commentary*, n. 38).
[75] *Councils and synods with other documents relating to the English Church*, ed. F. M. Powicke and C. R. Cheney, Oxford 1964, ii. 34, 88, 89, 190, 197, 234, 377, 636, 644.

the proposed union, the contract shall be expressly forbidden until there has been established from clear documents what ought to be done about it. If any persons presume to enter into clandestine marriages of this kind, or forbidden marriages within a prohibited degree, even if done in ignorance, the offspring of the union shall be deemed illegitimate and shall have no help from their parents' ignorance, since the parents in contracting the marriage could be considered as not devoid of knowledge, or even as affectors of ignorance ... Likewise the offspring shall be deemed illegitimate if both parents know of a legitimate impediment and yet dare to contract a marriage in the presence of the church, contrary to every prohibition. Moreover the parish priest who refuses to forbid such unions, or even any member of the regular clergy who dares to attend them, shall be suspended from office for three years and shall be punished even more severely if the nature of the fault requires it. Those who presume to be united in this way, even if it is within a permitted degree, are to be given a suitable penance ... Anybody who maliciously proposes an impediment, to prevent a legitimate marriage, will not escape the church's vengeance.[76]

The banns were a potentially effective publicity mechanism, for both the rules and for actual impediments. Certainly the penalties decreed for not following this publicity mechanism were intended to act as an incentive for parishioners. A marriage within the degrees would make any offspring illegitimate. Ignorance was to be no excuse. Given that one of the social purposes of marriage was the creation of heirs, this ought to have been an effective provision if it operated in practice.[77] In addition, the penalties on priests and clergy who did not forbid, or who attended, a marriage within the degrees ought also to have ensured a level of obedience. The banns were certainly regarded as important by contemporaries. The need for the banns to be read is a repeated feature of English conciliar legislation.[78] Also, there is an example of a tract on penance for confessors that suggested that the question of impediments should be raised before marriage.[79] These laws were a matter of conscience as well as penalty.

Naturally, however, clandestine marriages did take place. Not everyone married *in facie ecclesiae* (which the rules did not mandate, rather they required the announcement of the marriage in the public forum of the church). In England, the records of disputes in the church courts concerning marriage show that clandestine marriages were not unusual.[80] Equally, cases where

---

[76] X 4.7.5; translation from Donahue, *Law, marriage, and society*, 678–9 (*Texts and commentary*, n. 52).

[77] There is evidence to suggest that it did to some extent, in the form of a common law mnemonic discussed at pp. 74–5 below.

[78] M. M. Sheehan, 'Marriage theory and practice in the conciliar legislation and diocesan statutes of medieval England', in Farge, *Marriage, family, and law*, 118–76 at pp. 145–54.

[79] Ibid. 129.

[80] Helmholz, *Marriage litigation*, ch. ii; Donahue, *Law, marriage, and society*, 31, 71, 230.

couples tried to avoid the banns by marriage in another parish, where they had prior knowledge of an impediment, are indicative that the system was effective enough, although Michael Sheehan found that the banns sometimes occurred after the formation of an informal marriage and were used as a means of gaining public approval for the relationship.[81]

For couples who were within the outer reaches of the kindred as defined by the canon law, there was a further option. They could purchase a papal dispensation – an exception from the normal operation of the law – to allow marriage in the third or fourth degrees. This was possible because these reaches of the kinship system were acknowledged to be a matter of human law and ecclesiastical legislation rather than divine or natural law. Canonists used discretion based on their understanding of how wrong such a marriage would be. The close degrees were more scandalous and thus not suitable for dispensation.[82] Consistent with the pattern suggested by the dispensations of Alexander III, a fourteenth-century register of the bishop of Coventry and Lichfield did not contain any dispensations below the third degree. It also contained more dispensations for the fourth degree rather than the third.[83] Finally, dispensations were recorded sometimes in bishops' registers.[84]

It was not only before marriage that the rules of canon law kinship might come into play, although, without doubt, that would be the best time to save souls. These issues could also come before the church courts as people sought to enforce or dissolve a marriage. By the mid-thirteenth century a system of consistory courts had developed in England, such that nearly every bishop had a court.[85] These courts were presided over by officials and were served by bodies of attorneys who acted as advocates, proctors and promoters. Below this level many archdeacons had courts.[86] Above it there were courts belonging to the archbishops. A litigant could appeal through the hierarchical levels of the system, ultimately reaching the pope (for example, through his judges delegate), a possibility that had been open even before the thirteenth-century.

Cases *ex officio*, were ones where the canon law courts enforced their laws in a manner flavoured with criminal jurisdiction. They most often proceeded by inquisition. They could be founded on accusations (which were rare), denunciations (an alternative route for a wronged party) and the common knowledge (*fama publica*) of a group of worthies. The judge and officials would investigate, for example using sworn inquests of local worthies, and

[81]  Sheehan, 'Formation and stability of marriage', 48–54.

[82]  W. J. Sparrow Simpson, *Dispensations*, London 1935, 73.

[83]  *The register of John Catterick, bishop of Coventry and Lichfield, 1415–19*, ed. R. N. Swanson (Canterbury and York Society lxxvii, 1990), 24–33.

[84]  R. H. Helmholz, *The Oxford history of the laws of England, I: The canon law and ecclesiastical jurisdiction from 597 to the 1640s*, Oxford 2004, 543 n. 87; d'Avray, *Medieval marriage*, 121.

[85]  Helmholz, *Oxford history*, i. 99; Donahue, *Law, marriage and society*, 33.

[86]  Donahue, *Law, marriage, and society*, 34.

questioning of the parties; however, the key method of proof was compurgation.[87] The frequency of such cases in court business varied with the level and type of court. Thus, a visitation might consist mainly of such cases, as might the business of a lower ecclesiastical court, for example that of a deanery, but in grander courts, such as episcopal courts, they were less common, and in archbishop's courts they were significantly less so.[88] Archdeacon's courts tended to be staffed by less expert lawyers, although some proctors (who appeared for the parties and could appear at local courts) had degrees in canon or civil law.[89] The records suggest that the application of office jurisdiction was uneven.

Cases *ad instantiam* used civil law procedure, which involved numerous more or less formal stages, from the citation that summoned the parties, through the libel that stated the plaintiff's claim, to the *litis contestatio*, the clarification of the issue prior to proof. Many stages in an instance case were written.[90] The parties involved would have been well advised to seek the advice of a legal expert where one was available. By the thirteenth century there were professional canon lawyers, some of whom had studied at universities.[91] Witnesses would be summoned and examined in court before judgement.

There were three principal routes by which canonical kinship could come before the courts. It could be raised as an impediment and ground for divorce in an instance case, where litigants were appealing for a *divortium a vinculo*. It could be raised as a defence against an attempt to enforce a putative marriage. Or it could be raised as part of an office case, where the court was pursuing its duty to investigate alleged incest and save participants in a potentially sinful marriage or sexual relationship. Canon law kinship rules were raised in all these contexts, although not so commonly as might be anticipated given the wide reach of the kinship system. 'Divorces' on grounds of kinship were actually extremely rare.[92] In fact, annulments of any sort were not very common. By far the most frequent cases to come before the church courts in England aimed to enforce marriages, raising questions about clandestine marriages such as imprecise words of consent and the existence of prior contracts. In court, if the issue of kinship arose, the witnesses had to set it out and reckon

---

[87] On procedure see Helmholz, *Oxford history*, i. 604–24.
[88] On the archbishop's court in York, for example, see Donahue, *Law, marriage, and society*, 65.
[89] Helmholz, *Oxford history*, i. 216, 223.
[90] Ibid. i. 317–42.
[91] Ibid. i. 222; P. Brand, *Origins of the English legal profession*, Oxford 1992, ch. ix.
[92] Helmholz, *Marriage litigation*, 77–87; *Select cases from the ecclesiastical courts of the province of Canterbury, c. 1200–1301*, ed. N. Adams and C. Donahue, Jr. (Selden Society xc, 1981), 81–4; F. Pedersen, *Marriage disputes in medieval England*, London 2000, 137; d'Avray, *Medieval marriage*, 112–16; Donahue, *Law, marriage, and society*, 71, 230 and ch. xi.

the degrees as far as possible. The following example of a count is given in canon law treatises:

> When you want to know about the kinship of some people (how distant they are between themselves), revert to the common person from whom they descended thus: 'Petrus begat Seius and Titius, who were brothers, behold the first degree'. If, however, it is not possible to know who their father was, you should say: 'Seius and Titius were brothers.' I say exactly this because brothers should always be put in the first degree, as should brother and sister, or two sisters. Next proceeded in the count: 'Seius and Titius were brothers, who, as was said, make the first degree. The same [Seius] begat A, behold the second degree. A begat B, behold the third degree. B begat C, behold the fourth, with whom I now deal'. You should return to the other brother and proceed thus: 'Titius and Seius were brothers and in the first degree, as was said. Titius begat G, behold the second degree. G begat H, with whom is dealt, behold the third degree.'[93]

The key to this count is marking the generations and the connection to the common ancestor. Proof was not so easy as a simple statement, of course.[94]

Infrequently litigated or not, the rules of canon law kinship could be exercised and accessed through a court system that could extend to a very local level. These courts (and the international canon law legal system) were maintained and serviced by a coterie of experts. They were staffed by judges and advocates, many of whom had learned their law in universities. A canon law education was a valuable route into ecclesiastical administration for bureaucrats and other potentially powerful and influential men.[95]

### Education and kinship in books

Although canon law education was international, this discussion will focus upon the material available in England's universities. From the late twelfth century, there was a flourishing school of canonists in England.[96] The canon law curriculum, taught at both Oxford and Cambridge, was demanding, involving many years of study of the key texts. To become a bachelor of canon law at Oxford required seven years of study; a doctorate (pre-1333) required fifteen.[97] Such an education could be time-consuming and expen-

---

[93] Appendix 4.25–9.
[94] For further discussion of what was needed for kinship to be adequately proven under the canon law legal system see chapter 4 below.
[95] L. E. Boyle, 'Canon law before 1380', in J. I. Catto (ed.), *The history of the University of Oxford*, Oxford 1984, i. 531–64 at p. 539.
[96] S. Kuttner and E. Rathbone, 'Anglo-Norman canonists of the twelfth century: an introductory study', *Traditio* vii (1949–51), 279–358.
[97] Boyle, 'Canon law', 542–5.

sive, but the numbers attending law courses at universities show it to have had value.[98] Both Oxford and Cambridge also required candidates for a canon law degree already to have completed at least three years of study of the civil law.[99] Only clergy were exempt from this, following a decretal of Honorius III in 1219 which had forbidden them civil law studies; instead they had to complete additional years of canon law.[100] There were civil law faculties in Oxford and Cambridge (at Oxford maybe from the early thirteenth century) with numerous students.[101] At Oxford the canon and civil law faculties were closely allied, canonists had to have studied civil law and civilians, to gain their doctorate, had to know a certain amount of canon law.[102] Both faculties studied texts that included kinship law: the *Decretum* and *Liber extra* for canon law students, and the *Institutes* and *Digest* for civil law students.[103] Thus, it is not surprising that canon lawyers should have known of civil law kinship, and civilians of canon law kinship, as evidenced by references to the canon law in civil law lectures and in the *Glossa ordinaria* on the *Institutes*.[104]

Canon law was taught through lectures. Neither Oxford nor Cambridge maintained a permanent faculty at this period. Students at both were taught by a succession of bachelors and doctors who were teaching to meet the requirements of their own qualifications.[105] In the morning there would be lectures on the *Decretum*, in the afternoon on the *Liber extra*.[106] Helmholz describes canon law teaching at Oxford according to the university statutes. The curriculum was based on the texts of the laws, that is, on the *Decretum* or *Liber extra*, which would be read verbatim. Students were required to have copies of these texts and were meant to memorise them. Next the *Glossa ordinaria* would be read; this was the standard gloss written around the core texts of the manuscripts in question. Then the lecturer would give further explanation of the text, 'defining difficult words, relating the text to other relevant portions of the *Corpus*, solving apparent inconsistencies between them, and also raising points of special interest'. They did not

---

[98]  Boyle was able to identify 2,359 law students from the higher faculties of Oxford in A. B. Emden, *A biographical register of the University of Oxford to A.D. 1500*, Oxford 1959, 561–2.

[99]  Ibid. 545. See also S. L'Engle and R. Gibbs, *Illuminating the law: legal manuscripts in Cambridge collections*, London 2001, 31.

[100]  L'Engle and Gibbs, *Illuminating the law*, 31.

[101]  J. L. Barton, 'The study of civil law before 1380', in Catto, *History of the University of Oxford*, i. 519–30 at p. 525.

[102]  Boyle, 'Canon law', 539.

[103]  C.35; X 4.14; *Institutes* 3.6; *Digest* 38.10.

[104]  F. De Zuleta and P. Stein, *The teaching of Roman law in England around 1200* (Selden Society s.s. viii, 1990), 75–6. See also Accursius, 'Gloss' on *Institutes*, 3.6 'Adicit', from *Institutiones imperiales [with the gloss of Accursius]*, ed. J. Chappuis, Paris 1503, fo. 117r.

[105]  Boyle, 'Canon law', 535; L'Engle and Gibbs, *Illuminating the law*, 31.

[106]  L'Engle and Gibbs, *Illuminating the law*, 31.

discuss practice in the courts.[107] This fits also with evidence for Cambridge teaching.[108]

Canon law patterns of education made it a learned system (in contrast to the common law), an important consideration for an understanding of the canon law kinship system. The canon law produced academic specialists and experts, although no really notable authors in England due to the pattern of teaching at the universities.[109] Common law historians are apt to call the combination of the canon and civil laws the 'learned laws', while canon lawyers call them the *ius commune*.[110] The canon law kinship system was studied, taught, argued and elaborated in three main genres of texts. There were books of authority that set out the canon law: the *Decretum* and *Liber extra* which were at the heart of studies in canon law faculties. There were academic texts that discussed the canon law in more detail, the product of the canon law faculties and specialist academics of the continent. And there were beginners' texts, the genre of short treatises.

Thirteenth-century students began with Gratian's *Decretum*. This was one of the key scholastic texts of the Middle Ages, being both a teaching text and a practitioners' handbook. The initial recension was written in Bologna, the heart of legal studies, probably in the late 1130s. A later recension, probably written between 1139 and 1158, included various additions and quickly became the key text for canon law students as the academic study of law blossomed.[111] Even in the thirteenth century it remained vital to the canon law curriculum.[112] The *Decretum* was also called *Concordia discordantium canonum*. It gathered and reconciled sources of authority including the Bible, the writings of church Fathers like St Augustine, the decisions of church councils and various forgeries and real decretals of the popes.

*Causa* 35 in the *Decretum* was concerned with kinship law and marriage (thus with consanguinity and affinity). In this section Gratian asked and answered ten questions. For example, he rehearsed the authorities on whether a man could marry a woman from his own kindred and answered no, although various biblical authorities would seem to allow and even promote kindred marriage, such as the Mosaic rule that no one ought to take a wife except from his own tribe and family.[113] Gratian resolved his discordant authorities by concluding that the rule about marrying family was to protect the Hebrews from marriage to the infidels. He then discussed the extension

---

[107] Helmholz, *Oxford history*, i.189–90.

[108] D. M. Owen, *The medieval canon law: teaching, literature and transmission*, Cambridge 1990, 4.

[109] L'Engle and Gibbs, *Illuminating the law*, 31.

[110] In this book this term will be avoided where possible to avoid confusion over the translation.

[111] A. Winroth, *The making of Gratian's Decretum*, Cambridge 2000, ch. iv.

[112] Helmholz, *Oxford history*, i. 186–206.

[113] 'nullus duceret uxorem, nisi de propria tribu et familia': C.35 q. 1 Gratianus.

of the prohibitions beyond those given in the Bible.[114] Gratian harmonised his conflicting authorities, the very foundation of the scholastic canon law. Other canons in the *Decretum* explained that a man could not marry an affine, established the limit at seven degrees and explained why that limit was chosen.[115] The *Decretum* also taught how to count in degrees of consanguinity. It listed what person was in which degree, with reference to 'Isidore', although in fact the section quoted did not come from Isidore and can be traced back to the *Sententiae* of Paul, from the third or fourth century.[116] It included Alexander II's canon that gave the authority for preferring the canon law method of counting over the civil law method.[117]

Collections of canon law authority were made after Gratian's *Decretum* as the canon law changed and developed, for example those in the *Quinque compilations antique*.[118] These were superseded by the *Liber extra*, a collection of decretals made by Raymón de Penyafort at the behest of Pope Gregory IX, promulgated in 1234. *Liber extra* book 4, title 14 'extra de consanguinitate et affinitate' was another key text on canon law kinship. Here could be found the decretal that resolved that the more remote degree was preferred for deciding whether people at different distances from the common ancestor could marry.[119] Here also was guidance on incestuous marriages of infidels.[120] Most important, here was canon 50 of the Fourth Lateran Council: the decision that removed the prohibition on the second and third types of affinity; on children of a second marriage (who could not previously marry kinsmen of the prior husband); and on marriage to consanguines beyond the fourth degree.[121] After the *Liber extra*, collections continued to be made, such as the

---

[114] C.35 q. 1 c.1 Gratianus.

[115] C.35 q. 2 & 3; C.35 q. 4 c.1. The latter was based on Isidore, *Etymologies* 9.6.29, which put the limit at six degrees. However, the method of counting attributed to Isidore put the parents and children together in a degree, meaning that these six degrees were equivalent to the seven that was, by Gratian's time, the normal limit.

[116] In fact, Gratian says that C.35 q. 5 c.1 and C.35 q. 5 c.6 were both from Isidore. C.35 q.5 c.1 was in Burchard of Wurms's *Decretals*, attributed to Isidore, but not in the *Etymologies*: Burchardi Wormaciensis Ecclesiæ Episcopi, 'Decretorum libri viginti', *PL* cxl.781 at bk VII, c.10. C.35 q.5 c.6 can be traced back to the *Sententiae* of Paul: 'Sententiarum receptarum libri quinque qui vulgo Iulio Paulo adhuc Tribuuntur', in *Fontes iuris romani antejustiniani, II auctores*, ed. Johannes Baviera, Florence 1940, bk IV, c. 11 at pp. 381–3. In the west it was included in various early legal collections, for example Pauli, 'Sententiarum', in *Lex romana visigothorum: ad LXXVI librorum manu scriptorum fidem recognovit septem eius antiquis epitomis quae praeter duas adhuc ineditae sunt, titulorum explanatione auxit, annotatione, appendicibus, prolegomenis*, ed. G. Haenel, Aalen 1962, Lib. iv tit. x (at pp. 408–9). It is also in Burchard, *Decretals* cxl. 784–6 at bk VII c. 28, again attributed to Isidore.

[117] C.35 q.5 c.2.

[118] *Quinque compilationes antiquae nec non collectio canonum Lipsiensis*, ed. A. Friedberg, Leipzig 1832, 50, 93–4, 128, 145–6, 207.

[119] X 4.14.3, 9.

[120] X 4.14.4.

[121] X 4.14.8.

*Liber sextus* of Pope Boniface VIII (1294–1303) and the *Clementinae*, which was a collection of the decretals of Clement V (1305–14), published in 1317. However, for the purposes of canon law kinship structures in the thirteenth and fourteenth centuries these did not add significantly, although they did hold that conditional betrothals did not give rise to the impediment of public honesty, that those who knowingly married a kinsman were automatically excommunicate, and clarified details around spiritual kinship.[122] Such collections of authority were central to the study of canon law at the universities, and formed the authorised basis of the canon law kinship system. For example, approximately 600 manuscripts of the *Decretum* survive.[123] Some of these are workmanlike and some are beautiful.[124]

University education and faculties allowed for specialists who produced specialist texts, over and above collections of authority. Examples of such texts were the glosses. These tended to be written in manuscripts of authority. Manuscripts of the *Decretum* and various decretal collections were organised with the main text at the centre of each page, surrounded by a box of gloss. The glosses were linked to the text through references to key words which they expanded upon in the order dictated by the central text. The glosses to both the *Decretum* and *Liber extra* had been standardised: these were called the *Ordinary glosses*.[125] Other, more internally coherent works, known as *Summae*, were popular among canon lawyers. They discussed canon law problems and questions with reference to the authorities in the *Decretum*, *Liber extra* and even other learned law sources and they argued among themselves. They covered the basics but also dealt with more difficult and obscure questions, and used the law on marriage to draw out ideas of greater sophistication.

One of the most important texts on canon law kinship was Raymón de Penyafort's *Summa de matrimonio* (written c. 1235).[126] This was an adaptation of the *Summa de sponsalibus et matrimonio* of an earlier canonist, Tancred (written c. 1214).[127] Raymón's *Summa* took into account the changes made at the Fourth Lateran Council. It circulated widely and was popular and useful. It was a lucid, comprehensible and influential guide to the canon

---

[122] 'Liber Sextus Decretalium Bonifacii P. VIII' 4.1.1, 4.3.1–3, and 'Clementintis P. V Constitutiones' 4.1.1, *Corpus iuris canonici*, ii.

[123] Winroth, *Making*, 135.

[124] L'Engle and Gibbs, *Illuminating the law*, 105–237.

[125] See Johannes Teutonicus and Bartholomew Brixiensis, 'Ordinary Gloss', in *Decretum Gratiani cum glossis Domini Johannis Theutonici prepositi albertatensis et annotationibus Bartholomei Brixiensis etc*, Basle 1512, fos 382r–385r for C.35 q.1–5, and Bernard of Parma, 'Ordinary gloss to the Liber Extra', in *Decretales Gregory IX*, Venice 1489, fos 324r–326r for X 4.14.

[126] Raymundus de Peniafort, *Summa de poenitentia et matrimonio* [a facsimilie of the Rome edition of 1603], Farnborough 1967.

[127] Tancred, *Summa*. Dates and such details from J. A. Brundage, *Medieval canon law*, London 1995, 227–8.

law of marriage, and included a section that explained canon law kinship.[128] Hundreds of manuscripts are still extant, and Raymón 'if perhaps not one of the most original, was certainly one of the most influential canonists of his age'.[129] His text was printed in Rome in 1603. Other academic treatises also included sections on kinship. Among the most prominent were those of Geoffrey of Trani (d. 1245) who taught civil law at Naples and canon law at Bologna, and became a papal chaplain and a judge. His treatise, the *Summa super titulus decretalium* (written 1241–3), was based on the *Liber extra*.[130] Another influential canonist was Henricus de Segusio (d. 1271), also known as Hostiensis, who trained at Bologna, taught at Paris and was later an archbishop and cardinal-bishop. His *Summa aurea* (written in 1253) and *Lectura* (finished c. 1271) on the *Liber extra* were important works on canon law.[131]

The questions addressed in these *Summae* include such academic examples as the status after 1215 of a marriage contracted illicitly in the sixth or seventh degree before the change to a four-degree prohibition. First, there was the question of whether such a marriage should stand. There was a general consensus that it should not: the constitutions that changed the law did not refer to past marriages, so the couple must be judged by the old law, and the law should not be adjusted for their fault. The controversy came with the question of whether they could remarry each other. Geoffrey of Trani said that they could; the marriage would be in order if there was new consent.[132] Hostiensis disagreed: 'for the first consensus was illegitimate, and thus cannot be confirmed retroactively'.[133] This would seem to be a working out of the practicalities of marriage law. And yet, it may not have been very practical. Geoffrey was writing around 1241–3, Hostiensis in 1253. This is quite a time from the change in the law: twenty-six/twenty-eight years and thirty-eight years. Although Hostiensis was clearly reacting to Geoffrey's argument, it is hard to believe that it was still a live issue. Rather it had become a theoretical question, an issue upon which to pit their understandings of the scope of law and leniency, and of the implications of consent and fault. The question is both chimerically practical and actually academic.

Another dispute was on whether affinity was joined by marriage only or by fornication also. As early as the start of the thirteenth century Bernard

---

[128] Peniafort, *Summa*, 533–44, 555–8.

[129] Kuttner, 'Barcelona edition', 53.

[130] Brundage, *Medieval canon law*, 211–12; Geoffrey of Trani, *Summa in tit.decretalium*, Venice 1519, 367–73.

[131] Hostiensis, *Summa*, Lyons 1548, and *Lectura*, in BL, MS Royal 10 E VI. On Hostiensis see Brundage, *Medieval canon law*, 214, and K. Pennington, 'Henricus de Segusio (Hostiensis)', repr. in his, *Popes, canonists and texts, 1150–1550*, Aldershot 1993, XVI, 1–12.

[132] 'Posset tamen satis tolerari ut si denuo et de novo consentianti valeat matrimonium ut ex nunc non ut ex tunc': Geoffrey of Trani, *Summa*, 369.

[133] 'Primus enim consensus illegitimus fuit: et sic non potest confirmari ex post facto': Hostiensis, *Summa*, fo. 211v. He makes a similar argument about affinity at fo. 213v.

of Pavia (d. 1213) wrote that affinity was joined by concubinage as well as marriage.[134] Geoffrey of Trani explained the problem: some people thought that it was absurd that affinity, 'a bond affirmed by law', arose from 'a sexual union that has been condemned'.[135] These people said affinity came from weddings. Geoffrey seemed to agree; he said that affinity did not arise without marriage. But he compromised and conceded that if marital affection happened, as was possible with a betrothal for the future and subsequent 'extraordinary pollution', the impediment of public honesty arose and would prohibit matrimony.[136] Hostiensis reviewed the past literature and reached his own compromise: civic, natural, legitimate affinity only arose from marriage; but natural and illegitimate affinity could be contracted by fornication in such a way that it was a diriment impediment.[137] Practical questions with real implications for people's lives were played out in this academic arena: a prohibition arising from sexual relationships covered a significantly wider range of people than one arising from marriage or betrothal only.

Less learned, but fundamentally important for their role in introducing beginners to the *arbores* and thus to the canon law kinship system, were the types of short treatises like *Quia tractare intendimus*. They belonged to a teaching context and were linked to the tradition of the gloss. They were dominated by a central picture and were often copied around a picture of the trees of consanguinity and affinity.[138] Many of the early monographs on consanguinity and affinity were glosses on the trees. There was a gloss on the trees of consanguinity and affinity by Johannes Teutonicus (1170–1245), although that never seems to have been very popular.[139] There were glosses by the canonists Vincentius Hispanus (d. 1248) and Damasus (teaching in Bologna c. 1210–20).[140] This genre expanded and became popular until a wealth of short treatises on consanguinity and affinity circulated in the thirteenth century, explaining the structures of canon law kinship in the light of the changes introduced by the Fourth Lateran Council.[141] The most common was *Quia tractare intendimus*. A more unusual treatise was the *Arbor*

---

[134] 'Iam nunc de affinitate, quae contrahitur per concubinatum': Bernardus Papiensis, *Summa decretalium*, ed. E. A. T. Laspeyres, Regensburg 1860, 172.

[135] 'Quidam tamen absurdum reputent quod affinitas quæ est legitimum vinculum oriatur ex damnato coitu': Geoffrey of Trani, *Summa*, 366.

[136] 'Sed si maritalis affectio interuenit ut pote cum sponsalia de futuro præcedunt & postmodum sequitur extraordinaria pollutio, ex hac oritur publicæ, honestatis iustitia': ibid.

[137] 'Affinitas ergo civilis et naturalis et legitima non contrahitur, nisi nuptiis intervenientibus; sed naturalis et illegitima bene contrahitur per coitum fornicarium adeo quod matrimonium impediet et dirimet': Hostiensis, *Summa*, fo. 213r.

[138] L'Engle and Gibbs, *Illuminating the law*, 147–8.

[139] Schadt, *Arbores*, 204–5.

[140] A. García y García, 'Glosas de Juan Teutónico, Vincente Hispano y Dámaso Húngaro a los arbores consanguinitatis et affinitatis', *Zeitschrift der Savigny-Stiftung Für Rechtsgeschichte* xcix (Kanonistische Abteilung lxviii, 1982), 153–85.

[141] Schadt, *Arbores*, 202.

*versificata* of Johannes de Deo.[142] De Deo, a Spanish priest, who died in 1267, wrote a substantial body of canon law material.[143] He was born at Silves in Portugal, studied in Bologna in the 1220s and was teaching there between 1229 and 1255, and possibly later. His treatise seems to have been directed at his students. It explained consanguinity and affinity with the aid of twenty-four mnemonics. For example:

> Nullus cum trunco connubia iungere possit.
> Atque gradum quartum nemo transcendere posset.
> [None with the *truncus* is able to join in marriage
> And no one is able to overstep the fourth degree][144]

The verses are difficult and obscure, but seem to have been intended as handy doggerel mnemonics for canon law students (useful in a culture more accustomed to feats of memory than our own). The work was successful judging by the number of copies that survive.[145] The treatise was even mentioned by the eminent canonist Johannes Andreae in his kinship monograph, although he did not regard it favourably. He said that Johannes de Deo had too many rules and too much obscure verse, which made 'known things unknown to some people, and unknown things even less known to others'.[146] Andreae (*c.* 1270–1348), one of the most esteemed canonists of the period, wrote a kinship treatise which has been quoted extensively in this chapter. Written in about 1303, it contained the standard material, and in many ways – including the attitude to Johannes de Deo's verses – seems very sensible. There were many more minor works, including numerous anonymous tracts.[147] The genre was diverse and widespread. It was united by its usual home in canon law manuscripts and the consistent set of contents.

The most typical home for these treatises was to be copied, often around the trees of consanguinity and affinity, into canon law manuscripts of the

---

[142] 'Ad honorem summe trinitatis et individue unitatis patris et filii et spiritus sancti et ad stabilitatem universalis ecclesie et ad utilitatem audientium, incipit commentum arboris de consanguinitate et affinitate per compendium versificatum et per iura probatum a magistro Iohanne de deo yspano, per xviii regulas declaratum [...]' and 'Ideo quia ego magister Iohannes de deo sacerdos yspanus elegi de omnibus sentenciis qui potiora et breviora cognovi et causa brevitatis per versus declaravi.': Bibliotheca Apostolica Vaticana, MS Palatini Latini 629, fo. 260v.

[143] J. F. von Schulte, *Die Geschichte der Quellen und Literatur des canonischen Rechts*, Stuttgart 1877, ii. 94–107.

[144] BL, MS Harley 653, fo. 42r.

[145] Some are listed in Schadt, *Arbores*, 205, n. 71.

[146] 'sed propter multitudinem regularum et versuum obscuritatem aliquibus notum ignotum, aliis ignotum ignotius reddidit': Andreae, 'Declaratio arboris consanguinitatis', and 'Declaratio arboris affinitatis', prol. col. 1427.

[147] Some are listed in Schadt, *Arbores*, 202 n. 43. An example is the anonymous 'Arborem consanguinitatis describas hoc modo', in BL, Cotton Roll XIV.12 (on the outside, near the top). Schadt lists this as one of the works related to *Quia tractare intendimus*: *Arbores*, 209 n. 98.

*Decretum* and *Liber extra*. The *Arbor versificata* usually occurred in manuscripts with sets of papal decretals of the kind that canon law students needed to know.[148] *Quia tractare intendimus* also occurred most frequently with sets of decretals.[149] Some treatises occurred with academic *Summae* and other intellectual works that may have been associated with the universities.[150]

There were great similarities in the contents and structure of these treatises and their popularity and consistency speak strongly for their usefulness. They were brief, averaging approximately 4,300 words.[151] They tended to be in two parts: consanguinity and affinity (they did not include spiritual kinship). They followed the pattern of *Quia tractare intendimus*: defining standard terms; teaching how to count; providing examples; teaching how to draw the trees; and exploring interesting facts, often the same interesting facts. The definition of terms was consistent across many treatises. One, unusual, example offered several definitions of consanguinity: as a 'bond [*vinculum*] of people'; as a 'natural bond', perhaps in the sense that the lifting of the canon (human) law could not change the underlying natural law; and as 'a relationship [*habitudo*]' joined only by fleshy propagation. As it commented, 'all these definitions come back to the same thing'.[152] For the most part, the treatises were relatively simple. They included only the basics of marriage law and supported this with references to the authorities (*see* appendix 1).

---

[148] In a sample of ten manuscripts (according to the catalogues), three contained the *Decretals* of Gregory IX; one the *Decretals* of Gregory IX and those of Innocent IV; two the *Liber sextus* of Boniface VIII; one contained both of the above; and two contained unidentified decretal collections.

[149] In a sample of twenty-six manuscripts (according to the catalogues) ten contained the *Decretals* of Gregory IX; two the *Decretals* of Gregory IX and various constitutions; four the *Decretals* of Gregory IX and *New constitutions* of Innocent IV; three the decretal collections of Gregory IX, Innocent IV and Gregory X and other material; and one an unidentified decretal collection; one within an *Omne Bonum* (BL, MS Royal 6 E VI); one with the *Volumen parvum* (BL, MS Royal 11 D I); one with various texts including works on confession; one with a book of questions on mortal sins from the *Summa Raymundi*; one with various lectures including those of Johannes Andreae; and one with Johannes Predicator's *Super titulus decretalium*.

[150] For example, 'Lectura arborum consanguinitatis et affinitatis Magistri Ioannis Egitaniensis' (ed. I. da Rosa Pereira, *Studia Gratiana* xiv, Collectanea Stephan Kuttner iv [1967], 155–82), occurs alongside Raymón's *Summa de casibus* and *Summa de matrimonio*; Gratian's *Decretum*; Azo's *Summa codicis*; and a miscellany of university type material including some of the *Sentences* of Peter Lombard.

[151] These totals (including both the consanguinity and affinity sections) are tentative since they are based on a word count of personal transcriptions: *Arbor versificata* = 2,755 words; *Ad arborem* = 6,610; *Sciendum est* = 4,627; and *Quia tractare intendimus* = 3,168 words.

[152] 'Consanguinitas est habitudo persone ad personam, carnali tantum propagatione contracta. Vel sic: consanguinitas est vinculum personarum ab eodem stipite descendentium, carnali propagatione contractum, et hee [*correctly* hec] omnes diffinitiones in idem redeunt. Vel sic: consangui[ni]tas est naturale vinculum personarum ab eodem stipite descendentium, carnali p[ro]pagatione contractum': BL, MS Add. 41258, fo. 38r.

The similarity of the contents, particularly of the way in which key terms were defined, suggests a standard basis in canon law education, particularly in the teaching involved in understanding the trees of consanguinity and affinity. The contents overall fit well with the pattern for canon law lectures. They represent accreted layers of learning and questioning about canon law kinship, particularly about the trees.

So many short treatises on canon law kinship survive because kinship was significant, to everyday life, politically (in *cause célèbre* marriages), symbolically and in ordering society. Structure and order and patterns and technicalities are attractive to a certain type of mind: the 'exuberant learning' of canon lawyers has been remarked.[153] On a more prosaic level, canon law kinship was difficult and technical. The popularity of these treatises was also linked closely with the popularity of the image of the trees of consanguinity and affinity. These pictures were useful visual shorthand for a mass of ideas and material about kinship, but could be difficult to understand and apply without fuller explanation. Finally, kinship treatises filled a gap in the educational process. They stood between the key textbooks and the more academic works and might be compared to other similar genres of useful short treatises, for example, on procedure in court.[154] Kinship treatises can 'lack the charm of novelty'.[155] Yet their virtue was that they were simple and accessible, and their very basic nature made them a potentially more widespread source for knowledge about canon law kinship than the more intellectual work of the experts. Civil law kinship, which was not so relevant in practice, particularly in England, had nothing similar.

The canon law kinship system was based on a formal understanding of a biological connection (for consanguinity), or an analogy with that connection (for affinity and spiritual affinity). It was systematic and internally ordered, it had an in/out boundary and had an internal reasoning that supported this structure, organised by the closeness of relationship to the common parent. It had a rich terminology and was both relative (in that it could apply to anyone) and focused on actual people (ego and a kinsman who wished to marry). Finally, and most important, it was aimed at the social purpose of determining which marriages were safe for participants' souls and which were illicit and not allowed. Even the wide boundary on kinship appears to have been understood to have a social purpose, which was to encourage harmony by creating bonds through marriage. That this system may appear unusually extensive to meet the purposes of an incest prohibition, should not distract from the fact that it operated in England. The banns, the dispensations, the court cases, the degrees and the books are all evidence of that. The system

---

153 Pollock and Maitland, *History of English law*, ii. 386.
154 Helmholz, *Oxford history*, i. 215.
155 Ibid. i. 186.

was applied and it was thought. It could be artificial, but it was not wholly or particularly marked as a 'maze of flighty fancies and misapplied logic'.[156] It was the most important general way of thinking about the wider family in medieval Europe.

[156] Pollock and Maitland, *History of English law*, ii. 389

# 2

# Common Law Kinship Structures

Common law kinship determined inheritance of real property for the wealthy. It both reflected and shaped noble concepts of how the family should be ordered; its symbolic importance hence extended more widely than simply to those whose land descended according to its rules. The common law kinship system, specifically that part that concerned the structure of kinship, was a powerful force in people's lives (some practical matters such as dower or curtesy or bastardy will not be dealt with in detail here).[1] It may seem more natural and instinctive to modern readers than that of the canon law, as the inheritance patterns of the nobility in England are relatively well known in comparison to canon law kinship, yet it was artificial in the way that any formal legal kinship system will inevitably be. The focus of this chapter will be on parentelic kinship, although other kinship systems did operate locally, for example inheritance according to gavelkind in Kent and several other counties.[2]

The common law was the justice of the king's courts: the Common Bench, the King's Bench, in the eyres and such. It was the law that was written about in books of English law like Bracton's *De legibus et consuetudinibus Angliae* and argued about by lawyers as the profession emerged. It was that mass of writs, pleas, customs, statutes and common learning that English lawyers regard as the common law. Common law kinship was, for the most part, a matter of inheritance law and disputes about ownership of land or, more accurately, of rights to land. The importance of these rights, and land as a source of wealth and power, can hardly be overstated.[3] There was no allod in England, no complete title as such. Instead, the Conquest meant that, by fact or fiction, men held ultimately from the king. Below the monarch was, in theory at least, the whole panoply of the feudal pyramid, with some men (often more powerful lords) holding land direct from the king, and others holding land from them in subinfeudation down to the people who worked the land at the very bottom. Certain concepts underlie the discussion of kinship.[4] Men held, one from another, according to tenure (they were tenants, at least theoreti-

---

[1] For further detail see P. Brand, 'Family and inheritance, women and children', in C. Given-Wilson (ed.), *An illustrated history of late medieval England*, Manchester 1996, 58–81.
[2] R. J. Faith, 'Peasant families and inheritance customs in medieval England', *Agricultural History Review* xiv (1966), 77–95. Gavelkind is also explained at p. 41 below.
[3] S. F. C. Milsom, *Historical foundations of the common law*, 2nd edn, London 1981, 99.
[4] Ibid; J. H. Baker, *An introduction to English legal history*, 4th edn, London 2002.

cally reliant on their lord to enforce their title). This way of dividing rights arising from connection with land apportioned certain things to the lord and tenant. A simple illustration of this would be that the tenant who held by military tenure had possession of the land while the lord was in possession of the tenant's services and had a right to certain incidents such as wardship of the tenant's heir should the tenant die before his heir was of full age, and the reversion of possession of the land should the tenant's line fail.[5] There was potential for chains of subinfeudation until the statute *Quia emptores* in 1290, following which a vendor tenant could only substitute his purchaser into his own position. By the thirteenth century, the reality was not so feudal as this discussion might seem to imply, but the structure had been hardened by the developing legal system.

Different types of tenure brought different patterns of inheritance or succession. If a tenure was heritable it was a fee.[6] There were several types of tenure, both lay and spiritual. Among lay tenures there were base and free tenures. Base tenures were held by villeins for unfixed services and were not enforced in the royal courts but, according to custom, in manorial courts. Free tenures could be chivalrous or non-chivalrous. Chivalrous tenures included those held in return for military services. Knight service, requiring services such as castleguard and scutage (a tax), was the typical example and was the principal military tenure. Other examples were tenures that involved rendering some service to the king's person (such as grand-serjeanty). Free socage was the principal free, lay, non-chivalrous tenure: a tenure for fixed agricultural duties.[7] Socage tenure could be common, in which case it would follow the standard common law inheritance pattern; or customary, which included such special types of inheritance as gavelkind and burgage. The relevance of this for kinship is that all these types of tenure, except spiritual, villein (i.e. base tenure) and customary socage, followed the classical inheritance patterns of common law kinship.

An important final point to note is that the common law held a distinction between right and seisin. This is not quite the modern distinction between ownership and possession, but that is a suitable parallel, although seisin was something more than mere possession, it was possession flavoured with the right.

## Parentelic inheritance

Common law kinship provided a way of ordering kinsmen to find the nearest heir of the *propositus* (the last person who had died rightfully seised). This

---

5   For a full account of incidents see Pollock and Maitland, *History of English law*, i. 307–29.
6   Milsom, *Historical foundations*, 103.
7   Baker, *Introduction*, 223–9, 246–7.

inheritance system can be summarised by a set of rules. As given in Maitland the rules are that a living descendant excluded his own descendants;
a dead descendant was represented by his own descendants; males excluded
females of equal degree; among males of equal degree only the eldest inherited; females of equal degree inherited together; the rule of representation
overrode the preference for the male sex.[8]

The parentelic system (Maitland called it 'lineal-gradual') exhausted each
*parentela* before moving to the next one up.[9] So the deceased's descendants
should be called to the inheritance, following these rules. If they were all
dead, then the deceased's brother and his descendants should be called. If
they were all dead, then the deceased's father's brother and his descendants
should be called (this is supposing the land comes from the paternal line),
so on up the ascending line, with the ascendants themselves excluded from
the inheritance (in practice the vast majority of ascendants would be dead
ancestors anyway). In practice this system could raise difficult questions. For
example, which lines of ascendants should be chosen?[10] If the land had been
inherited, it was held that it should go back up the line it had come down,
i.e. if the land was inherited from the mother then it would ascend the
maternal line. It was less clear where the land should ascend when it was
purchased or newly acquired.

There were other possible legal patterns of inheritance in medieval
England. Gavelkind is perhaps the most well known. In Kent and several
other counties it was a pattern of landholding by which sons shared in
parage, meaning that they shared equally (although, in fact, in Kent one son
was somewhat more equal than others as the youngest son, the hearth-child,
would receive the parents' home and hearth). Gavelkind also included other
differences to the normal pattern of tenure, for example that the children of
a felon would still inherit.[11] It seems to reflect older patterns of customary
inheritance and where it was recognised as customary it could be enforced in
the king's courts. In some towns a system of ultimogeniture (inheritance by
the youngest) operated, known as Borough English. This pattern may have
had its origins in unfree tenure.[12]

In late medieval England common lawyers did not express the rules quite
so clearly as Maitland. Nor did they simplify kinship like their contemporary canonists. An example of the contemporary approach can be found
in the sections 'Of the proximity of heirs' and 'Of succession and inherit-

8  Pollock and Maitland, *History of English law*, ii. 260.
9  Ibid. ii. 297.
10  This was discussed by Maitland, ibid. ii. 297–302.
11  Ibid. ii. 271–3.
12  Ibid. ii. 279–83; Faith, 'Peasant families and inheritance customs'.

ance' in *Britton*.[13] *Britton*, a book that set out to explain the common law, was an Anglo-French translation, abridgement and updating of an earlier common law treatise, Bracton's *De legibus* (also known as *Bracton*). *Britton* was written about 1291-2.[14] The author may have been John le Bretton, a judge of Trailbaston and administrator, or possibly an anonymous clerk.[15] It was popular: approximately fifty manuscripts survive, including fragments.[16] It is an important source for the common law at the end of the thirteenth century and contains original and interesting thinking on kinship.

Several sections are concerned with the questions tried in a writ of right including central questions of inheritance and descent. The chapter 'Of proximity of heirs' tells the reader that 'inheritance is the succession of the heir to every right of which the ancestor died seised. And from inheritance [*heritage*] is derived heir [*heir*], who is the successor to every right which the ancestor had at the time of his death.'[17] This first point is telling: barring alienation inheritance was absolute; there was no testament of land. *Britton* continued that the inherited right: 'sometimes descends like a weighty body, and sometimes ascends'.[18] Typically common lawyers did not concede that a right could ascend. According to *Bracton* the right descended 'like a weight' and never re-ascended.[19] At common law the right was said to descend to children and siblings, while, if it went to any kinsman more distant, for example, to an uncle, it was said to resort. *Britton*'s statement may reflect the author's unusual view that direct ascendants could inherit or claim land, as where he suggested that a grandfather or father could use the action of cosinage based on a deceased son or daughter's seisin.[20] *Britton* defined a cousin as including those in the 'right line descending' as well as those in collateral lines.[21]

By the early thirteenth century common law kinship was systematic. The descent of the right to the correct next heir happened automatically, as shown by *Britton*'s comment that 'although the possession does not always follow the mere right, yet in the end it will return to it, if the right heir

[13] *Britton: the French text carefully revised with an English translation, introduction and notes*, ed. F. M. Nichols, Oxford 1865, ii. 310-26. All references to *Britton* will be to this edition.
[14] Ibid. i, p. xviii.
[15] Ibid. i, pp. xxi-xxii.
[16] Ibid. i, pp. xlviii-liii. See also J. H. Baker, *A catalogue of English legal manuscripts in Cambridge University Library; with codicological descriptions of the early manuscripts by J. S. Ringrose*, Woodbridge 1996, 63.
[17] *Britton*, ii. 310.
[18] Ibid.
[19] *Bracton*, ii. 184. See also A. W. B. Simpson, *A history of the land law*, 2nd edn, Oxford 1986, 57-8.
[20] *Britton*, ii. 163-4.
[21] Ibid. ii. 163. He was not alone in this understanding of who was a cousin. For the dispute surrounding this definition and its implications see pp. 107-10 below.

proceeds in a proper manner'.[22] The common law supplied remedies when possession did not follow this pattern. Since the system demanded one heir, and it was possible for a *propositus* (the landowning ancestor who died rightfully seised) to have many children, the section considered different types:

> All children however are not admissible to the inheritance, for some are natural and legitimate; and of those who are both legitimate and natural, some are sons and heirs, others sons and not heirs; and some are heirs of their fathers, some of their mothers, and some on both sides, and others are not heirs to either, although they are both legitimate and natural; and some begin by being heirs and afterwards perhaps cease to be so, and others not. And of natural and legitimate heirs, some are near and some again nearer, and some remote and others more remote ... But in all cases that person is next heir at law to whom the mere right soonest descends.[23]

The rules of the system determined the nearest heir and, from *Britton's* somewhat unsystematic analysis, it is apparent that this system was contextual. There was a hierarchy of nearness to, or remoteness from, the *propositus*, combined with a grouping which naturally classified all those in a generation as being of the same type: thus all brothers were near heirs, but the eldest was the nearest by primogeniture. *Britton* again emphasised that if the correct pattern of inheritance did not happen, between brothers for example, they could enforce their right legally. Thus, in practice, the system was potentially filtered through the possibilities of the forms of action: one brother could not use a possessory action against another and only the writ of right could try proximity between them (the forms of action are discussed further below). *Britton* implied a distinction between the operation of heirship and the law, when in practice they were deeply entangled. It was the biological (called 'natural') family and the law that were less closely entwined. *Britton's* classification strongly implied a contrast with illegitimate children. Bastards could not inherit at common law.[24] Even illegitimate brothers by the same parents were, legally, strangers to each other, as *Bracton* said: 'his bastard brother is completely foreign to him with respect to succession, though not with respect to blood relationship'.[25] It should also be noted that, while *Britton* talked of heirs as being male this was only because that was the normal pattern; daughters could and did inherit too. *Britton* began his chapter 'Of succession and the law of inheritance' with an explanation of parentelic inheritance:

> All those who first descend from the common stock [*commun cep*] from degree to degree in the direct line [*par dreite line*] for ever are lawful and true heirs;

22  Ibid. ii. 310.
23  Ibid. ii. 310–2.
24  For a more complete discussion see Brand, 'Family and inheritance'.
25  *Bracton*, ii. 76.

and when default is found in the direct line, then those who are found to be the nearest in the collateral degrees for ever are the right heirs; and lastly, when default is found in the transverse line descending, those who appear to be nearest in any transverse line ascending shall be admissible. But although the heirs so ascending for ever are lawful and right heirs, yet they are not all admissible at the same time to the succession, because the eldest, being nearest, excludes the youngest who is near, and he who is near excludes the remote, and the remote one more remote.[26]

If this description of the system seems to have some flavour of the canon and civil law systems, it is because there was a way of thinking about kinship that was shared, if only approximately. Like the learned systems there was a common parent, lines and degrees. Yet there were important differences. In *Britton*, as for other common law authors, degrees were hands the right passed through rather than a way of measuring distance. *Britton's* 'direct line' was the line of direct descendants coming from the right heir; descending transverse lines (it is implied), were where a resort was made between lines that had descended from the *propositus* (the landowning ancestor who had died rightfully seised).

*Britton's* discussion shows that this was not a corporate inheritance system (in the sense that family members other than the *propositus* did not have any right in the inheritance – not even the heir – unless explicitly granted it). In discussing the relevance of the form of the gift to finding the next heir, *Britton* had said that because land was alienable 'strangers [*estraunges persones*]' could be 'admissible to the succession in preference to the next heirs, who are excluded by the feoffors'.[27] In the early post-Conquest period heirs often affirmed their parents' gifts, suggesting that there was once a sense that family retained an interest.[28] Ultimately, however, no *retrait lignager* ever developed in England (no corporate right vested in heirs or kin allowing them to regain a parcel of sold land) . Kin members did not have residual rights over land, although they may have retained the hope of a reversion if, for example, they had made a gift of land to a collateral line. Instead there was a winner-takes-all lottery of birth order (or nearness to the *propositus*) and there were no residual rights among potential second ranks of heirs. Residual rights of a sort instead belonged to the lord, as he would have the escheat and regain the land if the line failed 'either by their blood becoming extinct, or by their right being forfeited by judgement of felony'. [29]

*Britton* went on to discuss what constituted proximity, i.e. what rules ordered who should succeed: 'to wit, sex, age, line, a partible inheritance,

[26] *Britton*, ii. 312–13.
[27] Ibid. ii. 316.
[28] J. C. Holt, 'Politics and property in early medieval England', in his *Colonial England*, 113–59 at pp. 124, 128.
[29] *Britton*, ii. 313.

plurality of female heirs, form of gift, and blood'.[30] This was more piecemeal than systematic, but showed some attempt at classification. Sex was the first issue:

> Sex, because the male is to be received and the female rejected, so long as there is a male heir apparent of the father by the same mother; but the daughter begotten on the first wife is to be preferred in the succession to the marriage [settlement] granted with her mother to the male begotten by the same father on the second wife.[31]

For *Britton*, two things could trump the powerful preference for a male heir: nearness to the *propositus* (the landowning ancestor who had died rightfully seised), expressed as the systematic preference for direct descendants over collaterals; and the origin of the right.

The second issue was age:

> Age is material; because he who is the first born is admissible before the younger son of the same father and mother . . . And if the elder brother dies without heir of his own in the lifetime of his father, the younger brother will take his place, and begin to be next heir to their common father [*commun pere*], and the other younger ones will be near; and so of those more remote, without end.[32]

Inheritance could take place at common law so long as there were heirs. The kinship system was potentially infinite. *Britton's* discussion of age also justified the rule of representation:

> if the elder brother dies in his father's lifetime, having begotten an heir, this issue remains under the authority of the grandfather, and shall be next heir to the grandfather by reason of the mere right which descended to him by the death of his father, the grandfather's son, although the son did not live to attain any estate; and the uncle or aunt [to the child] shall be only near heir, although he is one degree nearer than the grandson, who is next heir.[33]

This rule required some justification. It was not unnatural to view a younger son as having more right to his father's inheritance than a grandson. However, the hierarchical rule implied by the structure trumped the preference for nearness of generation. There had been difficulty with this problem, called the *casus regis*, whereby cases where an uncle had gained seisin and the nephew wanted to claim had been left undecided for some decades in the early thirteenth century because the courts could not hold contrary to

---

[30] Ibid.
[31] Ibid.
[32] Ibid. ii. 313–14.
[33] Ibid. ii. 314.

King John's own inheritance in preference to his nephew.[34] By *Britton's* time this had been resolved. *Britton* went on to discuss how the 'exception of proximity' would bar an uncle or aunt who tried to claim at law against the grandson, and how the grandson could always use the writ of right to recover 'by pleading his descent'.[35] The next issue was line: 'Line is material; because the daughter found in the direct line descending is to be preferred before the male found in the transverse line.'[36] Here structure trumped the preference for a male heir.

The next issue was a partible (divided) inheritance, which could occur between males where it was the accepted customary pattern: 'the younger son ... shall have as great a share as the elder; and in this case the custom of the place shall be observed'.[37] The more common partible inheritance was between sisters, and *Britton* discussed this as plurality of female heirs. Sisters 'all present themselves in the place of one heir, and no one of them is to be preferred before another, neither can one be heir to the others; for that would imply a nearer proximity in one than in another, which there is not, since they are all equally nearest'.[38] *Britton* stated that if one died the others' shares increased by accruer (i.e. not by succession); however, in practice the right was said to descend between sisters.[39]

The final issue was right of blood. *Britton* used his favourite counter-intuitive example to tell how it 'sometimes causes the female to exclude the male'.[40] In brief, *Britton* gave an example involving children by a second marriage. A man begot a son and daughter on his first wife, and a son on his second. If the eldest brother died, his full sister would be his nearest heir in preference to his half brother. *Britton* said children of the first wife could only inherit land from the second wife if it had descended to their half sibling (although this was, in fact, controversial). He also considered children born to the same mother by different fathers where the same pattern applied, and how a full blood sister would succeed to the purchase of her full-blood brother before a half-blood elder brother.[41] The inheritance rights of half-blood siblings was an area of kinship law that was still being settled in the late thirteenth century. The relative importance of factors such as seisin, method of acquisition, relatedness to the *propositus*, gender and position in the hierarchy of heirs was uncertain as the half-blood did not fit naturally into the structure of the common law kinship system.

---

[34] J. C. Holt, 'The *casus regis*: the law and politics of succession in the Plantagenet dominions, 1185–1247', in his *Colonial England*, 307–26.

[35] *Britton*, ii. 314–5.

[36] Ibid. ii. 315

[37] Ibid.

[38] Ibid.

[39] Ibid. ii. 316.

[40] Ibid.

[41] Ibid. ii. 316–19.

A series of five cases from the 1270–90s concerning half-blood siblings shed some light on this area and reveal how this confusion was shared.[42] In two cases the land in question had been acquired. In one of these the descendants of a half blood were allowed into the inheritance in preference to more distant kin. In the other the right of a full blood sibling was preferred to the half-blood kin so long as any in the full blood line survived. These different results might be attributed to the fact that in the second case there was a line of direct descendants of the full-blood sister, while in the first case the claimant full-blood kin were joined via a resort to a great-uncle. It had been accepted by this point that if the purchaser died without descendants the land would be inherited by collateral kinsmen, for preference on the paternal side.[43] Yet the grandson of a sister probably felt closer than the grandson of a great-uncle. Interestingly, in the second case it was decided that the right of a line descended from a full-blood sister barred half-blood sisters, contrary to the pattern *Britton* expected where all sisters would share equally.[44]

There were also cases where the land had been inherited. In one there was a preference for whole-blood sisters over half-blood brothers if the elder brother had gained possession; this was the rule in *Britton* too. In another it was asserted that the half-kin were allowed to succeed in absence of whole-blood kin provided that they were from the side the land had descended, but the court did not affirm or deny this. In the final case the actual decision was that half-blood kin were postponed to the full-blood kin, but it was said *obiter dicta* that even if there was no surviving descendant of 'the first branch of the family tree' (the line descending from the first wife), none of the line descending from the second wife could inherit. They could not claim by same descent 'because none of their ancestors were seised'.[45] Clearly, the law in this area was developing and changing. *Britton* captured only a moment and only an opinion. The point he made, that a half-blood could inherit before more distant relatives, was not clear.[46] Eventually the common law was to exclude the half-blood from the inheritance altogether, but in the thirteenth century this was as yet undecided.[47] This difficult area of law provides a good insight into both the lack of authority of these common law texts and into the problems common lawyers were working through at the edges of their system and structures.

*Britton* completed his section on succession with a discussion of inheritance between three full-blood brothers when a younger brother had purchased

---

[42] *The earliest English law reports*, ed. P. A Brand (Selden Society cxi, cxii, cxxii, cxxiii, 1996–2007), iv, pp. clxiv-clxvii.

[43] Ibid. iv, pp. clxvii–clxviii.

[44] *Britton*, ii. 315.

[45] *Earliest English law reports*, iv, p. clxvii.

[46] Ibid. iv, p. clxiv. See also Pollock and Maitland, *History of English law*, ii. 303–5.

[47] Pollock and Maitland, *History of English law*, ii. 302.

land and died seised. In this case: 'the eldest brother shall be his next heir, and shall exclude the father and mother, although they are nearer in blood, because the brother is found to be the nearest in the same degree, which the father and the mother are not; and he shall also exclude the other brothers and sisters, although they are found in the same degree'.[48] Whether this was often the case in practice is doubtful. However, the quotation provides an insight into *Britton's* structuring within the nuclear family, which reckoned parents to be closer in blood than siblings. Here *Britton* made the unusual statement that if all brothers and sisters and their descendants failed 'then it [the right] shall go to the common father, or if the father be dead, and no other be found in any degree nearer on his side, to the common mother and so of all the other degrees ascending'.[49] He may not have meant that any paternal kinsman no matter how distant excluded the mother, but he does seem to imply that any sibling of the father (or presumably any of his descendants) would. The preference for paternal kinsmen was stronger than the generational preference in this speculative example. Inheritance by the parents was not the usual common law pattern.

*Britton* promised a figure: 'In what manner the degrees branch out will appear by the following tree of kindred [*l'arbre de parentee*]'.[50] In the next chapter, 'Of degrees of kindred', the author went on to discuss the degrees with reference to a 'figure'. *Britton* was unusual among common law authors in promising and describing such a tree, or indeed any formal image of common law kinship at all.[51]

Common law texts from the thirteenth century that discussed parentelic kinship in any detail did so in a meandering, contextual manner; however, their contents were clear enough to be understood. The structure was developing and changing, particularly at the edges. Notably, of all the issues which decided proximity, the dictates of the kinship structure were among the most important, overriding even the preference for the male sex.

The common law at this time was not so much a law of books (when compared with the canon law). Within *Britton* there was a somewhat uneasy mingling of theory (the underlying structure and rules) and the need to be able to apply this in practice (the repetition of which form of action could be used to enforce which point, and the shaping of the discussion of the structures of kinship around a count of descent). The common law kinship system was at heart a series of rules for finding the nearest heir, but it was closely tied to the patterns of actions and the rules as to which action could be used in what circumstances. There were other sections in *Britton* that touched

---

[48] *Britton*, ii. 319.

[49] Ibid. ii. 319–20.

[50] Ibid. ii. 320.

[51] For these unusual trees, which were heavily influenced by the canon law model, as they appear in manuscripts of *Britton* see pp. 78–80 below.

on kinship, explanations of the actions of mort d'ancestor and cosinage, as well as the underlying structures that were enforced with the writ of right.[52]

## Origins

The fundamentals of the parentelic pattern of inheritance were well established by the early thirteenth century, but they had been less clear before. In post-Conquest England heritability could not necessarily be taken for granted. During the development of the common law there was a pattern of inheritance among a limited kin, if not the full parentelic system.[53] The Normans came to England 'accustomed to inheritance', but the fact of the Conquest, which meant that all land was essentially (or theoretically) granted, meant that inheritance could be less certain.[54] If land was a gift from a lord for service the heir was not automatically entitled; the different claims and justifications of the lord and the heir can be seen poetically in the French chanson *Raoul de Cambrai*.[55] However, inheritance was the normal pattern for passing on land at death, and close heirs usually gained the inheritance, although lords retained discretion, for example if the heir was unsuitable. More distant heirs were more likely to have problems, and, among the higher nobility, the vagaries of politics may have mitigated against certainty or system.[56] John Hudson constructs a categorisation of close and distant heirs in this context that is revealing. He draws a pattern from cases that shows grandchildren, brothers and sisters 'generally succeeded', and nephews and nieces 'often' succeeded, although at, and after, that point succession was less certain.[57] This is not a large group, and it is not clear from the case evidence that the parentelic system was operating systematically in twelfth-century England. Nor was the kinship system originally and entirely a legal beast. The system that identified an heir was a set of social norms, the development of which was closely linked to the emerging legal system,[58] probably inextricably so in the enforcement of inheritance by more distant collaterals.

---

[52] *Britton*, ii. 52–64, 162–8.

[53] J. Hudson, *Land, law, and lordship in Anglo-Norman England*, Oxford 1994, especially chs iii, iv.

[54] Holt, 'Politics and property', 115. On Norman inheritance patterns see idem, 'Feudal society and the family in early medieval England, II: notions of patrimony', in his *Colonial England*, 197–221 at p. 208.

[55] S. D. White, 'The discourse of inheritance in twelfth-century France: alternative models of the fief in *Raoul de Cambrai*', in G. Garnett and J. Hudson (eds), *Law and government in medieval England and Normandy: essays in honour of Sir James Holt*, Cambridge 1994, 173–97. For a review of the ideas of legal historians about the tension between inheritance and homage see also J. Biancalana, 'For want of justice: legal reforms of Henry II', *Columbia Law Review* lxxxviii/1 (1988), 433–536 at pp. 487–90.

[56] Holt, 'Politics and property', 129.

[57] Hudson, Land, law, and lordship, 109, 114.

[58] Holt, 'Notions of patrimony', 219.

Thus in the early post-Conquest period 'de facto succession' turned into 'de jure inheritance'.[59]

In 1187–9 the 'Treatise on the laws and customs of the realm of England commonly called Glanvill' was written, probably by a clerk in the king's court or possibly by a justice.[60] Magister Godfrey de Lucy has been suggested as a strong candidate. It has also been hazarded that the current text might be a series of treatises by several authors, brought together and polished.[61] The learned author was very knowledgeable about the workings of the royal court and was educated (he apologised for writing his text in plain language, in implied contrast to the civil law). He based his prologue on the preface to the *Institutes* of Justinian, emphasising the role of the king.[62] This was the law of the king's courts. It was relatively popular: more than thirty manuscripts survive today.[63]

*Glanvill's* section on inheritance detailed the order of heirs and shows that by this point the parentelic system was developing, although not yet fully fixed.[64] *Glanvill* wrote that heirs could be nearest or more remote. The near heirs were the heirs of a man's body: his sons and daughters. The more remote heirs were their lineal descendants *ad infinitum*. Following them, the brother and sister were called to the inheritance, with the people descending from them collaterally; then the uncle on the father's side and on the mother's side and aunts likewise and their descendants.[65] This does seem to be the core of the parentelic system, but there were ambiguities. For example, it does not seem that the rule that a dead descendent was represented by his descendants had been settled. This can be seen in *Glanvill's* discussion of the problem behind the *casus regis*.[66] The common law would eventually hold that the younger son would inherit, but this caused legal problems for at least two generations after King John and the Chief Justice had gained their land by alternate inheritance patterns.[67] These problems may be mainly a consequence of the exercise of royal power in a particular instance, but the result where a younger son was preferred to a grandson was not *outré*. In fact there were pressures in favour of the 'hearth child' (the younger son) even

---

[59] Idem, 'Feudal society and the family in early medieval England, I: the revolution of 1066', in his *Colonial England*, 161–78 at p. 174.

[60] *The treatise on the laws and customs of the realm of England commonly called Glanvill*, ed., intro., notes and trans. G. D. G. Hall; guide to further reading M. T. Clanchy, Oxford 1993, pp. xxx–xxxiii.

[61] R. V. Turner, 'Who was the author of *Glanvill*? Reflections on the education of Henry II's common lawyers', *Law and History Review* viii:i (1990), 97–127.

[62] *Glanvill*, p. xxxvi.

[63] Ibid. p. xl.

[64] Ibid. at p. 184 *per* Hall.

[65] Ibid. VII. 3 at p. 75.

[66] Ibid. at pp. 77–8

[67] Holt, 'The *casus regis*'.

in the late thirteenth century.[68] This issue implies a view of the generations as steps, and it is not difficult to see why a younger son/brother would view himself as having a greater right to his father's land than a grandson. The author's comment that only God made an heir suggests that the process of selecting one was inscrutable, yet this was clearly a 'system' in development.[69] But it does seem apparent that a version of the *parentela* structure was in existence before the inheritance of close heirs was quite decided.

Once primogeniture was accepted as the normal pattern of inheritance, the parentelic system may not have been so difficult to extend. Primogeniture meant that one heir received the land. They were immediately made distinctive; a hierarchy of brothers was implied that could extend very easily to the more distant lines. If, on failure of the eldest son, the younger son got all, it is not such a great leap that on the failure of all a man's sons, his father's younger son should get all. The question of representation (for example whether the child of a deceased elder son should stand in his place and thus inherit before a younger son) and the role of women were obviously more difficult.

Primogeniture was not, on the face of it, a fair system or one that parents would necessarily desire. Prior to the Conquest land in England seems to have been shared in some system of parage between co-heirs and on the continent Norman inheritance came to favour a system of parage.[70] Custom in some English counties, such as Kent, continued to favour shared inheritance. Frequent *inter-vivos* gifts testified to parents' desire to establish their other children. Examples of the kind of settlements people made to mitigate the effects of primogeniture and establish their children were gifts in *maritagia*, a category which included gifts in frankmarriage, or entails. Such gifts were sometimes made by parents on the marriage of a younger child to establish the couple in a household. They meant that the initial donees, often family members, did not have to perform services or give homage and could not sell the land. These gifts appear to have been regarded as limited in scope, for example as conditional gifts, and there was initially dispute about how far inalienability and absence of services extended.[71]

In the classical feudal sense land was not only a matter of property rights and wealth, but was also a matter of force, lordship and manpower. The system, at least in the first generations post-Conquest, began with lordship at a time when lords wanted to reward or gain the service of fighting men. For example, Henry I once intervened in a descent to put in a half-blood

---

[68] *Earliest English law reports*, iv, pp. clxii–clxiv.

[69] *Glanvill*, VII.1 at p. 71.

[70] F. W. Maitland, *Domesday book and beyond: three essays in the early history of England*, London 1969, 182; Holt, 'Politics and property', 148.

[71] J. Biancalana, *The fee tail and the common recovery in medieval England, 1176–1502*, Cambridge 2001.

who was 'a better knight'.[72] Primogeniture and preference for the male heir was the pattern most likely to guarantee fit fighting men. By the thirteenth century this may seem very much like a just-so story, for by that time the rights of the lord had retreated to a great extent. Incidents such as wardship and marriage and the payment of relief that allowed the heir to enter the land when he came to his inheritance (a fixed sum rather than a service) no longer had the same flavour and, like homage, had become more of an expression of a bundle of economic rights than any personal connection. Rights of inheritance had become so extensive that the land only returned to the lord 'for want of any other direction in which it can go'.[73] The world had changed, but the fundamentals of the common law kinship system, such as primogeniture, had been frozen in a feudal age. Ironically, female inheritance was initially by a single female heiress, a rule which appears to have been deliberately altered to the Norman model of parcenery in about 1130–5. There were practical reasons for this, most obviously the access to a portion of land it allowed to all heiresses' husbands.[74]

The canon law kinship system was universal in the sense that it was church law; parts were even divine law. This was not the case for the common law kinship system. It did not, for example, apply where individuals held by gavelkind, Borough English or such types of traditional tenure. Indeed, King John caused hesitation around the rule of representation (that a child of an elder brother would stand to inherit the patrimony before a younger son). The common law kinship system was bound up with particular tenures and thus need not have applied beyond them (for example, the king need not have followed the system). That it was, by and large, followed must reflect the importance of the system as a set of social norms. The common law kinship system was, at its core, the practice of a social class, regularised and extended by the operation of the legal system and legal thinkers. The relationship between law and norm in this area is delicate. It is reasonable to see the structure as polished and systemised out from several basic shared concepts, the most fundamental of which was primogeniture. Although many landowning parents wanted to provide for their other children too, the dynamics of power and pride, closely tied to land in this period, and the pressure to conform and consolidate the family's position, were overall powerful drivers to retain whole patrimonies and, as a consequence, hierarchies of heirs.

Kinship was not limited to structures. The rules around bastards were among the most important aspects of everyday disputes about family at common law. The common law also recognised the affine, although in a limited sense. A widow had right to dower and a widower, who had fathered

---

[72] Holt, 'Politics and property', 124.

[73] *Britton*, ii. 313.

[74] Holt, 'The heiress and the alien', 251–5.

live children on his wife, had the right to curtesy.[75] These claims on land lasted only a lifetime and can be viewed as existing over the underlying, fundamental kinship structures, but in practice they were very important.

## Kinship in practice: inheritance and actions

Ideally, parentelic inheritance operated automatically, presided over by the lord. When the tenant died the lord could take possession if he were first on the scene, although if the heir was resident with the *propositus* (the land-owning ancestor) he could take possession (a right that was included in the Assize of Northampton of 1176). If the lord was in first he could hold the land until he was certain of the right heir, that is until he had found the heir who was nearest and of age, and until the heir had offered homage, fealty and surety of the relief that he had to pay.[76] The precise procedures for discovering the nearest heir remain vague. Presumably if the lord and tenant had had an enduring relationship the matter ought to have been easy. Yet the many cases where one kinsman challenged the right of another show that the system did not always operate perfectly. In other cases some investigation or inquest was involved. The case of *John the son of Wigan de Cherbourg Senior* v. *Nicholas de la Huse and Others*, in 1289, mentions that the king 'like every other chief lord, after the death of his tenant had the said enquiry taken *ex officio*'.[77] This implies that an enquiry process was normal enough, although in that instance it may not have reached the right answer as the tenant settled the case. That other lords at lower levels followed the same process, or some echo of the same process, is probable. Disputed cases that reached the courts were a minority. Unfair or not, the system was regular enough that it worked.

If an inheritance was disputed the claimant could go to the king's courts to attempt to make and enforce that claim. Access to the king's courts required the purchase of a writ from the Chancery (although there were other, less formal routes). Initially a response to disputing parties' requests to the king for aid, writs became formalised and regularised and the common law grew around them – around the possibilities that this means of access provided and the questions that they raised.[78] The language of the writs limited what enquiries were possible, although lawyerly inventiveness, sophisticated pleading and special exceptions widened the range.

---

[75] See further Brand, 'Family and inheritance'.

[76] Idem, *Kings, barons and justices: the making and enforcement of legislation in thirteenth-century England*, Cambridge 2003, 55.

[77] *Earliest English law reports*, iv. 438.

[78] R. C. Van Caenegem, *The birth of the English common law*, 2nd edn, Cambridge 1988, esp. ch. ii.

The courts where these issues could be tried were the King's Bench and the Common Bench. A central royal court had sat, with some interruptions, since the time of Henry II.[79] There were also itinerant justices who travelled in circuits to the regions. Such a visit was known as an eyre. The general eyres periodically visited the counties, bringing royal justice. Since the eyre circuit could be lengthy, special justices could be commissioned to take assizes in between times; this was regularised during the thirteenth century into a system known as the 'assizes'.[80] By early in the reign of Edward III, the gap between eyres was so long that the peripatetic King's Bench and the Common Bench based in Westminster had become more important as a source of royal justice.[81]

These courts were not deliberately given the wide jurisdiction now regarded as familiar. Communal justice was absorbed and feudal justice became a paper matter through accidents of demand. Most land law matters ought rightly, originally, to have been decided in a lord's feudal court. It was a provision in Magna Carta that writs of right for land should be considered in the king's court 'only if the immediate lord had waived his court or had failed to do justice'.[82] At the beginning of the thirteenth century there was a fear that the royal courts would encroach too far on this feudal jurisdiction. It was proved correct. There should be no surprise in this, since a clause allowing the case to be moved to the royal court if the lord had failed to do justice surely encouraged claimants to take another shot at winning the case, or to take their case to what could be considered a more effective forum. The lord's court ceased to have real power. The writ of right patent, which had been intended to make the lord's courts investigate a claimant's right, required the case to be removed from the lord's court through mechanisms known as tolt and pone. It was cumbersome and went out of use. It was replaced by a writ of right brought because the lord had waived his court ('quia dominus remisit curam suam'), and by the more attractive possessory writs and the writ of entry where they suited the matter.[83] If, where there was no customary opt out, any lord's court had been inclined not to follow the parentelic pattern (which seems unlikely as inheritance was also a matter of social convention), the logical extension of inheritance and the kinship system as enforced by the common law would soon have become regular by these means.

One of the reasons for the apparent disjunction between the kinship structures in the legal literature and those recited in court was the role of writs in the piecemeal development of the common law. In a dispute, someone

---

[79] Baker, *Introduction*, 18–20.
[80] Ibid. 20–2.
[81] Ibid. 20.
[82] Magna Carta 1215 cl 34: ibid. 22.
[83] Ibid. 229–37.

had first to buy a writ to initiate the case.[84] Writs determined access to the king's courts and shaped the possible actions. Some actions were more final than others and actions had different procedures, costs, delays, methods of pleading, essoins (valid reasons for non-appearance), exceptions, availabilities of warranties, etc. For the litigant, choosing a form of action was not merely a consideration of which one fitted: he (or she) and his lawyer would also have to act tactically. Writs *de cursu* (the writs 'of course' which initiated cases in the king's courts) were purchased from the Chancery, where they were written and sealed. From the time of Edward I senior Chancery clerks advised the litigants on which writs to buy.[85] The writ would 'invariably' be addressed to the sheriff; it 'authorised the initiation of proceedings' in the appropriate court.[86] Some writs were returnable, meaning that the sheriff had to send them to court with a report on the action that he had taken. The writ gave the justices jurisdiction, but, because the king's courts were initially extraordinary, the justices' jurisdiction was bound by the writ, hence the wording of the writ and its agreement with the plaintiff's count were fundamentally important.[87]

Some writs and actions were more likely to raise issues of kinship than others. The most fundamental context for the application of parentelic kinship was where the heir's right was at issue, such as in a case arising from a writ of right (the fundamental writ of the common law). The discussion of common law kinship in *Britton* was founded around the assumption that the claimant would be counting descent in a writ of right. Other writs, however, also led to cases where parentelic kinship was applied and one class of possessory actions developed over time that were inextricably bound with common law kinship patterns: the possessory assizes that developed from the action of mort d'ancestor.

The writ of right tried who had the right to land. The claimant in such a case would found their claim on a connection to the *propositus*: the last landowning relative who had died rightfully seised and in possession (the writ could also found claims based on the claimant's own right, or on the right of a vendor). In court the plaintiff would assert that they or their ancestor had been seised in demesne as of fee, meaning that they asserted their right and their seisin. A descent from the ancestor would be traced to the plaintiff (this was called a count of descent), which needed to show that the plaintiff was the nearest living heir of the *propositus*. The issue put to the jury was, at its most basic, the defendant's blank denial of the plaintiff's right. Plain-

---

[84] This chapter will not explore the less formal methods of access such as bills and plaints.

[85] D. A. Carpenter, 'The English royal chancery in the thirteenth century', in K. Fianu and D. J. Guth (eds.) *Écrit et pouvoir dans le chancelleries médiévales: espace Français, espace Anglais*, Louvain 1997, 25–53 at p. 35.

[86] Baker, *Introduction*, 54.

[87] There were also other kinds of writs, for example judicial writs.

tiffs could only use the writ of right within certain time limits.[88] Because of its finality, it was slow, cumbersome and expensive, with many delays and advantages to the defendant.[89] There were two main modes of proof between non-related litigants: battle, although this was already a 'ghost' by the time of Edward I; and a type of jury known as the grand assize.[90] Between kinsmen, battle and the grand assize were not possible as neither could wholly deny the other's right, so their claims were tried by a reckoning of the descent. The records of claims via writs of right are full of pedigrees. Knowledge of kinship structures would have been vital for a common lawyer.

Mort d'ancestor and the related writs arising from it were more expedient for litigants. They were thus popular and very important for common law kinship law. They were a class of actions to claim seisin (possession) only, designed to be used by specific kinsmen of a *propositus* (the landowner who had died seised). Mort d'ancestor was created by Henry II, probably at the Assize of Northampton in 1176.[91] Initially the action was quick and cheap. It was meant to be a solution to recent wrongs against property. It was a claim for seisin of the land based on the seisin of a restricted range of close kinsmen: parents, uncles, aunts and siblings. It was limited to the close family where the norms of inheritance were clear, so it did not even extend to the grandfather's seisin.[92] The action had to be within time limits, and specific questions were asked of the jury: had the ancestor been 'seised as of fee [i.e. hereditarily] and in his demesne [i.e. directly exploited by him and not handed to another tenant or vassal]' at the time of their death or going on crusade or entry into a monastery?[93] And was the claimant the nearest heir? It was not permitted between litigants of the same blood.

Over time the pressure to extend the possessory actions to a wider group of kinsmen was powerful. Some time in the 1230s the actions of cosinage and aiel were created to allow claims based on the seisin of more distant (but still relatively close) ancestors or kinsmen who had died seised. Cosinage was a claim for seisin of the land of a dead 'cousin', similar in some respects to mort d'ancestor, but with some variations. For example it was in the form of writ

---

[88] P. Brand, "Time out of mind': the knowledge and use of the eleventh- and twelfth-century past in thirteenth-century litigation', *Anglo-Norman Studies* xvi (1993), 37–54 esp. pp. 37–44, 54. Legislation in 1237 excluded claims based on seisin prior to 1154; legislation in 1275 excluded claims based on seisin prior to 1189.

[89] For a different explanation of the development of the writ see Pollock and Maitland, *History of English law*, ii. 62–3, 77; cf. Milsom, *Historical foundations*, 124–34. On the process see also S. F. C. Milsom, 'Legal introduction', in *Novae narrationes*, ed. E. Shanks, completed with a legal introduction by S. F. C. Milsom (Selden Society lxxx, 1963), pp. xxx–ccxiv at pp. xxxi–xxxix.

[90] See Pollock and Maitland, *History of English law*, ii. 632. Battle was, however, offered in a criminal case in 1818.

[91] Ibid. i. 138.

[92] Biancalana, 'For want of justice', 484–514 at pp. 486, 507–8.

[93] Van Caenegem, *Birth of the English common law*, 47.

*praecipe quod reddat* and had various procedural differences: there were no pre-set questions for an assize jury, and a continued default (failure to appear or make good previous defaults) by the tenant led to judgement by default not verdict in absence. In a case where the tenant continually defaulted the land would be awarded to the plaintiff and the tenant would have to begin a new action by writ of right to regain the land.[94] The limits on this action may initially have been very wide. A note in the collection of cases known as *Bracton's note book* says that the justice William of Raleigh created the action of cosinage in 1237 (although the earliest known writ is from 1235).[95] William of Raleigh is also a good candidate for authorship of *Bracton*; it has been suggested that he 'played a major part in the production' of the composite text.[96] The treatise *Bracton* said that cosinage lay on the death of the grandfather (a claim for seisin based on the entitlement and seisin of a dead grandparent was later to be called aiel), was available to cousins ascending to a *tritavus* (great-great-great-great-grandfather), and descending to a *trinepos* (great-great-great-great-grandson), and could go beyond those bounds if the time limit permitted.[97] These were not the kinsmen who could use cosinage according to later case law. *Bracton* was written in the 1220s and revised and edited up to the 1230s, so the cosinage section may have been a late addition, written while the action was still being explored and designed. Later law showed conflict about the limits of the kin who could claim by this action.[98] Some set the limits very narrowly, not allowing claims by kinsmen linked beyond the grandparents or great-grandparents.[99] Over time there was pressure to extend this and eventually the action was to extend to kinsmen related through a great-great-grandfather. The other possessory actions for specific kin were also extended. Initially, possessory actions could also be mixed in nature. *Bracton* gave an example where a *propositus* had two daughters, one of whom died leaving a son, who then joined with his aunt to claim seisin of his grandfather's (and her father's) land. The author said that this action combined mort d'ancestor (for the daughter) and cosinage (for the

---

94 Brand, *Kings, barons and justices*, 55.

95 *Bracton's note book: a collection of cases decided in the king's courts during the reign of Henry III, annotated by a lawyer of that time, seemingly by Henry of Bratton*, ed. F. W. Maitland, London 1887, iii. 1215. On the earliest known writ see Brand, *Kings, barons and justices*, 54 n. 43.

96 P. Brand, 'The age of Bracton', in J. Hudson (ed.), *The history of English law: centenary essays on 'Pollock and Maitland'*, Oxford 1996, 65–89 at pp. 78–9.

97 *Bracton*, iii. 250–1, 283, 318.

98 Brand, *Kings, barons and justices*, 54 n. 45. For an overview see Milsom 'Legal introduction', pp. cxvii–cxix.

99 'E le bref de Cosinage ne passe nient le Ael; e au frere e la soer iekes al ael est le bref bon, e sil passe donkes est le bref abatable': 'Fet Asaver', in G. E. Woodbine, *Four thirteenth century law tracts: a thesis presented to the faculty of the Graduate School of Yale University in candidacy for the degree of doctor of philosophy*, New Haven 1910, 53–115 at p. 99.

grandson).[100] The earliest known writ based on aiel is from 1239;[101] later still, the action of besaiel allowed a claim based on the seisin of a great-grandparent. It is not certain exactly when besaiel was created, although it was well established under Edward I,[102] and was mentioned in the Statutes of Gloucester c.1 (1278) and II Westminster c.20 (1285). There were also some cases where a writ was based on the seisin of a *proavus* or *proavia* (using a special writ) from 1287 to 1288.[103]

What happened once a claim reached court depended partly upon the case, but a frequent element in claims founded on a kinsman's right and seisin was the necessity to make a count of descent to link the claimant to that person. Only mort d'ancestor was based on such a restricted range of kinsmen that a count as such was not necessary (or, at least, not recorded on the plea rolls). Getting the count right was of vital importance: it was part of the foundation of the claim. If the claimant made a mistake and omitted someone who should have been included in the count he could lose that action and, if he was using the writ of right, be barred from future actions.

There were many other claims at common law that involved pedigrees. A pedigree could be recited in court in almost any action in which the tenant who had died rightfully siesed could be a kinsman. The plaintiff (or a representative) and the original writ had to appear in court. Then the defendant (or a representative) had to appear. This could take some while; there were whole hierarchies of essoins potentially available. Both could employ representatives and through them the plaintiff would make his count (*narratio*), which was a statement of his case; the defendant would reply with a plea (*placitum*); the plaintiff would reply, and pleading would continue until an issue was reached. The process of pleading could be long and complex and most of it did not appear on the record (in the rolls), although it did come to be reported in year books. Pleading has been described as 'lightning chess'.[104] Lawyers (known as *narratores* or pleaders, later called serjeants) advanced tentative pleas, 'not legal arguments but formulaic statements of fact on which the party relied', which were discussed and dismissed and could be withdrawn.[105] Only very rarely did a court decide on an issue of law. This required a *demurrer*, effectively an admission of the facts, and was a very dangerous tactic.[106] Instead, the lawyers played their game of pleading until they reached a triable 'issue' that could be put to the jury.

---

[100] *Bracton*, iii. 250.

[101] Brand, *Kings, barons and justices*, 54 n. 43.

[102] Milsom, 'Legal introduction', p. cxvii.

[103] CP 40/69, mm. 8, 50d, 64d, 113d; CP 40/70, m. 62d; CP 40/75, m.9d. My thanks to Paul Brand for providing me with these references.

[104] J. H. Baker, 'Case-law in medieval England', repr. in his *The common law tradition: lawyers, books and the law*, London 2000, 133–64 at p. 162.

[105] Ibid. 135.

[106] Ibid. 161.

A typical example of a count of descent, as recorded in the plea roll, is from a writ of right case in 1280:

> They says [*sic*] that one Godwin, the ancestor of the said Isabel, was seized of the said tenements in time of peace and in the reign of the lord king Richard, the kinsman of the present lord king, as of fee and right, receiving profits to the value etc. From the same Godwin the right descended to one Edmund as son and heir; and from the same Edmund to one William as son and heir; and from the same William, because he died without an heir of his body, the right descended to one Adam as brother and heir; and from the same Adam to one John as son and heir; and from the same John, because he died without an heir of his body, the right descended to this Isabel and to Christine, her sister, as sisters and heirs; and from the same Christine, because she died etc., the right of her purparty descended to the same Isabel as sister and heir.[107]

The right and seisin of the *propositus* was set out, and the claimant was connected to the *propositus* step by step. Following some questions of jurisdiction, the defendants denied Godwin's right and seisin and attempted to put themselves on the grand assize (jury). The plantiffs replied that there could not be a grand assize between them because they were kinsmen and recited this descent. The defendants offered an alternative count. In fact, according to the record of this case, the details of the pedigree were explored at least three times. The eventual issue was the choice between competing computations of descent, although no result was recorded.[108] In general, counts could be challenged on several fronts including omitting a person or people who should have been included, or when the defendant could offer an alternative account of the kindred. Counts could also be challenged if the descent differed from the writ, for example if someone claimed by a writ of cosinage when rightly they should have used a writ of mort d'ancestor.[109] Counts of descent were a weapon for a skilful pleader to use to shape the eventual question that would determine the outcome of the case.

Once issue was reached, the jury would be summoned, or the issue would go to a jury in the county, which would establish the facts and make the decision. Their thinking, reasons or what kind of evidence they typically relied upon, are unknown, too often obscured in their blank verdicts, as recorded in the plea rolls. Judgement was 'merely the formal decision as to whether the plaintiff succeeded'.[110]

---

[107]  *Earliest English law reports*, iv. 576.
[108]  Ibid. iv. 574–7.
[109]  *Year books of the reign of King Edward the first: years XXX and XXXI*, ed. and trans. A. J. Horwood, London 1863, 98, no. 2.
[110]  Baker, 'Case-law', 135. Any further procedures would also be recorded on the plea roll.

## Education and kinship in books

The reports, principally in the year books, show lawyers formally expressing the way in which facts could be manipulated to fit the actions and pleas available. Such technical tricks, often driven by the litigants' desire for victory, were part of the 'common learning' of the legal profession.[111] Common lawyers were an interest group that shared a common learning and method of practice that belonged distinctly to the common law. There was a group of common lawyers and justices that can be called professional by the early 1220s.[112] The beginning of legal education for fledgling common lawyers was closely linked to the development of a profession of common lawyers and justices, and the increasing scope and activity of the common law courts.[113] Common lawyers were educated in a manner very different from canonists and civilians. Their education was based around apprenticeship to the bench and attendance in court. There was a 'crib' – an enclosure for apprentices – in the Common Bench early in the reign of Edward II.[114] Apprentices attended court, listened to cases and took notes. There was a whole genre of records of arguments about pleading (the year books), many of which seem to have been written by apprentices. Occasionally the judges directed an explanation explicitly at the learners.[115] These reports often show a sophisticated legal understanding, for example in finding the key arguments of a case, although different reporters could be interested in different points. In addition some sporadic lecture series survive.[116] A number of the better-known short treatises on aspects of the common law are of a length and format that might reflect lectures and some treatises may reflect students' or teachers' notes, or aggregations of such notes from lectures.[117]

Common law kinship structures, as with so much else, would have been absorbed via a practical learning process, through the powerful filter of observing the actions. This perhaps explains why written discussions of

---

[111] Idem, *The Oxford history of the laws of England*, VI: *1483–1558*, Oxford 2003, 467–72. Although the concept as Baker discusses it is from a later period, and is rooted in the moots and lectures of later legal education, the idea of a shared 'common learning' based on discussion and attendance at court, between the very small numbers of increasingly professional justices and serjeants is appealing for the late thirteenth and early fourteenth centuries too.

[112] Brand, *Origins*, 55.

[113] Ibid. See also idem, 'Courtroom and schoolroom: the education of lawyers in England prior to 1400', in his *The making of the common law*, London 1992, 57–75. See also J. S. Beckerman, 'Law-writing and law teaching: treatise evidence of the formal teaching of English law in the late thirteenth century', and P. Brand, 'Legal education in England before the Inns of Court', in J. A. Bush and A. Wijffels (eds), *Learning the law: teaching and the transmission of law in England, 1150–1900*, London 1999, 33–50, 51–84.

[114] Brand, 'Courtroom and schoolroom', 60, and 'Legal education', 62–4.

[115] Baker, 'Case-law', 146 n. 62; Brand, 'Courtroom and schoolroom', 61 n. 15.

[116] Brand, 'Courtroom and schoolroom', 61–3, and 'Legal education', 66–7.

[117] Beckerman, 'Law-writing and law teaching', 36–8.

common law kinship can seem to be dominated by the structures of the actions rather than the underlying structures themselves. Yet books were not unimportant to common law education (and thus to common law kinship). *Britton*, for example, promised an illustration of his kinship section explicitly to help apprentices ('en eyde des prentiz').[118] Such big texts did not, however, play a sustained and formal role in learning and many seem to have been owned by experts, probably for personal interest, reference and as status symbols. Common law kinship, discussed in a formal structured context, is found in two types of text: short treatises and *Summae* (in contrast with collections and records of reports where it can be seen on a case by case basis).

Short common law treatises, in general, did not contain much evidence of underlying common law kinship structures, focusing instead on the practicalities of the legal system. The second half of the thirteenth century saw the creation of a number of such treatises and collections (often based on writs or procedure), many of which can be associated with education. They often included discussions, or cases, which illustrated which kinsmen could use claims of limited descent, such as cosinage, rather than explaining the parentelic system. An example is the *Modus componendi brevia*, a short Latin treatise, written in about 1285.[119] Unlike *Britton* it did not contain a section on common law kinship, but it did discuss the actions. First the author detailed those deaths on which mort d'ancestor could be brought. Then he explained that, if several people shared the heritage, one in a more remote degree could plead so long as the other was among the relatives who could bring mort d'ancestor. Then he discussed claims on the seisin of a grandfather (aiel) or great-grandfather (besaiel). Finally, he discussed claims based on the seisin of a cousin (cosinage).[120] This hierarchy of actions was typical for practical discussions which touch on common law kinship. Other short treatises included a little such similar law.[121]

Much of the kinship discussed so far has been predicated on the explanations used in the big books of the common law which attempted to be comprehensive. One of the most important is *Bracton* (*De legibus et consuetudinibus Angliæ*), which was an impressive attempt to summarise the common law at an early stage of its development. It is a massive text. The modern edition, with translation and textual analysis, runs to four hefty volumes.[122] It is not unusual for the manuscripts to consist of more than 300 folios so

---

[118] *Britton*, ii. 323.

[119] 'Modus componendi brevia', in *Four thirteenth century law tracts*, 143–62. For a discussion of the date and context see Brand, 'Courtroom and schoolroom', 64.

[120] 'Modus componendi brevia', 147–8.

[121] 'Fet Asaver', 100. See also *Brevia placitata*, ed. G. J. Turner, completed with additions by T. F. T. Plucknett (Selden Society lxvi, 1951), 179, and *Casus placitorum and reports of cases in the king's courts, 1272–1278*, ed. and intro. W. Huse Dunham, Jr. (Selden Society lxix, 1952), 9/39, 19/83, 23/6, 24/46.

[122] The introduction and textual analysis occupies the whole first volume.

it would have been an expensive and time-consuming text to produce.[123] Today, more than fifty manuscripts survive, written between about 1250 and 1350, with most clustered around 1300.[124] They encompass an impressive amount of textual variation. The annotations, changes, interpolations and updatings (apparently done by knowledgeable scribes, probably lawyers and judges) reflect the popularity and practical importance of this book, as do later adaptations such as Gilbert of Thornton's *Summa*, *Fleta* and *Britton*. It was originally believed, due to manuscript attributions, that the Justiciar Henry of Bratton (Justice of the King's Bench, 1247–57, d. 1268) wrote *De legibus* some time in the 1250s.[125] This is no longer the general view (although the name *Bracton* is used as a convenient shorthand). Samuel Thorne, in his excellent edition, dated the original to some time in the late 1220s or early 1230s, and makes it clear that Henry de Bratton was not the author.[126] (The first record that the text was in circulation comes from 1278, so it seems possible that *De legibus* was not in circulation before 1268 when Henry of Bratton died.[127]) The treatise, within which there are layers of revision and editing, seems to have been written in the early 1220s by a clerk in the service of Martin of Pateshull, then revised over thirty years or so by a succession of clerks in the service of William of Raleigh (one of Pateshull's clerks who went on to a distinguished legal career), before being edited.[128] Raleigh is a 'plausible author'.[129] Henry of Bratton himself was probably one of the revisers and editors.

When examining English legal kinship systems, *Bracton* is a vital source: it was the first common law text to articulate a wide and relatively developed common law kinship system. It is not, however, the only source for the common law in the first half of the thirteenth century, nor is it always the most reliable. It can be idiosyncratic and argumentative and it was certainly often influenced by civil law ideas and frameworks. Still, in the late thirteenth century it continued to be a useful text: in 1294 Chief Justice Mettingham told a lawyer to look to his *Bracton*.[130] The kinship structures it contains were presented in a planned, literary way, and with a complete-

---

[123] For Woodbine's description see *Bracton*, i. 5–20.

[124] Baker, *Introduction*, 176. For a list of the manuscripts see *Bracton*, i. 5–20, *per* Woodbine, and Baker, *Catalogue*, 68.

[125] For example Pollock and Maitland, *History of English law*, i. 206–7.

[126] When the treatise does mention decided cases it almost exclusively uses those of Pateshull (retired 1229) and Raleigh (retired 1239). Its final, dateable instance is from the mid 1250s. The various manuscripts have been heavily annotated after their first draft: *Bracton*, iii, pp. xxviii–xxx *per* Thorne; cf. J. L. Barton, 'The mystery of Bracton', *Journal of Legal History* xiv (1993), 1–142. Thorne's dating is now generally accepted: Brand, 'Age of Bracton', 66–73.

[127] Brand, 'Age of Bracton', 87.

[128] *Bracton*, iii, pp. xxx–xxxi *per* Thorne.

[129] Brand, 'Age of Bracton', 78–9.

[130] Idem, 'Courtroom and schoolroom', 73.

ness that no single case can show. It explained parentelic inheritance and how to make a count of descent. The section devoted to kinship in *Bracton*, however, is difficult to read and use. It borrowed heavily from the model of civil law kinship in Justinian's *Institutes* and possibly also from the visual image of the *arbor consanguinitatis*. There are confusions and conceptual difficulties that make it a difficult model for the detail of common law kinship.

*Bracton's* discussion of inheritance and his vision of the scope and certainty of the parentelic system were much more fully developed and extended than *Glanvill's* had been. Within the relevant sections, 'Degrees of kinship and succession' and 'Of those who ought to succeed others and the order of succession', the author began by noting the various *parentela* of kinsmen, above, below and in the collateral line, and by defining some terms.[131] He then detailed who would be in the ascending line, and mirrored this with a discussion of the descending line. He elaborated who would succeed in various situations. For example, when all the heirs in the right line had failed the land would go to the collateral line; if they failed then the land would go to an heir in the higher collateral line. He noted that the computation of descent might be split, if two sisters inherited, and discussed who should be included in a computation, giving examples (a frequent issue in this text was whether an elder brother who died before he could inherit should be mentioned in a count of descent). He then stated that he had 'discussed the degrees and would go on to discuss the persons of the successors'.[132] He reiterated the degrees in which close family members sat (parents to grandchildren) and then began what was essentially an elaborated list of terminology, detailing the beginning of each collateral line and explaining that their heirs could be called *in infinitum* until the line was exhausted, first dealing with the paternal side, then the maternal. His discussion of kinship extended from the *trinepos* (great-great-great-great grandson) to the *tritavus* (great-great-great-great-grandfather). The essential parentelic design emerges clearly enough.

The common law kinship material in these manuscripts could have been read by a wide range of men with a connection to the common law. The amount of textual variation in the surviving manuscripts shows that they were probably copied by lawyers, presumably at Westminster, where they were loaned and exchanged.[133] Such copyists were not concerned with reproducing a perfect facsimile of whatever they had before them. They added, reordered and subtracted material (from a few lines, to whole sections) and sometimes argued with the core text when they disagreed with it. There was intelligence behind this: common lawyers' inquiring minds, rather than careful, standardised, institutionalised production. It is not necessary to assume that the busy masters of law did all this copying and comparison.

---

131  *Bracton*, ii. 195–200.
132  Ibid. ii. 199.
133  Ibid. i, p. xv *per* Thorne.

Juniors, apprentices and clerks are possible candidates too, although these manuscripts were not used in formal education. Copies were owned and used by men with an interest in common law such as John de Longeville, an MP for Northamptonshire who died in about 1324 and who glossed and arranged the *Bracton* and *Britton* in CUL, MS Dd.7.6 (or at least, who provided the original for a gloss that was later copied).[134] A lawyer, tax collector, an assessor and collector of the subsidy from Northampton, de Longeville appeared in London to demand that Northampton be free of all tolls and custom.[135] He was a prominent regional government man. He also served as a justice, investigating sheriffs and crown officers. He was knowledgeable about the law and his range of interests was wide, judging from the many treatises in this large manuscript.[136] Another example is CUL, MS Dd.7.14, which has a connection with John de Solers, a tax collector for Hereford and Gloucestershire in 1313 and 1319, and lawyer for the abbey of Winchume.[137] It is also possible that de Solers had a university connection.[138] The manuscript is also connected to Walter de Langton (d. 1321), bishop of Coventry and Litchfield, and treasurer to Edward I and Edward II (his arms appear on a figure).[139] Annotations in such manuscripts – notes referring to cases, or marking interest, doodles and hands pointing out key passages, legal records and forms included in the flyleaves and among the contents – confirm that the text, despite being somewhat out of date by the late thirteenth century, was not moribund.

*Bracton's* section on kinship, although confusing, was retained in later versions; kinship was understood to have a role in the legal system. *Fleta* was an adaptation, apparently written in the 1290s in the Fleet prison, possibly by Matthew of the Exchequer. In it, the sections 'Degrees of kinship and succession' and 'Of those who ought to succeed others and the order of succession' were retained and barely changed, save that they were moved to the section on the count in a writ of right.[140] Only one manuscript of *Fleta* survives today, so it may not have been very influential, although it

---

134 Baker, *Catalogue*, 68. See also *Britton*, i, pp. lxii-lxiii, *per* Nichols, and D. Oschinsky, *Walter of Henley and other treatises on estate management and accounting*, Oxford 1971, 24.
135 For references to his career see Oschinsky, *Walter of Henley*, 26, 24 n. 1, and *Britton*, i, pp. lxii–lxiii.
136 Baker, *Catalogue*, 48–68.
137 *Earliest English law reports*, i, pp. xxxii-xxxiii, cf. Oschinsky, *Walter of Henley*, 26. Brand's interpretation is to be preferred.
138 Two John de Solers are listed in Emden, *Biographical register*, iii. 1726. One was a master by 1309, a canon who was engaged at the papal Curia and on papal service. The other was not listed as having a degree; rather he was a subdeacon and later deacon (1313, 1314) to St Frideswide's Priory in Oxford.
139 Baker, *Catalogue*, 83.
140 *Fleta*, ed. and trans. H. G. Richardson and G. O. Sayles (Selden Society lxxii, lxxxix, lxxxxix, 1955–84), iv. 110–13. Sayles doubted that Matthew of the Exchequer was the author (at pp. xxiv–xxv). His distaste seems unreasonable.

seems to have been a source for *Britton*.[141] Chief Justice Gilbert de Thornton wrote another adaptation (his *Summa*, written in 1292), which seems to follow the same pattern.[142] *Britton* adapted the kinship material in *Bracton*. Clearly, even though underlying kinship structures were not studied as such at common law, they had a function that justified their repetition and were part of an overarching scheme by which the law was categorised and ordered (in *Bracton* they were in the section on succession, in the 'book' 'Of acquiring dominion of things', one of a series of ways of gaining title to land).[143]

The underlying kinship structure was part of the common law, and it seems that authors and copyists felt it necessary to explain this formally under the inspiration of learned law models. Both *Glanvill* and *Bracton* had been inspired by the civil law model via the *Institutes* of Justinian. Thorne's edition of *Bracton*, with its hundreds of references to learned law texts, has revealed the author as a competent Romanist.[144] The civil law within was used 'to rationalize and reduce to order'.[145] In *Glanvill* there was very little of this influence in his discussion of kinship; in *Bracton* there was much. The author of *Bracton* tried to adapt the section on cognates from *Institutes* 3.6. His early division of the *parentelae* into three types: above, below and from the side, echoed the introduction to *Institutes* 3.6, although he went on to discuss them in that order, above, below, from the side, while *Institutes* 3.6 discussed them above, below, from the side within each degree.[146] His concluding promise of a tree echoed that in *Institutes* 3.6.[147] *Bracton* spoke of kinsmen as cognates, as did the *Institutes*.[148] The author's preference for a six-degree extent (beyond which 'the memories of men' would be exceeded), also reflected the limit given in *Institutes* 3.6 where the *tritavus* and *tritavia* (the great-great-great-great-grandparents) were the last named ascendants,

---

141 *Britton*, i, p. xxvii; *Fleta*, iv, p. xxv.

142 T. F. T. Plucknett, 'The Harvard manuscript of Thornton's *Summa*', *Harvard Law Review* li (1937–8), 1038–56 at pp. 1051–6.

143 'Book' here is used to refer to the divisions within the text, not to Thorne's four volumes that make up the modern edition.

144 *Bracton*, i, pp. xxxvi–xxxvii. The first third of *Bracton* quoted almost 200 different sections of the *Digest*, as well as other learned law sources.

145 *Bracton*, iii, p. xl *per* Thorne. See also P. Brand, 'Westminster hall and Europe: European aspects of the common law', in J. Boffey and P. King (eds), *London and Europe in the later Middle Ages*, London 1995, 55–85 at p. 63.

146 *Bracton*, ii. 195–200; cf. *Institutes* 3.6. See also H. G. Richardson, *Bracton: the problem of his text* (Selden Society s.s. ii, 1965), 100–5.

147 'Et qualiter gradus cognationis computentur, et quoto gradu quis distet ab alio in linea descendente vel ascendente, in figura inferius depicta manifestius quasi ad oculum apparebit': *Bracton*, ii. 200; cf. 'Sed cum magis veritas oculata fide quam per aures animis hominum infigitur, ideo necessarium duximus, post narrationem graduum etiam eos praesenti libro inscribi. Quatenus possint et auribus et inspectione adulescentes perfectissimam graduum doctrinam adipisci': *Institutes* 3.6.9.

148 *Bracton*, ii. 195–6; cf. *Institutes* 3.6. prol. However, the author of *Bracton* also used *parens, parentis* a term found in Isidore, *Etymologies* 9.5.4 (which also used *cognatio*, for example at 9.5.10).

and the *trinepos* and *trineptis* (great-great-great-great-grandchildren) were the last named descendants.[149] In some ways *Bracton's* author was building his parentelic kindred on civil law foundations; however this influence can be seen in the description of kinship in *Bracton*, not in the parentelic system itself. Legal studies had blossomed in the English universities in the twelfth century, and it is clear that the author of *Bracton* had had a learned law education of some sort.[150] A tempting and intriguing possibility is that his work was the product of a law school at Westminster that worked on 'a synthesis' of common law and civil law and was closed down by a royal order to prevent the teaching of 'laws' in the city in 1234.[151]

Adopting elements from the learned laws was not, in *Bracton's* case, particularly successful. The author added much peculiar kinship terminology, similar to his learned law exemplars, but distorted (there was no 'abavunculus magus' in traditional learned law terminology).[152] His discussion was complicated because his focal person was not always clear. *Bracton's* discussion did not use an ego character to whom all the others referred, nor could his discussion of the various lines descending from the father (the usual *propositus*) follow the pattern in such schematic representations as the *arbor consanguinitatis* which showed one single line of descendants, since in common law inheritance it was necessary to distinguish between the various descending lines. This caused some confusion in *Bracton* between collateral lines.[153] *Bracton* also used the concept of degrees in a different way from canonists or civilians. In *Bracton* degrees were generations, hands that the land passed through (like degrees of entry), steps on a ladder or convenient markers, rather than a system of measuring distance.[154]

This learned law patina was not necessary to the practice of common law. Yet something about formal legal kinship structures was thought necessary in the big books of the common law and when common lawyers wanted to write such a section in such a book they turned to models from the learned law. *Britton*, following *Bracton*, was also influenced in his discussion of kinship by the learned laws. In that instance, however, the author chose the canon law as a model. This suggests a perception amongst common lawyers of a gap in their own law, not in the actualities of kinship, but in the formal expression of it. Perceiving this gap, they turned to the dominant model for formal kinship.

The common law had its own kinship system, the parentelic system described so succinctly by Maitland and in so piecemeal a manner by *Britton*. This

---

[149]  *Bracton*, ii. 196; cf. *Institutes* 3.6.6.
[150]  Brand, 'Westminster hall', 62.
[151]  Ibid. 63–4, and 'Legal education', 57–8.
[152]  Worby, 'Kinship in thirteenth-century England', 255–60.
[153]  See ibid. 71–3.
[154]  See ibid. 73–9.

was a system based on formally recognised biological connection (only the legitimate could be heirs), with blood kinship providing the connection necessary for heritability. Whether it had an in/out boundary is more difficult, because theoretically the common law parentelic system could extend forever. However bastard brothers were regarded as 'completely foreign [*extraneus est*] … with respect to succession, though not with respect to blood relationship',[155] which suggests that in practice, common law kinship was not thought to extend infinitely, particularly when it was so closely linked to seisin or the descent of the right. The parentelic system provided a method of ordering and a simple internal reasoning, though sometimes common lawyers struggled to apply it, for example in the *casus regis* and at the boundaries where the rights of half-blood kin had to be decided. Common law kinship rules reflected non-legal senses of family in England; even so, the systemising effect of legal rules drove the development of the structure beyond the concepts with which some were comfortable. The system was focused on inheritance – a clear social purpose – and on the person inheriting or claiming, or on the *propositus* who had died rightfully seised. It even had a terminology, although not one as extensive as either of the learned law systems.

Common law kinship may not seem so systematic as canon law kinship Yet, perhaps due to familiarity, is is a system that is traditionally accepted as having operated more easily than that of the canon law. Common law kinship was applied at the point of inheritance and was enforced and reinforced in the courts. It was without a doubt a system in practice. When focusing upon the kinship system as set out in common law books, it is understood that such books reflected practice, rather than necessarily determining it. They are valuable because they were attempts to be general and they included explanation of parentelic kinship in a manner that a bald scrutiny of the forms of actions would not supply. In particular they show that models for formal discussions of common law legal kinship, although never the core of the contents, were supplied by the learned laws.

---

155 *Bracton*, ii. 76.

# 3

# The Dominance of Canon Law Kinship Ideas

Among the literate and learned, canon law concepts were foremost in thinking about kinship in thirteenth- and fourteenth-century England. This does not mean that the canon law was applied in legal contexts outside its remit. It was not applied or used where the parentelic system of common law kinship ought to have been employed. Rather, non-canonists turned to canon law ideas of kinship. The kinship of the canon law, in the form of ideas, *arbores* and treatises, was found more widely in such contexts than that of other systems (such as civil law kinship). Canon law kinship material can be seen in manuscripts other than the usual *Decretum* and decretals collections, or collections of canonist *Summae*. It can even be seen outside a university and clerical context, in the manuscripts of secular common lawyers. Knowledge of the canon law kinship system attained different levels of sophistication, and it was absorbed and integrated into people's thinking about kinship to different degrees. There is evidence of plain copying, of a patina of knowledge and awareness and, tellingly, of attempts to integrate more detailed canon law concepts with knowledge of other kinship and even to adapt canon law kinship into other contexts. This shows the dominance of the canon law as a general, common way of thinking about kinship structures.

## Canon law kinship among common lawyers

The canon law kinship system was widespread and known among the learned including some common lawyers in thirteenth- and fourteenth-century England. Several introductory treatises on canon law kinship and *arbores* were copied into common law manuscripts in the first half of the fourteenth century. Such material occurred in approximately 10 per cent of surviving *Bracton* manuscripts. While this figure is not large enough to posit a significant influence on common law kinship, it is large enough to reveal the importance of the canon law in conceptualising kinship generally.

There was no other body of extraneous material in *Bracton* manuscripts quite like this group of canon law treatises and trees, although many *Bracton* manuscripts contained 'extraneous' material. In his edition, George Woodbine listed fourteen manuscripts with notable additions, including four that contained consanguinity treatises.[1] Most of these contained other

---

[1] *Bracton*, i. 5–20. BL, MS Add. 41258 can be added to the total.

common law material, such as *Britton*, or short common law treatises such as *Cum sit necessarium*, *Cadit assisa* or *Iudicium essoniorum*. Many included statutes and records. Among these assorted additions the canon law kinship material stands out; saving references to the statutes of Edward I, it seems to be the most common or consistent substantial body of extraneous material to be included in these manuscripts.

This relative prominence is given added force by the fact that the material clearly belonged to another legal system, and also by the common law's reputation for insularity,[2] a reputation justified insofar as the learned laws had limited practical impact on the common law. The thirteenth century was a high point for the influence of the civil law, yet this, maxims excepted, seems to have been more a feature of literary texts like *Bracton* than of reality and pleading in the courts.[3] Analysis of general canon law influence has revealed that there was conflict, cooperation and reciprocal influence but that this was sporadic and based on actions of individual lawyers, or restricted to certain areas of law.[4] Kinship law was one of these areas: there was a consistent (although limited) incursion of canon law learning into common law texts. Moreover, the subset of *Bracton* manuscripts that contained this material was not made at the same date or in the same place or style. They were not a coherent group in any way other than through various canon law kinship treatises. Thus this influence was not organised or focused, but reflects a general attention to an important set of concepts.

The copyists who included works of canon law kinship in *Bracton* manuscripts were conscious of their difference, however; the inclusion of such material was deliberate, planned and purposeful. In most instances the treatises were headed with rubrics, yet the material was not marked as otherwise unusual.[5] Given the usual pattern for *Bracton* manuscripts, it seems likely these were copied by common lawyers, or men knowledgeable in the common law.[6] The canon law trees might more readily have been added by

---

[2]  See J. H. Baker, 'Roman law at the third university of England', *Current Legal Problems* lv (2002), 123–50 at p. 145. The main focus of this article, however, is later than the thirteenth and fourteenth centuries.

[3]  D. J. Seipp, 'Roman legal categories in the early common law', in T. G. Watkin (ed.), *Legal record and historical reality: proceedings of the eighth British legal history conference Cardiff 1987*, London 1989, 9–36 at p. 35.

[4]  R. H. Helmholz, 'Continental law and common law: historical strangers or companions?', *Duke Law Journal* xl/6 (1990), 1207–28; *The ius commune in England: four studies*, Oxford 2001; and *Canon law and English common law*, London 1983. J. Martínez-Torrón, *Anglo-American law and canon law: canonical roots of the common law tradition*, Berlin 1998, p. ix, has argued for 'substantial and sustained influence'. His work is too brief to do justice to that claim.

[5]  For more detail see Worby, 'Kinship in thirteenth-century England', 87–92.

[6]  On the production of *Bracton* manuscripts see *Bracton*, i, p. xv *per* Thorne.

illuminators to set patterns, yet in the most complete example the trees were completed by the same hand that had copied the text.[7]

Inclusion was haphazard and appears to have been a matter of individual impetus rather than a coordinated effort, a pattern that suggests a relatively wide knowledge of canon law kinship among men who owned common law manuscripts (although at least one manuscript with these contents belonged in the fourteenth century to an archdeacon).[8] This is shown by a survey of the main canon law kinship material that was included in five common law manuscripts.

First, British Library, MS Additional 41258, which dates to c. 1300. This contains two trees of consanguinity, one of seven degrees (which was by then out of date), and one of four; a tree of affinity (of seven degrees and three types, so again out of date); a note on affinity; and the start of the anonymous treatise *Sciendum est*.[9] *Sciendum est* dealt with canon law kinship and contained much the same material as *Quia tractare intendimus*. This treatise may have originated outside a canonist context as it contains an unusual introduction which rehearsed the history of canon law kinship (see appendix 2), and an unusual section including quotations from the Bible.

Second, Bodleian Library, Oxford, MS Rawlinson C 160, which dates to the first quarter of the fourteenth century. This contains a frame for a tree of affinity in which the cells were not filled and the treatise *Sciendum est*, incomplete at the beginning.[10] Neither of these first two manuscripts appear to be the source for the other, nor are the two closely enough related to indicate that they came for a common source.[11] Probably other *Bracton* manuscripts now lost contained this same treatise.

Third, BL, MS Harley 653, which dates to the early fourteenth century. This contains an untidy tree of consanguinity drawn by a fifteenth-century annotator and three treatises: *Quibus modis*, *Triplex est* and the *Arbor versificata* of Johannes de Deo.[12] *Quibus modis* and *Triplex est* are somewhat unusual. The *Arbor versificata* was one of the more popular canon law treatises.

Fourth, Worcester Cathedral Library, MS F 87, which dates to the late thirteenth century. This contains *Quibus modis* and *Triplex est*.[13] Again, these two manuscripts were not related, so it is likely that other manuscripts now lost contained the same paired treatises.[14]

---

[7] For more detail see Worby, 'Kinship in thirteenth-century England', 93–7. The manuscript with the most complete set of trees is BL, MS Add. 41258, fo. 37rv.

[8] WCL, MS F 87 belonged to an archdeacon: R. M. Thomson, *A descriptive catalogue of the medieval manuscripts in Worcester Cathedral Library*, Cambridge 2001, 56. Ironically it contained a common law adaptation of canon law treatises.

[9] BL, MS Add. 41258, fos 37r–38v.

[10] Bodl. Lib., MS Rawlinson C 160, fos 36r–38r.

[11] Worby, 'Kinship in thirteenth-century England', 105–6.

[12] BL, MS Harley 653, fos 40v–43r.

[13] WCL, MS F 87, fos 28v–29r.

[14] Worby, 'Kinship in thirteenth-century England', 105–6.

Finally, Cambridge University Library, MS Dd.7.6, which dates to very soon after 1307. It contains the treatise *Ad arborem*.[15] Again, this is not a conventional canonist treatise. It belonged originally to theology studies, although it was within the genre of short introductory treatises concerning canon law kinship as it followed the standard structure and contained much of the usual set of contents.

In all the manuscripts except CUL, MS Dd.7.6 the treatises were placed directly after *Bracton's* own confusing section on kinship, as if to illuminate or resolve it.[16] *Bracton's* kinship section, not an easy read, by the early fourteenth century was not even a synthesis with the 'right' kinship system. The importance of canon law kinship eclipsed that of the civil law, and was more interesting to the common law experts who copied these manuscripts.

*Bracton* manuscripts were not the only common law context into which canon law kinship material was copied. For example, Winchester Cathedral Library, MS 18, a plain and somewhat scruffy portable statute book which dates to the first quarter of the fourteenth century, contains a copy of the popular canon law treatise *Quia tractare intendimus*.[17] BL, MS Hargrave 433, a small, portable and neat statute book which dates to very early in the fourteenth century, contains an adaptation of the same popular canon law kinship treatise.[18] Bodleian Library, Oxford, MS Douce 17, which dates to the second quarter of the fourteenth century, another small, neat statute book, contains an identical adaptation of *Quia tractare intendimus*.[19] It was probably produced by the same *scriptorium* as MS Hargrave 433, as the contents are almost identical.[20] Other examples of this adaptation may once have been copied.

Statute books (*statuta Angliae*) were the most prolific common law genre. In fact, they are among the most common surviving secular manuscripts: approximately 400 survive today.[21] They ranged in quality and size, but most were small and serviceable. They were written from the late thirteenth century until they were printed in the fifteenth. Most of the manuscripts

[15] CUL, MS Dd.7.6, pt III, fos 66r–68v.

[16] In CUL, MS Dd.7.6 the treatise was at the end of a section containing common law treatises, almost immediately before *Bracton*: Baker, *Catalogue*, 67–8.

[17] Winchester Cathedral Library, MS 18, fos 190v–194v. It is described by N. R. Ker and A. J. Piper, *Medieval manuscripts in British libraries*, Oxford 1992, iv. 597–601.

[18] BL, MS Hargrave 433, fos 99r–100r.

[19] Bodl. Lib., MS Douce 17, fos 161v–163r.

[20] Worby, 'Kinship in thirteenth-century England', 296–302.

[21] Baker, *Catalogue*, p. xxii. See also D. C. Skemer, 'From archives to the book trade: private statute rolls in England, 1285–1307', *Journal of the Society of Archivists* xvi/2 (1995), 193–206 at p. 194; 'Sir William Breton's book: production of *statuta Angliae* in the late thirteenth century', in P. Beal and J. Griffiths (eds), *English manuscript studies, 1100–1700*, London 1997, vi. 24–51 at p. 24; and 'Reading the law: statute books and the private transmission of legal knowledge in late medieval England', in Bush and Wijffels, *Learning the law*, 113–31 at p. 113.

belonged to the reigns of Edwards I and II.[22] Pre-1327 collections, which include the manuscripts above, are known as *vetera statuta* or *statuta antiqua* (the later collections are *nova statuta*). A statute book might draw together a collection of nearly all the practical texts that a common lawyer could need: statutes, a register of writs, tracts on procedure and so on.[23] They tended to contain a core consisting of Magna Carta, the *Carta de Foresta*, the Statute of Merton, the Statute of Marlborough, the Statute of Westminster I, the Statute of Gloucester and the Statute of Westminster II, frequently accompanied by a table of *capitula* and a list of contents. This was supplemented by various other statutes and selected treatises; a great range of material could be included and there really was very little consistency.[24] It is likely that statute books were produced in *scriptoria*, and the contents appear to have been prescribed by the purchaser,[25] who was not always a common lawyer. Some were owned by landowners great and small, by monasteries, merchants and even the future Edward III.[26] Winchester Cathedral, MS 18 seems very likely to have belonged to a common lawyer since it included a register of writs.[27]

From the common law perspective the incursion of canon law kinship material into common law manuscripts was not extensive and, even including the relatively numerous trees, might not tip the scales. Yet the fact that this material was not limited to more learned texts like *Bracton* shows a wide reach for canon law kinship texts and images into secular contexts. Several facts make this body of material significant. First, that there appears to have been no specific group or tradition among common lawyers that looked towards canon law kinship. Second, that the variety of consanguinity treatises was wide and peculiar and included several treatises that were not popular or authoritative. There is a sense that the scribes were including what interested them. They may have compared manuscripts, and been inspired to find a consanguinity treatise to include. Some copied each

[22] Skemer, 'Sir William Breton's book', 24. His survey of 350 *Statuta Angliae* revealed that 57% pre-dated 1327.

[23] 'a vade mecum': H. G. Richardson and G. O. Sayles, 'The early statutes', *Law Quarterly Review* 1 (1934), 201–23, 540–71 at p. 544.

[24] Broad patterns can be discerned. Some treatises and statutes are much more common than others. For a comparison of the contents of three statute books see Worby, 'Kinship in thirteenth-century England', 296–302.

[25] A. Bennett, 'Anthony Bek's copy of *statuta Angliae*', in W. M. Ormrod (ed.), *England in the fourteenth century: proceedings of the 1985 Harlaxton symposium*, Woodbridge 1986, 1–27 at p. 2. See also Skemer, 'Reading the law', 18, and 'Sir William Breton's book', 29–37.

[26] For example M. A. Michael, 'A manuscript wedding gift from Philippa of Hainault to Edward III', *Burlington Magazine* (Sept. 1985), 582–99. See also V. H. Galbraith, 'Statutes of Edward I: Huntington library ms. H.M. 25782', in T. A. Sandquist and M. R. Powicke (eds), *Essays in medieval history presented to Bertie Wilkinson*, Toronto 1969, 176–91 at pp. 176, 181. For a more complete list of examples see Skemer, 'Reading the law', 114.

[27] Ker and Piper, *Medieval manuscripts*, iv. 597–601.

other; some found something original. This speaks of a continuing curiosity about the subject among common lawyers. It was not traditional to add this material; it was interesting to the compiler and hence of significance.

The common lawyers who copied this material were outside the canonist norm, but possible routes of transmission can be glimpsed. A profession of common lawyers was emerging by the end of Henry III's reign.[28] A number of justices and lawyers can be found to have had a university education, while some had even trained and practised as canon lawyers.[29] Some common lawyers owned canon and civil law books.[30] There could be contact and interaction between the laws. *Bracton* stands as a monument to just how close and productive that interaction could be, although its success in the area of kinship law is questionable. Less formal routes of transmission are also plausible. The secular men who included this material would have been among the literate and educated with access to manuscripts. They may have read the material, and found it in fellows' libraries. After all, these treatises were introductory texts, and the images of the *arbores* were common. The treatises copied show that canon law kinship was noted outside its normal sphere, and that it was regarded as interesting by a legal culture that typically had little time for formal frameworks, preferring instead the learning of practice.

Some references to canon law kinship in common law texts show how thinking about canon law structures was integrated into the general way people regarded kinship. For example, there are several references which suggest that canon law terminology was widely known. When Glanvill in the twelfth century had written about 'divorces' on the ground of consanguinity, he had done so using common law terminology, with an explanation that the *divortium* was because the couple were in the same *parentela* (which was not actually the same as consanguinity).[31] In later texts this pattern changed and canon law terminology was applied in common law areas. In *Casus placitorum* there was reference to people who were in the 'same stock of consanguinity [*meime le cep de sa consanguinite*]'.[32] In *Modus componendi brevia* the author even said that he would order pleas on the seisin of a dead ancestor by degrees of consanguinity.[33] He did not actually do so because common law actions did not fit canon law degrees. The point is that by the second half of the thirteenth century even the down-to-earth authors of small common law texts were accustomed to thinking of kinship in terms of

[28]  See Brand, *Origins*, 63, and his chapter iv more generally.
[29]  Ibid. 155.
[30]  The recorded book collection of Matthew of the Exchequer (in 1293) included the *Decretals* and several civil law books: R. J. Whitwell, 'The libraries of a civilian and canonist and of a common lawyer, an. 1294', *LQR* xxi (1905), 393–400 at pp. 399–400.
[31]  *Glanvill*, ed. Hall, vi. 17 (at p. 68).
[32]  *Casus placitorum*, 26/72.
[33]  'Et si modo praedicto obiit seisitus, videatur quo gradu consanguinitatis ipse antecessor attingat petentem': 'Modus componendi brevia', 147–8.

canon law language and concepts. This may have been lazy thinking, but it is revealing of a patina of knowledge about canon law kinship.

In some contexts the operation of the canon law could impinge on the common law. In the areas of bastardy and dower it is no surprise that common lawyers should have been interested in canon law concepts including kinship. A 'divorce' could affect whether a child was regarded as legitimate and thus whether they would receive their inheritance. Bastardy was one of the more common responses (exceptions) to a claim in which the plaintiff had to be the nearest legitimate heir, because it was not always clear if the parents had been validly married in the absence of a system of marriage registration.[34] Thus, the law around divorce in this area would have been worth knowing. A divorce also affected whether a wife would receive her dower. In fact, there was a common law mnemonic on 'divorce'. Examples survive in some statute books;[35] and it was included in the *Summa on bastardy*, which was a short treatise that circulated fairly widely in the thirteenth century.[36] The mnemonic gave a list of canon law grounds for 'divorce' which was neither complete nor traditional by canon law standards. It listed seven types and detailed whether the wife got her dower and the son his inheritance in each: consanguinity, prior contract, adultery, spiritual kinship, impotence, affinity and chastity (probably covering the canon law grounds of vow or clerical order).[37] The mnemonic stemmed from an understanding of divorce

---

[34] Clandestine marriages were not uncommon and disputes about prior contracts were the most common form of matrimonial litigation in canon law courts: Helmholz, *Marriage litigation*, ch. ii; Donahue, *Law, marriage, and society*, chs iv–vi.

[35] Listed in Baker, *Catalogue*, 354, art. 78a.

[36] There is a transcription of the *Summa* on bastardy in W. Hooper, *The law of illegitimacy: a treatise on the law affecting persons of illegitimate birth, with the rules of evidence in proof of legitimacy and illegitimacy; and an historical account of the bastard in mediæval law*, London 1911, 227–33.

[37] 'Nota quod septem modis fit divortium, scilicet causa castitatis, causa consanguinitatis, causa prioris contractus, causa adulterii, causa affinitatis, causa frigiditatis, causa comparternitatis. Causa castitatis: mater habebit dotem et filius hereditatem. Causa consanguinitatis: mater carebit dote et filius habebit hereditatem in casu et in casu non. Et quo casu non? Ad hoc respondendum est quod ubi bannum inductum [*recte* indictum] fuerat in ecclesia parochiali et coram parochianis, in diebus festivis, per presbiterum parochialem puplice pronunciatum ante sponsalia celebrata, et in illo tempore non obiectum fuerit contra eos per aliquem ibidem existentem, quod sollempniter [*recte* sollempnitas] matrimonii non fuit obiecta aliqua consanguinitate occasione illa, filius habebit hereditatem. Ubi vero sollempnitas matrimonii fuerit antequam [bannum] proclamatum sit locis debitis, hoc est occulte et non in facie ecclesie, illo casu filius carebit hereditate. Causa prioris contractus uxor carebit dote et filius hereditate. Causa adulterii et compaternitatis, et frigiditatis et affinitatis: in omnibus istis casibus, ubi aliqua pars matrimonii, sive masculus sive femina, sciebat predictam affinitatem, adulterium sive consanguinitate [*recte* consanguinitatem] ante nuptiarum sollempnitates, et possit manifestari et intelligi, carebit filius hereditate, eo quod sancta ecclesia [*recte* scientia certa] alicuius partis matrimonii, quam [*recte* que] venerat ante sollempnitates, excluditur heres ab hereditate sua. Et mater carebit in omnibus dote ubi divortium factum fuerit, preter quam in casu

law among non-canonists. It said that after a 'divorce' due to chastity the wife got dower and the son got the inheritance. The other cases depended on circumstances: after a 'divorce' for consanguinity the wife would not get dower, but the son might get his inheritance if the local priest had read the banns in the parish church publicly before the wedding was celebrated and no objection had been made (otherwise if the wedding was clandestine). This reflects canon law thinking in this area, which would also add that the parents should have no knowledge of the impediment, else the child would be illegitimate, although the canon law applied its rules on clandestine marriages and the banns to affinity too.[38] According to the mnemonic, in the cases of adultery, spiritual kinship, impotence and affinity the wife did not get dower, and, if either the husband or wife had known about the aforesaid impediment before the wedding was celebrated, the son would be deprived of his inheritance. It is notable that consanguinity received the most attention in this discussion, although modern studies have shown that there were few divorces on that ground. The idea of blood-kinship was symbolically important.

Other canon law kinship concepts can be seen in common law texts, such as the four-degree limit on kinship. The point at which people could marry seems to have had a wide currency as that at which blood-kinship ceased. For example, *Britton* used four generations as a limit on kinship, subject to the usual restrictions on the actions of limited descent and the time limits. According to *Britton* a plea of rationabili parte (a plea for a division of land between parceners) extended as far as the *tresaiel* (the great-great-grandfather).[39] The ascending limit for cosinage was the *tresaiel*, although, if time allowed, it could descend 'to the remotest blood'.[40] A contemporary annotator to one *Britton* manuscript, in a discussion of whether a freeman holding land by villein tenure could become a villein, said that the fourth degree marked a break and that after that point the tenant would be a villein.[41] At common law, kinship could extend as far as necessary if it was within time in the context of a dispute over the right. When the structures and rules of the common law did not provide a natural limit, however, and one was needed, *Britton* and his annotator turned to their understanding of canon law kinship (in contrast, *Bracton* had used the civil law six-degree extent in his examples).[42] Similarly, a lecture on the statute *De donis* borrowed the canon law limit on kinship and explicitly referred to

castitatis': Bodl. Lib., MS Douce 17, fos 163r–164r. My thanks to Charles Donahue, Jr., for suggestions on the concept of 'castitas'.
[38] X 4.7.5.
[39] *Britton*, ii. 82.
[40] Ibid. ii. 163.
[41] Ibid. i. 195 n. q. He also said (ii. 164 n. r) that the seisin of the 'grandfather's grandfather' could only be counted on in a writ of right.
[42] *Bracton*, ii. 196.

marriage law: 'according to some in conditional gifts the blood of the feof-fees is not made pure and the estate does not return to its first nature until marriage could take place between the issue of the feoffor and the issue of the brother or sister to whom the tenements are thus given'.[43] The common lawyers who included this material lived and married under the canon law system and thus would have known the basic rules.

A deeper knowledge of canon law kinship can be seen where more specialist knowledge from canon law treatises was integrated into common law contexts. An idiosyncratic example is the *Mirror of justices*.[44] This treatise dates to 1285–90 and was written in law-French. Although long connected with Andrew Horn, it seems that he was not the author. The text does not appear to have been common, as only one manuscript survives.[45] The *Mirror* is an unusual and possibly unreliable text, which has inspired some strong reactions in its readers and editors and garnered an impressive collection of dismissals.[46] Maitland described it as a dream disguising 'dangerous opinions', or a young man's prank: it was full of 'fables and falsehoods and views and visions'.[47] However, this odd polemical treatise might not be so aberrant if medieval lawyers are acknowledged to have had a range of opinions.[48] It includes canon law kinship material. Some of it was a potentially plausible synthesis given the slight integration of such concepts at the fringes of common law kinship in other texts, but some is more doubtful.

Unlike many common law texts which touched upon kinship, the *Mirror* grouped the ideas of consanguinity and affinity with kinship (*parente*).[49] Affinity did not often figure in common law writing, beyond being a known canon law ground for 'divorce', or being a ground to challenge a juror.[50] The *Mirror* went further: it defined incest as the 'defiling of a person related by consanguinity or affinity'.[51] Incest was rarely (if ever) mentioned in other common law texts. It was included here, alongside a definition of rape, presumably because of the author's penchant for muddying the line between the religious and secular spheres. The author had clearly read a canon law treatise on consanguinity and affinity. He defined the terms: 'for as consan-

---

[43] Brand, 'Legal education', 66–7. Other common lawyers who borrowed this limit are discussed at pp. 110–12 below.

[44] *The mirror of justices*, ed. W. J. Whittaker, intro. F. W. Maitland (Selden Society vii, 1895).

[45] D. J. Seipp, 'The mirror of justices', in Bush and Wijffels, *Learning the law*, 85–112 at pp. 88–91.

[46] Ibid. 85–7.

[47] *The mirror*, pp. ix–lv at pp. xlvii, xlii, xlvii, lii.

[48] Seipp, 'Mirror of justices', 104, 112.

[49] 'cosine ou parente ou affin de la partie adverse': *The mirror*, 116.

[50] Challenges of jurors due to affinity occur in the year books: *Year books of the reign of King Edward the first: years XXXII–XXXIII*, ed. and trans. A. J. Horwood, London 1864, 338–41; *The eyre of Northamptonshire 3–4 Edward III (1329–30)*, ed. D. W. Sutherland (Selden Society lxxxxvii, 1983), i. 30, 350.

[51] 'Incest est a porgesir cosine parente ou affin': *The mirror*, 29.

guinity is a bond between divers parceners descending from one stock and arising from carnal engenderment, so affinity is the relation between persons established by carnal copulation where there is no common ancestry'.[52] As the text is in Anglo-French a direct parallel with a particular canon law treatise cannot be made, but this was clearly a translation of canon law definitions.

This knowledge was not merely background learning. The author attempted to integrate canon law kinship into common law practice concerning appeals for homicide, that is the manner by which a litigant could accuse another of murder. There were certain limits on who could bring such appeals: usually the heir, often a close male relative, or the wife if her husband died in her arms. The author of the Mirror suggested that 'all persons connected by consanguinity, affinity, or alliance' could be received to appeal.[53] Only one person could appeal at a time, and, if the man did not die in his wife's arms, the appeal belonged to the eldest legitimate son. According to the Mirror the order of appealers should follow a simplified parentelic system (descendants then collaterals, with a preference for the paternal line), going from degree to degree ('de degre en degre').[54] Then, if collaterals failed, affines should be allowed (an innovation). The order should follow the pattern of degrees in the 'figures' of consanguinity and affinity and stop at four degrees.[55] The author accepted and would have applied widely the canon law kinship system, as embodied in the canon law arbor and the canon law extent of the kindred. It seems most unlikely that the full extent of this synthesis was ever followed in common law courts, although there were instances where appealing kinsmen had to be sorted according to nearness of blood to a very limited extent: for example, sometimes an appeal was challenged because the appealer was alleged to have an older brother.[56] The attempted synthesis in the Mirror was peculiar and antiquarian. It stated that 'the appeal of homicide was restrained by King Henry the First within the four nearest degrees of blood'.[57] The text's editor could find no such legislation of Henry the First; and, given that the canon law limit was set at four degrees by the Fourth Lateran Council in 1215, it seems unlikely that Henry I chose that limit in 1110–35. This seems therefore to be a typical appeal to antiquity. From the perspective of operational common law, the veracity of this canon law-flavoured system is highly doubtful. However, it

[52] Ibid. 21.
[53] Ibid. 50.
[54] Ibid.
[55] Ibid.
[56] Year books 32 & 33 Edward I, 192–3; Year books of 1 & 2 Edward II (1307–1309), ed. F. W. Maitland (Selden Society xvii, 1903), 42–3; Year books of 11 Edward II (1317–1318), ed. J. P. Collas and W. Holdsworth (Selden Society lxi, 1942), 263–4.
[57] The mirror, 50.

is further evidence that canon law kinship ideas could have a deep impact on non-canonists' thoughts on the classification of kin.

More orthodox common law treatises than the *Mirror of justices* contain evidence of common law specialists having a relatively sophisticated knowledge of canon law kinship. *Britton* broke from its exemplar to discuss kinship under the influence of the canon law system (where *Bracton* had used the civil law). Trees illustrating kinship structures were important in *Britton*. The author promised three and gave guides to how to draw two, somewhat in the manner of a consanguinity treatise.[58] *Britton* called the tree 'l'arbre de parentee', a terminology which suggests that the author regarded it as a parallel adaptation of the *arbor consanguinitatis*.[59] These guides were meant for students.[60] The author of *Britton* was not only familiar with the model of canon law *arbores*, but had read and integrated a treatise on canon law kinship, most probably one of the introductory treatises of the sort that were copied into *Bracton* manuscripts. He wrote: 'How the degrees are placed in consanguinity, appears by the above figure, whereof the half might suffice, and then it would resemble a banner; but it is displayed on the one side to show the issue of male ancestors, and on the other to show the issue of female ancestors.'[61] This comment was a commonplace in introductory canon law treatises. *Britton's* statement is close enough to have been a translated quotation.[62]

Combined, such various incidents, from terminology to trees and quotations, are good evidence for widespread knowledge of canon law kinship, and even familiarity with some specialised canon law kinship texts, among educated non-canonists. The reach of this material suggests that knowledge of canon law kinship as an underlying structure for the family was not limited to the relatively small number of common lawyers who had attended universities and studied the canon or civil laws.

Adaptations of canon law kinship material show an even deeper engagement with the ideas and the system. The most common adaptations were variations on *arbores consanguinitatis* that survive in *Britton* manuscripts. In the section 'Of degrees of kindred' *Britton* gave instructions on how to draw a tree.[63] The pattern is familiar. A 'perpendicular line' was drawn, and a degree was left empty in the middle for the 'supposed plaintiff'; the father and mother were placed above – they made the first degree; the other ancestors were placed above 'and so higher and higher'. Interestingly, *Britton* wrote that this ascending line could stretch as far as the time limit of the writ of right allowed; thus his adaptation attempted to fit the tree to a common law

---

58 *Britton*, ii. 57, 164–5, 321, 323–4.
59 Ibid. ii. 320.
60 Ibid. ii. 323.
61 Ibid. ii. 326.
62 See appendix 1.20.
63 *Britton*, ii. 321, 323–4.

pattern. Next, the descending line was put below the plaintiff 'ad infinitum'. If there was 'no plaintiff in the direct line to who the right of succession could descend' the collateral lines were to be called.[64] There was a different type of tree in *Britton's* section 'Of the writs of cosinage, ael, and besael'.[65] Again, this tree was based on the model of the *arbor consanguinitatis*, but here it was significantly adapted. *Britton* began with the central line containing four cells (called the direct line). The first cell was filled with the great-grandfather and great-grandmother, the fourth with the son and daughter. Collateral lines extended 'from the three upper degrees', with male children on one side and female children on the other.[66] This tree had no ego. It was a common lawyer's innovative design to show who were cousins and who could claim by the actions of cosinage, aiel and besaiel. From a canon law model *Britton* had designed a new common law image and, although his originals do not survive, his description was to inspire creative common lawyers to a range of diagrams in *Britton* manuscripts.

In such manuscripts several trees do survive, based on the four-degree arrow-shaped exemplar of the *arbor consanguinitatis*. Those that followed it most closely were beside the sections 'Of succession, and the law of inheritance' and 'Of degrees of kindred'.[67] Some of these trees used civil law degrees although they followed the canon law shape, revealing knowledge of both learned kinship systems.[68] Perhaps more interesting, however, are the six surviving cosinage trees which were contracted versions of the *arbor consanguinitatis* (free of degrees or central 'egos').[69] Following *Britton* several common lawyers drew trees inspired by the canon law exemplar. These trees tended to occur in the more formal two-column *Britton* manuscripts, and although the trees were not all in the same hand as the surrounding text, none seem fine enough to have been decorated by illuminators. As a contrast, a third type of tree in *Britton* manuscripts was far removed from the canon law exemplar. It was a diagram that showed whose land could be claimed using an action

[64] Ibid. ii. 323–5.

[65] Ibid. ii. 164–5. Nichol's version of this tree is not the same as those in the manuscripts personally examined. He says that it is based on CUL, MS Dd.7.6, but it seems instead to be a composite.

[66] *Britton*, ii. 164.

[67] Bodl. Lib., MS Bodley 562, fo. 98r; MS Rawlinson C 898, fo. 154v; BL, MS Harley 3644, fo. 164r; CUL, MS Dd.7.6, pt III, fo. 47v. See further Worby, 'Kinship in thirteenth century England', 181–3, 246–7.

[68] CUL, MS Dd.7.6, pt III, fo. 47v; Bodl. Lib., MS Rawlinson C 898, fo. 154v; BL, MS Harley 3644, fo. 164r.

[69] Bodl. Lib., MS Rawlinson C 898 fo. 126r; BL, MS Harley 3644, fo. 132v; Bodl. Lib., MS Bodley 562, fo. 78r; BL, MS Egerton 1842, fos 257r, 317rv. There are also several Anglo-French schemata: BL, MS Lansdowne 652, fo. 71v; MS Lansdowne 1176, fo. 101r; MS Lansdowne 574, fo. 118v. There is also a peculiar image at CUL, MS Dd.7.6, pt III, fo. 37r. See further S. Worby, 'Kinship: the canon law and common law in thirteenth-century England', *Historical Research* lxxx (2007), 443–68 at pp. 465–6, and 'Kinship in thirteenth century England', 183–6, 240.

of mort d'ancestor (that of a brother, sister, father, mother, uncle or aunt).[70] This simple schematic diagram was by far the most popular image and was included in 91 per cent of the *Britton* manuscripts examined.[71] Most of these images were little more than lists and roughly drawn cells, among them only one figure referred back to the canon law model and named the central cell in the diagram *protheus* after the canon law ego, rather than the usual *filius* or *fiz*.[72] Common lawyers thus sought diagrammatic illustrations of kinship, arguably under canon law inspiration.

A final example of an adapted 'arbor consanguinitatis' occurred in CUL, MS Dd.7.14, a *Bracton* manuscript that dates to the late thirteenth or early fourteenth century.[73] Although the tree survives apart from the text of *Bracton* it was clearly linked to it and, although it was titled 'arbor consanguinitatis', it showed the kinship structure detailed in the sections on the 'Degrees of kinship and succession' and 'Of those who ought to succeed others and the order of succession' in shape, size and terminology.[74] This tree can be connected to Walter de Langton (d. 1321), bishop of Coventry and Litchfield, and treasurer to Edward I and Edward II, whose arms occur on the figure.[75] It is surprising to see the arms of a bishop on such an unorthodox tree of consanguinity, even a bishop so famously devoted to secular matters as Walter of Langton.[76] It may have belonged to someone in his employ.[77] Most likely it belonged to a common lawyer who wanted to make a Bractonian tree inspired by the canon law exemplar – even though this exemplar was not easily adaptable to common law purposes. The *arbor consanguinitatis* image of canon law kinship had wide currency.

More informative than adapted trees are the adapted treatises that are to be found in common law contexts. Three survive that show a deep but peculiar engagement with canon law kinship ideas. *Quibus modis* and *Triplex est* were paired treatises that occurred in the *Bracton* manuscripts BL, MS

---

[70] *Britton*, ii. 57.

[71] Bodl. Lib., MS Douce 98, fo. 336r; BL, MS Lansdowne 574, fo. 96r; Bodl. Lib., MS Rawlinson C 898, fo. 106v; BL, MS Harley 3644, fo. 110r; MS Add. 25004, fo. 105r; MS Harley 324, fo. 127r; MS Harley 869, fo. 250v; MS Harley 5274, fo. 141v; CUL, MS Ff.2.39, fo. 83r; MS Hh.4.6, fo. 107r; MS Add. 3584, fo. 107r; MS Gg.5.12, fo. 141v; Bodl. Lib., MS Digby 136, fo. 91v; BL, MS Harley 529, fo. 156v; MS Harley 870, fo. 103v; MS Lansdowne 1176, fo. 84r; MS Egerton 1842, fo. 211r; MS Lansdowne 652, fo. 58r; MS Harley 4656, fo. 78v; CUL, MS Dd.7.6, pt III, fo. 30v.

[72] CUL, MS Dd.7.6, pt III, fo. 30v. See Worby, 'Kinship in thirteen century England', 26, 186–7, 240.

[73] CUL, MS Dd.7.14, fo. 410r.

[74] On the integrity of the tree as part of the manuscript see Baker, *Catalogue*, 81–3. On how the tree followed its Bractonian model see Worby, 'Kinship: the canon law and the common law', 461–2, which includes a reproduction of the tree.

[75] Baker, *Catalogue*, 83. The arms are identified (wrongly) in the figure in the hand of Francis Tate.

[76] ODNB xxxii. 523–5.

[77] Baker, *Catalogue*, 83.

Harley 653 and Worcester Cathedral Library, MS F 87 (*see* appendices 3 and 4). It seems likely that there were more in manuscripts of *De legibus* now lost, as there were important differences between the two manuscripts (such as distinct rubric titles), and because neither manuscript actually contained a tree to fulfil the promise they copied.[78] They show the potentially deep reach into secular contexts of canon law kinship ideas.

*Triplex est* (named here by the first two words of the treatise) was an adaptation of the section 'De cognatione carnali' in Raymón de Penyafort's *Summa de matrimonio*.[79] This was not the most difficult of *Summae*, although it was still a comprehensive introduction to marriage law. *Quibus modis* (named from the opening words of the rubric from BL, MS Harley 653), was an adaptation of a minor canon law kinship treatise, the 'Summa Magistri Iohannis Ispanii super arborem de consanguinitate'.[80] The author, Johannes Egitaniensis (John of Idanha), was a thirteenth-century Portuguese civilian, who, until fairly recently, had been mistaken for Johannes de Deo.[81] Virtually nothing is known about him.[82] His *Summa*, sometimes called his *Lectura*, on consanguinity was closely related to the very popular canon law kinship monograph *Quia tractare intendimus*.[83] It was part of the tradition of monographs on consanguinity and affinity that were so popular in the thirteenth century, but it was not a major work and was relatively rare.[84] It probably came to be adapted by a common lawyer because it occurred in a manuscript along with Raymón's *Summa de matrimonio* and attracted notice that way.

These adaptations were made by a common lawyer, who integrated them into *Bracton*, some time in the late thirteenth or early fourteenth century.[85] The end of *Triplex est* reads: 'And how the degrees of kinship are computed and in how many degrees one person is distant from another in the ascending or descending line will appear more clearly to the eye in the figure given below', an ending virtually identical to that of *Bracton*'s section on parentelic kinship.[86] In fact, both manuscripts into which these treatises were copied omitted that line from their version of the *Bracton* section 'Degrees

---

[78] The tree in BL, MS Harley 653, fo. 42r, was a later addition and is associated with the treatise *Arbor versificata*.

[79] Peniafort, *Summa*, 533–6.

[80] The full version of the monograph has been edited: 'Lectura', ed. da Rosa Pereira, 165–182.

[81] Kuttner, 'Barcelona edition', 55 n. 10, identified him. Earlier writers mistook his identity. See, for example, von Schulte, *Geschichte der Quellen*, ii. 106.

[82] A. García y García, 'La canonística Ibérica (1150–1250) en la investigación reciente', *Bulletin of Medieval Canon Law* n.s. xi (1981), 41–75 at pp. 62–3.

[83] Schadt, *Arbores*, 210–11.

[84] 'Lectura', ed. da Rosa Pereira, 54–5, 159–60.

[85] The *terminus post quem* is about 1235 when Raymón wrote his *Summa*. The *terminus ante quem* is around the early fourteenth century when the manuscripts were copied. As the original adaptation was written to be put in *Bracton* it presumably dates to the late thirteenth century, when there is evidence that *Bracton* was in circulation.

[86] See appendix 4.33 below; cf. *Bracton*, ii. 200.

of kinship and succession'.[87] Furthermore all the references to canon law authorities were removed, showing that the treatises were adapted and used outside a university context.[88] In addition, the lack of clarity over the identity of the authors in the rubrics to both treatises shows that they were out of context.[89]

The changes made by these common law adaptors reveal precisely what aspects of canon law kinship they were interested in: the skeleton of the canon law kinship system, the structure divorced from its intended purpose. Much material was removed, in particular the references to authority. This change is reminiscent of removing all the footnotes from a modern academic text. It was a drastic device that cut the contents of the treatises adrift from their original context and purpose. Another change was equally drastic: both Raymón's Summa and Johannes Egitaniensis's Lectura contained sections on affinity.[90] Neither of the adaptations did. These common lawyers were not interested in canon law authority or in affinity rules, they were not really interested in marriage law at all. Almost all the marriage law was omitted, including, for example, the rule that the canon law used the more remote degree to determine whether marriage was allowed (when the distance from the common ancestor was not the same for both parties contemplating marriage).[91] What was left was essentially a guide to drawing the tree and counting in the canon law manner with definitions of terms and a series of examples.

The adaptors did not only remove material, they reorganised the treatises and added material relevant to their understanding of kinship. The contents of Quibus modis were rearranged to make them easier to use and to focus on the structure of the tree.[92] The adaptors also added material, notably the quotation from Bracton discussed above. Most interestingly, there were some telling additions at the end of Quibus modis, notabilia that the reader is commanded to note. These could, perhaps, reflect the answers to student style questions, and could be a glimpse of a common law lecture on canon law kinship. This is a tempting proposition, but it is tentative. It is also possible that they are merely notes on difficult questions about the tree, added by the knowledgeable adaptor or later reader, who clearly had a sophisticated understanding of the differences between canon law and common law kinship.

The common lawyer who wrote this adaptation understood that the structures underlying the two kinship systems were not identical and that

---

[87] BL, MS Harley 653, fo. 40r; WCL, MS F 87, fo. 28rv.

[88] For example, appendix 3.13, 17, 23, 27, 32; appendix. 4.11, 17, 22.

[89] Appendices 3.1; 4.1.

[90] Peniafort, Summa, 556–8 (admittedly this was not directly after the consanguinity section), and 'Lectura', ed. da Rosa Pereira, 176–82.

[91] For example, appendix 4.30, 32. .

[92] Appendices 3.13–4, 23.

the differences between them could cause confusion. The notes discuss the function of 'ego'. Common lawyers often, in their images and discussions of kinship structures, conflated the ascending and descending lines and removed ego. This could be problematic (for example, the difficulties arising from the lack of a central reference character are part of what made the kinship section in *Bracton* confusing). The reader is instructed to

> Note that the same line is called ascending and descending, being made higher or lower, in relation to different computations. But if only one line were to be put in the tree, which would be ascending, on account of the changing of people's names, something would be lacking, and it could not be called ascending and descending in respect of the *truncus*. Therefore, two lines were put there, so that the defect might be avoided and thus this one was called ascending and that descending in respect of the *truncus*.[93]

Later, the notes gave an explanation of the direct line that seems to fit with the pattern of a common law count rather than the canon law tree. This line 'proceeds from whatever cell of the ascending line up to the nearer cell and not beyond' (an echo of the common law division of heirs into near, nearer and more remote).[94] Elsewhere, the note acknowledges that the reality that families understood according to the common law pattern did not fit the schematic framework of the tree described in the canon law manner: there were more ascending and descending lines than the two in the tree, because each ascendant had two oblique lines (although the *truncus* did not) and these people were called ascendants if the computation began from someone below them.[95] The image of the *arbor* was a useful conceptualising tool, but it did not wholly fit a common law context.

An even more drastic adaptation was included in the two statue books BL, MS Hargrave 433 and Bodl. Lib., MS Douce 17. They include a version of *Quia tractare intendimus* so heavily abbreviated as to be almost a new treatise: it had been reduced from approximately 3,220 words to approximately 320.[96] All but the material most relevant to common lawyers had been pared away. As with other common law adaptations none of the affinity section was included and all references to canon law authorities were omitted. The adaptor also commented that the calculation of degrees was made 'ad mortem'.[97] There was no point calculating at death canon law degrees structured for the purposes of marriage. There was a reason to reckon kinship at death, however, in the context of inheritance. The material that remained in the abbreviated version, the canon law kinship that was interesting to

---

[93] Appendix 3.33–5.
[94] Appendix 3.38. For a more complete discussion see Worby, 'Kinship in thirteenth-century England', 163–4.
[95] Appendix 3.36.
[96] Cf. appendix 1.
[97] BL, MS Hargrave 433, fo. 100r.

common lawyers, was merely a brief plan; a definition of consanguinity; a definition of the *stipes*; the etymology of *consanguinitas*; a definition of a line; the note that there were three lines; an explanation of who was in each line; a definition of a degree; and a guide to how to draw the tree.[98] This was consanguinity at its most basic, more basic even than the similar adaptations in *Bracton* manuscripts. Common lawyers were not interested in who could marry whom (the treatise promises to include this but did not); only the definitions, the tree and perhaps the basics of counting, remained. They seem to have been interested in this material for its connection to the action of cosinage. The text did not explain the numbers in a canon law tree and, while it talked about degrees, it did not say how to count them in the canon or civil law manners, yet it was called 'Des Degrez de Cosinage' or 'Gradus Consanguinitatis'.[99] In Latin a writ of cosinage was a *breve de consanguinitate*. This may merely be a matter of parallel words each with a specific meaning within their legal context. However, the adaptation of these treatises and the choice of that title, which did not quite fit the contents, suggests otherwise. The structures of canon law kinship in this abbreviated treatise could

---

[98] 'Quia tractare intendimus de consanguinitate et eius gradibus, et de arboribus consanguinitatis expositione, ad eius evidentiam pleniorem videndum est primo et prenotandum quid sit consanguinitas, et unde dicatur; quid linea consanguinitatis, et quot sunt linee; et quid gradus, et qualiter computetur; usque ad quem gradum prohibeatur matrimonium. Consanguinitas est vinculum personarum ab eo stipite descendentium carnali progeneratione contractum. Stipitem autem dico illam personam a qua aliqui duxerint originem. Dicitur autem consanguinitas a communi sanguine, quare [*recte* quasi] communem sanguinem habentes vel de uno sanguine procedentes. Linea est ordinata collectio personarum consanguinitate coniunctarum, vel ab eodem stipite descendentium, diversos gradus continens, et eos stipites ab unitate stipitis secundum numerum distinguens. Linearum tres sunt species: descendentes, transversales; sicut triplex est diversitas consanguineorum vel propinquorum. Linea descendentium [*recte* ascendentium] que continet eos a quibus originem traximus, sicut pater, mater, avus, avia, et sic deinceps. [Linea] descendenter [*recte* descendentium] est illa que [continet] illos qui duxerint originem a nobis, sicut filius, filia, nepos, neptis, et sic deinceps. Transversarium autem a latere venientium est illa que continet illos qui [nec – *s.l.*] a nobis duxerint originem nec nos ab ipsis, ut super: soror et eorum progenies. Gradus est quedam habitudo sive distantia personarum, facta ad mortem, collectione ad communem parentem, qua cognoscitur qua generationis distantia due persone inter se defecerint. Arborem consanguinitatis sic describas: pretende a vertice prothei sursum lineam ascendentem continentem .iiii. cellulas, in quarum prima ponitur pater et mater; in secunda avus et avia; in tertia proavus, proavia; in quarto [*recte* quarta] abavus, abavia. Et similiter describo [*recte* describe] lineam descendentem a protheo continentem .iiii. cellulas, in quarum prima ponitur filius et filia; in secunda nepos et neptis; in tertia pronepos, pronepetis; in quarto [*recte* quarta] abnepos, abneptis. Restat videre de lineis transversalibus, quarum due oriuntur ex protheo, [immo – *non leg.*] a patre prothei secundum Petrum de Hispania, quia pater et filia in eodem gradu sunt. Et a quolibet suo superiori oritur tam a patre quam ex matre. Ab inferiori nulla oritur, quia omnes ab inferioribus descendunt recta linea, a protheo descendunt': ibid. fos 99r–100r.

[99] *Des degrez de cosinage* is the French title in BL, MS Hargrave 433, fo. 99r; *Gradus consanguinitatis* in Bodl. Lib., MS Douce 17, fo. 161v.

have had a practical value in an action of cosinage, which was, after all, concerned with claims based on the seisin of collateral kinsmen.

The kinship of the canon law clearly had a currency outside its own sphere. This reach was not shared by other kinship systems. While some common lawyers (i.e. *Bracton*) referenced civil law kinship, this borrowing was limited and unsuccessful. In contrast, the range of references to canon law kinship outside its normal context show that the canon law kinship system was the most widely considered formal kinship system in thirteenth- and fourteenth-century England. Common lawyers were not applying canon law kinship in place of their own parentelic kinship system. Rather there was a wide knowledge of canon law kinship among literate non-canonists, coupled with a perceived gap in common lawyers' presentation of their own kinship system, leading to attention among some to the powerful formal structure of the canon law. Clearly, the fact that these men were common lawyers and specialists leads to a bias in their works towards structures over marriage law and practice: the material reflects a range of particular, secular knowledge about canon law kinship.

There seems to be no evidence of reciprocal attention to the common law kinship system among canon lawyers. This is something of an argument from silence, and admittedly there was a dearth of specialist canon law authors in England. Yet it is suggestive that when canon lawyers wrote of an alternative kinship system they limited their references to the civil law system enshrined in the universities. The fact that canonists' learning was not country specific goes some way towards explaining the lack.

## Canon law kinship among theologians

One *Bracton* manuscript contains a treatise on kinship (*Ad arborem*, named here for the opening words) by Robert Kilwardby (d. 1279), who was, in later life, archbishop of Canterbury.[100] Kilwardby was an academic theologian who studied and taught arts and theology at Paris (c. 1237–45) and Oxford (c. 1250), and became a Dominican. He was not a canon lawyer and his treatise on kinship was usually associated with works of theology and university manuscripts.[101] Canon lawyers and theologians shared a common

---

[100] His works are listed in T. Kaeppeli, *Scriptores ordinis praedicatorum medii aevi*, Rome 1970–93, iii. 320–5. For biography see Robert Kilwardby OP, *On time and imagination: De tempore, de spiritu fantastico*, ed. P. Osmund Lewry, Oxford 1987, pp. xiii–xvii, and E. M. F. Sommer-Seckendorff, *Studies in the life of Robert Kilwardby OP*, Rome 1937. For a full discussion of the identification of Kilwardby as the author of *Ad arborem* see Worby 'Kinship in thirteenth-century England', 114–15, 131–3.

[101] CUL, MS Dd.7.6, pt III, fos 66r–68v (with *Bracton* and other common law texts); Bibliothèque Mazarine, Paris, MS 3642, fos 90v–95 (with works on astrology, algorithms, and natural history, and works by Aristotle, Boethius, Cicero and Seneca); Balliol

framework where kinship was concerned. One of the key texts for the study of theology at medieval universities was the *Sentences* of Peter Lombard and one of the questions this addressed was marriage.[102] In fact the *Sentences* contained some of the same authorities as the *Decretum*.[103] Kilwardby's treatise shows how canon law kinship was not just a set of practical rules but an intellectual system giving coherence to the social world at the highest level. The penetration of canon law kinship into original theological reflection in one direction, and into common law thinking in another, gives it a decisive claim to be the lynchpin of reflection about kinship in thirteenth-century England.

*Ad arborem* was part of the genre of introductory treatises on canon law kinship. While its discussion of the subject was somewhat unusual, for example in the redefinitions of the key terms, it was clearly about the canon law. Kilwardby explained why the canon law definitions were unsuitable and offered his own. He referenced mostly the same authorities as the canon law treatises, and the opinion of a canon lawyer, Geoffrey of Trani. His treatise was wider in scope and more scholarly than the usual canon law monographs, it attempted to discuss kinship in a broader context and it reworked some of the canon law commonplaces on the subject.

Ultimately, for Kilwardby, the canon law kinship system was part of a way of classifying and ordering the world. This can be seen in his discussion of the two *arbores*. He gave five specific uses for the *arbor consanguinitatis*. The first was 'to know [how] to find the distance of any person whatsoever in the blood-kin group'.[104] The second was to know by how many degrees of consanguinity the two people in question relate to each other.[105] Both of these were practical exercises to do with using the tree. The third use showed the context of this material. It was to know which people were able to be

College, Oxford, MS 3, fo. 172v (with other works by Kilwardby); MS 215, fos 39v–45v (with theology texts, including a table of contents for the works of Augustine); New College, Oxford, MS 106, fos 297–302 (with the *Sentences* of Peter Lombard); Magdalen College, Oxford, MS 114, fo. 216 (with the *Sentences* of Peter Lombard); BL, MS Royal 9 B VI, fos 247r–249v, and the fire damaged end of this treatise in BL, MS Royal App. 85, fo. 36 (with the *Sentences* of Peter Lombard); Bibl. Apost. Vat., MS Borgh. 296, fos 325r–328r (with the *Sentences* of Peter Lombard); Münster Universitätsbibliothek, MS 157, fos 186ra–189r (with theological texts including the works of Thomas Aquinus).

102 J. I. Catto, 'Theology and theologians, 1220–1320', in his *History of the University of Oxford*, Oxford 1984, i. 417–517 at pp. 472–3.

103 Peter Lombard, *Sententiae in iv libris distinctae, tomus ii, liber iii et iv*, ed. Collegii S. Bonaventurae, Grottaferrata 1981, Lib. 4 Dist. xl–i. 22 of the authorities were the same as in the *Decretum* (21 from C.35, 1 from C.36), but the *Sentences* did not include C.35 q.5 c.2, which is the chapter from the *Decretum* cited most frequently in *Ad arborem*

104 'Prima est scire invenire distantiam quarumcumque personarum in consanguinitate': CUL, MS Dd.7.6, pt III, fo. 66v.

105 'Secunda utilitas arboris est scire quoto gradu consanguinitatis sibi attineant due persone proposite': ibid. fo. 67v.

married according to the canon law.[106] All the people prohibited were in the tree, and all those not prohibited were permitted.[107] The fourth use was to see which people in the tree could marry which others in the tree – another canon law question.[108] Thus, for example, all the people in one part of the tree could marry all the people in the other, for example the right and left sides, except for the three inferior lines which descended from the father and mother of the *protheus*, through the *protheus* himself and through his brother and sister.[109] The fifth use of the tree reveals it as a conceptualising tool. It was 'to know the whole blood kin-group of any person insofar as it is an impediment to marriage'.[110] Kilwardby explained that the tree did not show all the people, but all the manners of relating (i.e. as grandparents, or great-grandparents, etc).[111] Nor was the whole natural family included; the constitutions upon which these limits were based addressed marriages; such human constitutions did not lift a law of nature.[112] Elsewhere he noted that the people in the tree were 'named only in respect of the family relationship which they have to the *protheus*' not in respect of all their other families.[113] While this treatise built upon canon law ideas it was more clearly about defining family and its place in the world.

*Ad arborem* also explained the uses of the *arbor affinitatis*. Unlike the common lawyers, this non-canonist was interested in affinity because he took a wide rather than a narrow view of the scope of this material. Even so, affinity was not put in a wider context of natural family. The subject was more technical so the uses of the tree he described were limited to technicalities, explained with rules and examples. The first use was to know how and from where affinity arose, which, he said, was partially clear from the definition of affinity, and from the rule that 'person added to person by mixture

---

[106] 'Tercia ultilitas arboris est scire que persone possunt matrimonialiter copulari secundum canones': ibid.

[107] 'Quot ergo gradus hodie [sunt] prohibiti patet ex arbore que continet congnationem [*recte* cognationem] prothei precise usque ad quartum gradum ex omni parte. Inde etiam constat qui sunt permissi quia omnis gradus non prohibitus est permissus': ibid.

[108] 'Quarta [utilitas] est specialiter de personis in arbore contentis videre, scilicet que illarum cum quibus copulari possit et que non': ibid.

[109] 'quod omnes que sunt ex una parte arboris possunt contrahere cum illis que sunt ex alia, hoc est sinistra pars cum dextra et econtro [*recte* econverso], exceptis lineis tribus inferioribus que a patre et matre prothei descendunt per protheum ipsum, et per fratrem eius, ac sororem': ibid.

[110] 'Quinta utilitas arboris est scire cuiuscumque persone totam consanguinitatem que matrimonium impedit': ibid.

[111] 'et dico totam. Non quo ad omnes personas, sed quo ad omnes modos attinentie': ibid. This was because the *protheus* had more than the two grandparents, for example, depicted in the tree.

[112] 'non continetur tota cognatio unius persone in arbore quia constitutio humana non tollit ius nature': ibid.

[113] 'quod cognati prothei positi in arbore non nominantur secundum omnem respectum cognationis quem habent [...] Sed nuncupantur solom [*correctly* solum] secundum respectum cognationis quem habent ad protheum': ibid. fo. 66v.

of flesh changes type of close relationship but not degree'.[114] The second use was to know 'between whom affinity universally arises'.[115] He gave a rule: 'Whatsoever two people are carnally joined, each of them joins affinity with the consanguines of the other, but their blood relations do not become related by affinity to each other.'[116] The third use was to know how to find the degrees of affinity.[117] The rule was to use the degrees of consanguinity.[118] The fourth use was to know how to reckon the degrees of affinity.[119]

Kilwardby's conception of kinship was more precise and scholarly than normal canon law examples. This can be most clearly seen in his intellectual approach to the usual canon law definitions of kinship terms and ideas. A standard canon law definition of consanguinity was 'a bond of people descending from the same *stipes*, joined by propagation through the flesh'.[120] This was quoted and reconstructed by Kilwardby, who disagreed because it seemed to exclude the *stipes* from the consanguinity. He departed from the tradition of the canon law treatises, and explicitly redefined the term:

Because, however, this description only contains descendants, excluding the common parent and consanguinity is hardly doubtful between father and son, not only between his sons, it seems that it is able to be defined more fittingly thus: consanguinity is a coming together in nature of people derived from one parent by propagation of flesh. This contains descendants and the *stipes*, however they are arranged in relation to one another. 'A coming together of people' excludes the coming together of irrational things; 'in nature' excludes a coming together in free will or friendship; the derivation of 'propagation' excludes [people who come together in] confined spaces. And the words 'from one parent' exclude people of different kindreds'.[121]

---

[114] 'Prima scire unde et quomodo oritur affinitas et hoc pro parte patet ex premissa descriptione affinitatis. Magis etiam declaratur ex regula: "illa persona addita persone per carnis commixtionem mutat genus attinentie sed non gradum"': ibid. fo. 68r.

[115] 'Secunda utilitas est scire inter quos universaliter oritur affinitas': ibid.

[116] 'Quecumque due persone carnaliter copulantur utraque illarum cum consanguineis alterius contrahit affinitatem, consanguinei tamen non sunt affines adinvicem': ibid.

[117] 'Tertia utilitas est scire invencionem gradus affinitatis': ibid.

[118] 'Quoto gradu consanguinitatis sibi attinent due persone, toto gradu affinitatis attinebit alteruter illarum que per carnis copulam alteri illarum admiscetur': ibid.

[119] 'Quarta utilitas est scire computare gradus affinitatis': ibid.

[120] 'Consanguinitas est vinculum personarum ab eodem stipite descendentium, carnali propagatione contractum': Peniafort, *Summa*, 533.

[121] 'Quia cum [recte tamen] ista descriptio non continet nisi personas descendentes, excluso parente communi, et consanguinitas habeant [recte haut] dubium est inter patrem et filios, non solum inter filios eius, videtur quod possit diffiniri conventius sic: consanguinitas est convenientia personarum in natura ab uno parente carnis propagatione derivata. Hec continet personas descendentes et stipitem qualitercumque comparentur adinvicem. "Convenientia personarum" excludit res irrationabiles; "in natura" convenientiam in voluntate vel gratia; derivatio "propagationis", angulos. Et quod dicitur "ab uno parente" excludit personas diversarum cognationum': CUL, MS Dd.7.6, pt III, fo. 66r.

For Kilwardby, the standard definition of a line – 'an ordered set of people joined by consanguinity, descending from the same *stipes*, containing different degrees'[122] – was not sufficient either 'because "set" sounds as if it were at the same time, and also because this only makes mention of descendants and not of ascendants, and because in it the common parent seems to be excluded from every line'.[123] Again, he offered a new definition:

A line is an ordered disposition or series of people mutually consanguineous, containing degrees. Nor is it necessary here to say 'from one parent' who would be the propagator, because this is understood when it says 'of consan-guineous people', just as is apparent through the definition of consanguinity. As for the fact that 'containing degrees' is added; it is appropriate to put it in, because a single degree is never a line, but only a beginning of a line, whence neither father to son makes a line of consanguinity, nor does son to father, nor brother or sister to brother, but [they make] a degree only and the beginning of a line, as is apparent in the tree from the numbers written in.[124]

He defined a degree as 'a positioning of person to person in a group related by blood, that is to say, a place above or below or alongside'.[125] He followed the same approach in his discussion of affinity:

But since not only joining of flesh makes affinity, but also blood-relationship (for the woman in the middle who is related to one person and joined to another by sexual union causes affinity between those persons on either side), it can perhaps be more completely described thus: affinity is a kind of prox-imity of certain persons who are not blood relations, connected through the intermediary role of a third person, who is a blood-kinswoman to one of them and [who has] carnally joined with the other.[126]

---

[122] 'Linea est ordinata collectio personarum consanguinitate coniunctarum, ab eodem stipite descendentium, diversos gradus continens': Peniafort, *Summa*, 533.

[123] 'sed quia collectio sonat insimul esse, et etiam quia hic non fit mentio nisi de descendentibus et non de ascendentibus, et quia hic videtur excludi communis parens ab omni linea': CUL, MS Dd.7.6, pt III, fo. 66v.

[124] 'linea est ordinata dispositio vel ordo personarum consanguinearum adinvicem gradus continens. Nec oportet hic facere mentionem "de uno parente" q[u]i sit propagator, quia hoc intelligitur in hoc quod dicitur "consanguinearum"; sicut patet per diffinitionem consanguinitatis. Quod autem additur "gradus continens"; congrue ponitur quia unicus gradus numquam linea est, sed solum incho[h]atio linee, unde nec pater ad filium lineam facit consanguinitatis, nec filius ad patrem, nec frater vel soror ad fratrem, sed gradum tantum et linee incho[h]ationem; ut patet [in arbore] ex numeris inscriptis': ibid.

[125] 'gradus est ordo persone ad personam in consanguinitate secundum aliquam differen-tiam situs scilicet supra vel infra vel iuxta': ibid.

[126] 'Quia vero non solam copula carnis facit affinitatem, sed etiam cognatio, media enim persona, uni cognita et alteri carnaliter copulata, causat affinitatem inter illas personas extremas, potest forte plenius sic describi: affinitas est propinquitas quedam personarum non consanguinearum per mediationem tertie persone contracta quedam [*recte* que] uni earum est cognita et alteri carnaliter copulata': ibid. fo. 67v.

These deconstructions and redefinitions are one of the most striking features of this text as they are so unlike the canon law norm.

This remarkable work also reveals some interesting attitudes to kinship and the canon law system. *Ad arborem* shows an awareness of underlying natural law, such as Kilwardby's reference to an argument between canonists which expressed discomfort about allowing marriages beyond the fourth degree when the parties were aware of their relationship or where one was a direct descendant of the other.[127] He also included a comment which is suggestive of a potentially vernacular sense of the ordering of the kindred. He asked 'why the common parent is excluded in the computation of legal [meaning civil law] degrees and no other person, when [the common parent] is the most dignified of all?'[128] This reveals an attitude that privileged the ancestor, which is not unnatural in a social system such as that which operated in medieval England. The answer to his question was because they could not inherit.[129] Again, his thinking about consanguinity was put in a context that was wider than the canon law. Although it is tempting to regard his answer as a reference to the common law, which conventionally barred direct ancestors from inheriting, it is more likely to be a reference to the civil law under which the father at the head of the family had control of the family property, especially as the civil law was the context of his question. Kilwardby's discussion was founded on canon law kinship, but reveals clearly how this was part of a wider suite of ideas and how several layers of thinking about kinship existed (from conceptual, to practical, to attitudinal).

At medieval universities the kinship system of the canon law was the foremost manner of thinking about kinship. Even civil law texts referred to the canon law system. Accursius' gloss on the *Institutes* gave definitions of degrees and contrasted two canon law definitions with a civil law defini-

---

[127] 'Ideo non committitur hodie incestus ultra quartum gradum: siquis copulatur sue consanguinee in quinto gradu vel ulteriori, ubi enim licite contrahitur matrimonium non committitur incestus. Dubitatur autem de verbo quod dictum est nuper quod tota consanguinitas unius persone impediens eius contractum continetur in arbore. Videtur enim quod licet ita sit de cognatione eius laterali quod non sit tamen verum de cognatione secundum lineam descendentem. Videtur enim quod in infinitum duret impedimentum matrimonii secundum lineam cognationis descendentem ut habetur .ff. *de ritu nupciarum* [*Digest* 23.2.0] et 35.q.1. *progeniem, de consanguinitate, in copula* [C.35 q.2 & 3 c. 16, 17 & 18]. Et illud concedunt aliqui dicentes quod hoc quod dicitur tota consanguinitas impediens matrimonium in arbore contineri ad lineam transversalem pertinet tantum. Alii tamen quibus consentit dominus Gaufridus de Crana Cardinal' dicunt quod hodie tam in ascendentibus quam in descendentibus et quam in collateralibus quartum gradum prohibicio non excedit ut habetur extra de consanguinitate et affinitate *non debet* [X 4.14.8]': ibid.

[128] 'quare communis parens excluditur in computatione graduum legalium et nulla alia persona cum illa sit omnium dignissima?': ibid.

[129] 'quod communis parens excluditur in computatione legali quia non sunt computandi nisi quibus deberi potest hereditaria successio': ibid.

tion.[130] A text of lectures on the *Institutes*, from England in the last quarter of the twelfth century, discussed *Institutes* 3.6 (on cognates) and noted the contrast with canon law degrees.[131] Even in the civil law schools the two systems had become entwined. For the purposes of formal thinking and the study of kinship, the canon law classificatory structures were dominant.

The creativity based on the canon law system tells its own tale. Outside a canon law context, among common lawyers and among the theologians in the universities, canon law kinship was the foremost formal way of thinking, depicting and writing about kinship structures. It superseded civil law structures, which were effectively obsolete in practice in England at this time. It did not replace the common law's own kinship system, but it could be an inspiration and *addendum*, or sometimes just a way of talking about kinship. The evidence suggests that the kinship of the canon law was in common currency, particularly among the literate.

From the common law side the absolute numbers and eventual influence of this material on practical common law kinship (for example on inheritance and disputes about inheritance) was not substantial; parentelic kinship applied. The material is interesting, however, because it shows common lawyers reaching for formal kinship structures. It is fascinating to see canon law kinship, not only referred to in passing, but quoted, integrated and even adapted for common law purposes. In contrast to Kilwardby's ivory tower clarity, the adoptions and attempts at synthesis also reflect the common law's struggle with the descent from structure, be it common law forms of action or canon law frameworks, to real, often inchoate kinship. The reach of the canon law kinship system into secular and university contexts in thirteenth- and fourteenth-century England was wide and often deep.

---

[130] 'Gradus est numeratio singularum personarum cognatione vel affinitate sibi coniunctarum quoto gradu una persona distat ab altera optime indicans': Accursius, 'Gloss' on *Institutes* 3.6 'Adicit', fo. 117r.
[131] De Zuleta and Stein, *Teaching of Roman law*, 75–6. They use the unusual phrase 'divine pagine' but the reference was clearly to the canon law manner of counting.

# 4

# Kinship Laws in Practice

In practice, the interaction of litigants with the rules, and thus with the two legal kinship systems, was more complicated than the books of either legal system suggested: canon law rules could not be applied completely and the common law encompassed several senses of kinship. It is clear that neither the canon nor the common law kinship system was limited to the bookish sphere and that, to a greater or lesser extent, both applied in practice, and cannot be properly understood without this dimension (although the application of the law in court is by no means the whole of the picture either). There was a nexus between formal concepts of kinship and how people acted in relation to these ideas, and a tactical link between structures, rules, practice and reality.

An important preliminary is an understanding that these cases were in some sense constructions. The shape of the law forced people into narratives that fitted with and enlisted the force of the rules. Some people lied or deceived themselves, and they presented facts in the manner most likely to succeed if they were well informed or had legal advice. Such narratives are powerful shapers of the presentation of underlying facts.[1] The close link between both marriage and inheritance and land could lead to strong pressures on the potential litigant and this should be recalled when considering specific cases.

## At canon law

Canon law kinship rules can be seen in court records in three main ways: as a ground for 'divorce'; a defence against an action to enforce a marriage, usually in litigation between parties; or as a matter of disciplinary action in an office case (where the canon law courts were exercising their quasi-criminal jurisdiction). The evidence that divorces on grounds of kinship were rare should not obscure the fact that canon law kinship law was applied in contemporary courts, although spiritual kinship and public honesty were comparatively unusual.

An example where the exception of affinity was successfully used was the case of *Alice La Marescal c Elias de Suffolk*, which came before the arch-

---

[1] Donahue, *Law, marriage, and society*, ch. ii.

bishop's court in Canterbury in 1292–3.[2] This was an appeal from an earlier hearing in the bishop's court in London (itself an appeal from a hearing in the church of Chelsea by the archdeacon of Middlesex). Alice attempted to enforce a putative marriage which she claimed had been formed by a present tense promise to marry. Elias resisted this and used the exception that he could not solemnise the marriage because he had had sexual intercourse with a relative of hers within the forbidden degrees (a female blood relative). The facts as stated may not have been true, and the evidence from the witnesses was initially patchy (although not exceptionally so). Several witnesses on Elias's behalf did not know of the consanguinity between Alice and Christine, Elias's alleged former lover, although they were able to supply details of the time that Elias and Christine had had intercourse. Then a witness who had been in service in the village where Christine's mother married and had passed through the village where Alice's grandmother had married was able to testify that Christine's mother and Alice's grandmother were sisters 'both by public report and by the way they greeted one another'.[3] Another witness supported this relationship and Alice's father, mother and brother testified to the kinship between their families. Alice's position looked very weak when her close family eventually gave testimony that undermined her case. Elias was successful; he and Alice could not marry as they were within the forbidden categories (in the first type and third degree of affinity). The court annulled the contract and absolved Elias.

Canon law kinship can also be seen in action in *ex officio* cases. In the court of the dean and chapter of Lincoln, between 1336 and 1343 there were seven records of action against Robert Basage and Emma Thorif who were cited repeatedly for adultery and incest: Emma was an unspecified relative of Robert's wife.[4] The warnings were reiterated so often that the record-maker reported that 'they are incorrigible' and that it was a matter of 'great scandal' in the parish and neighbouring countryside.[5] Entertaining as this is, the number of citations is not good evidence for the system operating efficiently. The suggestion of scandal, however, does indicate some public acceptance of the system among the scandalised.

Overall, cases involving canon law kinship did not form a large part of the business of the canon law courts in England.[6] In York, for example, marriage made up 38 per cent of the business of the court between 1301 and 1499.[7] Most of this was instance cases rather than 'criminal enforcement'.[8] Most

---

[2]  *Select cases from the ecclesiastical courts*, 350–65.
[3]  Ibid. 359.
[4]  *Lower ecclesiastical jurisdiction*, 11–12, 43, 48–9, 66, 78, 157, 162.
[5]  'et quod est incorigiblis de predictis et super hoc est magnum scandalum in parochia … et in tota patria vicinia': ibid. 157.
[6]  Donahue, *Law, marriage and society*, 564–5.
[7]  Ibid. 64.
[8]  Ibid. 65.

of the marriage actions were to enforce a putative marriage and only 14 per cent were actions to dissolve.[9] Pre-contract was the most common ground for matrimonial litigation in the fourteenth and fifteenth centuries (overall 46 per cent of matrimonial cases), and denial was a common response. Other grounds used to defend against marriages were force and/or non age at 13 per cent, then consanguinity and affinity at 12 per cent (a total of 9 cases) in the fourteenth century. While kinship was not a large proportion of the business of these courts it did occur more frequently than grounds such as crime, impotence and vow (i.e. a vow to stay celibate).[10] In the fifteenth century there were slightly fewer actions where the grounds of consanguinity and or affinity were raised than in the fourteenth.[11] Overall kinship was raised in 16 out of 178 cases.[12] In Ely, between 1374 and 1381, cases involving kinship were more common, perhaps because of the higher proportion of *ex officio* cases in the business of this court. Kinship was raised as a defence or ground for divorce proportionately more frequently (in 15 claims of incest). In Ely kinship was a more common defence than force and non age, but was still significantly less common overall than allegations of precontract.[13] There is reason to believe that the Ely court was active in relation to kinship as the Ely office cases tended to be brought at the start or in the early public phase of a relationship.[14] While neither set of figures show kinship to have been a major part of business, they both show that it was still a relatively usual part.

The canon law on kinship was variously ignored, followed and manipulated (these being alternatives in different times and places, for both the courts and the people subject to them).[15] Donahue has shown, for example, how one new judge of Canterbury diocesan court, Richard de Clyve, on visitation in 1292, fresh from the schools, began by prosecuting every case in relation to kinship, but faced some resistance as is shown variously by witnesses growing less certain and by a letter pleading mercy on behalf of a woman sentenced to whipping from a mutually acquainted royal clerk. He finished his circuit on a more flexible note and began to base his decisions on the degree of local scandal that the cases inspired. He also exhibited doubts about the application of the rules which held that affinity arose from mere sexual relationships.[16] Thus the courts could take an accommodating attitude to the rules about kinship, and sometimes finesse (or ignore) the strict application of the rules. Richard de Clyve's experience also confirms

9   Ibid. 70.
10  Ibid. 71.
11  Ibid.
12  Ibid.
13  Ibid. 230.
14  Ibid. 573.
15  Ibid. 565–6.
16  Ibid. 566–70. See also C. Donahue, Jr, 'The monastic judge: social practice, formal rule and the medieval law of incest', in P. Landau and M. Petzolt (eds), *De iure canonico medii aevi: Festschrift für Rudolf Weigand*, Rome 1996, 49–69.

that people were aware of the rules, made an effort to follow them (to a degree) and could be scandalised in certain circumstances by their breach. An example of such scandal is the deathbed warning of a father against his son's marriage. Though the kinship was distant, in the fourth degree, the father allegedly said 'they will never flourish or live together in good fortune because of the consanguinity between them'.[17] There were also cases where people 'hotly resisted' marriages that were within the forbidden degrees: one woman even said she would prefer to die rather than marry her kinsman.[18] Rhetoric or not, such a declaration in a court case would have been dramatic, and would not have been plausible were the rules not accepted. Equally, there were some cases that suggest a certain degree of cynicism in relation to the rules. It is not unreasonable to suspect that affinity through illicit intercourse may sometimes have been used collusively to escape marriages. In *Marion c Umphrey*, in Ely in 1377, the husband petitioned for divorce based on his prior intercourse with his wife's second cousin. The wife appeared and agreed to the 'divorce', the second cousin confessed the intercourse and five witnesses supported the case. This apparent unanimity and the fact that the relationship between the cousins was not very distant are suggestive pointers. This is enough to raise the question of collusion (successful collusion in fact, because the 'divorce' was granted).[19]

The evidence from York and Ely shows how far down the social scale obedience to the kinship rules of the canon law reached. Some of the cases were brought by or against relatively humble people but the 'middling' sort were not uncommon in these courts which suggests that some attempt was being made to apply the canon law kinship system across the classes.[20]

While the surviving case evidence does not often reveal 'divorces' on grounds of 'incest' it does show other aspects of the canon law kinship system at work. Several cases in the York and Ely samples, for example, reveal the banns system operating. One Ely example, *Borewell c Bileye*, arose from reclamation of the banns (that is from a response to the banns alleging an impediment to the proposed marriage) and led to the discovery of affinity by illicit intercourse between the woman and a kinsman of the potential husband within the fourth degree of consanguinity.[21] Of course, not all objections raised at the banns were genuine. In *Godewyn c Roser*, a York case of 1337, affinity by illicit intercourse was raised at the banns by the mother of the woman with whom the alleged illicit intercourse had taken place. Witnesses

---

[17] Helmholz, *Marriage litigation*, 80.

[18] Ibid. 79 n. 16.

[19] For example, Donahue, *Law, marriage, and society*, 259, 573, and p. 566 where he suggests that this may have occurred in other cases. My discussion of the cases that follow owes a great debt to the work of Donahue.

[20] Ibid. 65, 298–301, though cf. 572.

[21] As detailed ibid. 270–1. The Ely cases in relation to the banns are discussed in more detail by Sheehan, 'The formation and stability of marriage', 46–55.

only knew of the alleged kinship between the two women following the reclamation of the banns, which may have been a specious objection.[22] In addition to cases involving banns there were examples where a priest or official refused to officiate or allow a marriage on grounds of consanguinity or affinity. For example, in *Office c Bourn (vicar)*, in Ely in 1378, a vicar was cited for refusing to solemnise a marriage. He alleged that this was because five male parishioners had reclaimed the banns on grounds of consanguinity. Four testified and the putative marriage was held void.[23] In *Talbot c Townley*, a 1477 York case, a chaplain refused to solemnise a marriage because it was within the degrees, although clearly the forceful abduction of the woman by her putative husband also had an effect.[24] These cases show that there was a level of potential scandal around incestuous marriages.

There are also several cases that show people seeking dispensations, again suggesting that the system could operate effectively. In *Wistow c Cowper*, a York case of 1491, a papal dispensation (for spiritual affinity) overcame the attempted defence.[25] However, in several cases a papal dispensation was held to be, or appeared to be, insufficient. In the remarkable *Hiliard c Hiliard*, a York case of 1370, the couple had previously been cited for a consanguineous relationship, but the sentence had been deferred to allow them to obtain a papal dispensation. A priest had attempted this and failed. He testified that in the papal court he was told 'that he could not get such a dispensation for a hundred pounds'.[26] Since the relationship was in the fourth degree of consanguinity this statement is unlikely to be true.[27]

Kinship was often raised as a secondary issue, with some other impediment;[28] alongside, for example, force, absence, crime and impotence.[29] An impotence case from Ely, *Pyncote c Maddyngle*, is an interesting example because consanguinity in the fourth degree was only raised by the woman seeking to escape the marriage after her husband had avoided an examination for impotence and as a result had been excommunicated. In this case the proctor had objected to witnesses to the consanguinity but was overruled. The court may have allowed consanguinity to be used as a ground for divorce where there was impotence that they could not prove (because the husband would not be examined).[30]

Divorce cases on grounds of kinship were not the norm. Despite the occasional outlandish case, such as *Ask c Ask and Conyers* where a son alleged that his parents had divorced collusively on grounds of spiritual fraternity to

---

[22] As detailed in Donahue, *Law, marriage, and society*, 106–7.
[23] As detailed ibid. 290.
[24] As detailed ibid. 175–6.
[25] As detailed ibid. 202.
[26] As detailed ibid. 147–8 at p. 148.
[27] Ibid. 719 (*Texts and commentary*, n. 284).
[28] Ibid. 574.
[29] Ibid. 175–6, 263–4, 277–8, 287–8, 293–4, 572, 709.
[30] As detailed ibid. 277–8.

deprive him of his inheritance,[31] the case evidence reveals a very different world from that where Maitland had proposed that almost any marriage could be dissolved on grounds of kinship.[32] Clearly, consanguinity and affinity could be used or discovered to escape from marriages, but the records suggest that they were not often used to escape from current marriages; instead they were more common as a defence in marriage enforcement cases. In fact, the court records seem to show that the underlying system that was meant to prevent incestuous or harmful (i.e. non-dispensable) marriages operated with some level of success. It may be that a genuine sense that 'incestuous' marriages were wrong prevented kinship from being used as a casual route to escape marriage. There is evidence that shows that incestuous marriages were a matter of bad conscience. For example, both Donahue and Sheehan consider that John de Lile of Chatteris resisted cohabiting with his 'wife', Katherine, in the late 1370s, once affinity was discovered between them.[33] Some effort was made to observe the rules: people would not have paid for a dispensation or for a priest to travel and gain a dispensation if there were no need and no social pressure to conform. It may also have been that kinship sufficient to dissolve or defend against a marriage was difficult to prove to a level that satisfied canon law rules of evidence. Whatever the reason for the comparatively small role of kinship in litigation, it seems clear that the canon law kinship system operated in practice and that some people obeyed it and were (publicly at least) scandalised when it was disobeyed.

One vital element for the successful operation of the system was acceptance and knowledge of its rules among the population under its remit. People had some element of choice in the way that the rules affected them and in the way that they reacted under, against and around the rules: they could ignore them (but to do so they might want to believe that others would ignore them too); they could attempt to break them (by knowingly forming incestuous marriages); they could do just enough to follow the rules; or they could follow them wholeheartedly. There were numerous strategies available and most probably people in different positions used them all, but factors such as the ability to prove kinship would thus have influenced how people behaved in relation to the kinship rules.

A litigant's ability to prove the alleged kinship was one of the most important factors in court. In office cases, where the canon law courts enforced their quasi-criminal jurisdiction, proof was most often made through confession or compurgation and evidence of relationships could come from people sworn to the inquest. In instance cases (litigation between parties) the burden of proof was on the person who asserted the fact and there were several ways to

---

[31] *Ask c Ask and Conyers*, as detailed ibid. 572.

[32] Pollock and Maitland, *History of English law*, ii. 385–9.

[33] *Blofeld and Reder c Lile* as detailed in Donahue, *Law, marriage, and society*, 276, 744 (*Texts and commentary*, n. 487). See also Sheehan, 'The formation and stability of marriage', 73 n. 136.

satisfy it: confession by the party; presumptions of law; physical and written evidence; oaths of the parties; inquests by impartial sworn men; and, most commonly, depositions from sworn witnesses produced by the parties, who gave evidence under oath and were questioned by the judge.[34] Despite these several options, however, the classical canon law rules, if properly applied, made kinship difficult to prove.

As in the common law system an account of the alleged kinship was needed. The count in a canon law context as elaborated by a witness and recorded in a deposition, could be simple. *Richard de Bosco c Johanna de Clapton* was a case heard 1269–71 in the archbishop's court in Canterbury, on appeal from a sentence of matrimony. Richard claimed that solemnisation of the marriage should not be enforced because he had had sexual inter-course with a woman, Matilda Goderhele, who was related to Johanna (the actrix) in the third degree of consanguinity.[35] The record suggests that he had previously claimed that he was related to Johanna in the third degree of consanguinity, but either this was a mistake or it was unsuccessful.[36] Rich-ard's witness, John, testified that Richard's great-grandmother, Alice, was the sister of Johanna's great-grandmother, Socheta, and that he knew this because he too was a descendant of Alice – her grandson (thus he would be Richard's first cousin once removed). He counted 'that there were two sisters, namely Alice and Socheta: from Alice was born Matilda, from Matilda was born Richard Byssewod, from Richard [was born] Richard about whom the case is concerned; from Socheta was born Isabel, from Isabel was born Matilda, from Matilda [was born] Johanna about whom the case is concerned'.[37] This count did not include degrees, in contrast to the example counts given in canon law treatises which did. In practice, witnesses could be asked whether they knew in what degrees of consanguinity the parties were as part of the examination.[38] Such an examination would also go beyond mere knowledge of the degrees. For example, in this case John testified to various details: his own relationship to the appellant as a ground for his knowledge; the fact that he never saw the elderly sisters but did know their daughters; and the fact that he did not know the *stipes* (the common parent).[39] Kinship was not always easy to prove and, in fact, Richard failed even with what appears to be fairly substantial evidence of relatedness.

The witnesses in this case were asked such questions for a good reason. Canon 52 of the Fourth Lateran Council (included in the *Liber extra* and

[34] Helmholz, *Oxford history*, i. 328–39.
[35] *Select cases from the ecclesiastical courts*, 96–102.
[36] Ibid. 96.
[37] 'quod due sorores, videlicet Alicia et Socheta; de Alicia nascebatur Matillda, de Matillda nascebatur Richardus Byssewod, de Richardo Richardus de quo agitur; de Socheta nascebatur Ysabella, de Isabella nascebatur Matillda, de Matillda Johanna de qua agitur': ibid. 99.
[38] For example, ibid. 358.
[39] Ibid. 99–100.

so taught to any trained canonist) set requirements for proof of kinship at canon law. The previous distant limits of kinship at six or seven degrees had necessitated the use of hearsay evidence in court. With the restriction on kinship to the fourth degree of consanguinity this was no longer to be allowed:

> we have decided that in future witnesses from hearsay shall not be accepted in this matter, … unless there are persons of weight who are trustworthy and who learnt from their elders, before the case was begun, the things that they testify: not indeed from one such person since one would not suffice even if he or she were alive, but from two at least, and not from persons who are of bad repute and suspect but from those who are trustworthy and above every objection, since it would appear rather absurd to admit in evidence those whose actions would be rejected.[40]

Hearsay evidence was only allowed from two people above objection. Grounds for exception to witnesses included 'condition, gender, age, discretion, reputation, fortune and truthfulness'.[41] Thus it seems that the ideal witness would be a free, rich man of full age with a good reputation for discretion and truthfulness. Kinship could also be a ground to object to a witness, although *Alice La Marescal c Elias de Suffolk* shows that this was not always done and if the witnesses' testimony weighed against their kinsman there were good tactical reasons to use it.[42] The canon went on to say that the hearsay evidence of one who learned from several was not sufficient, nor was evidence of men of bad repute who heard it from men of good repute. It concluded that

> The witnesses shall affirm on oath that in bearing witness in the case they are not acting from hatred or fear or love or for advantage; they shall designate the persons by their exact names or by pointing out or by sufficient description, and shall distinguish by a clear reckoning every degree of relationship on either side; and they shall include in their oath the statement that it was from their ancestors that they received what they are testifying and that they believe it to be true. They shall still not suffice unless they declare on oath that they have known that the persons who stand in at least one of these degrees of relationship regard each other as blood-relations. For it is preferable to leave alone some people who have been united contrary to human decrees than to separate, contrary to the Lord's decrees, persons who have been joined together legitimately.[43]

For non-hearsay evidence – in this context meaning that the witnesses

40  Donahue, *Law, marriage, and society*, 676 (*Texts and commentary*, n. 39).
41  Helmholz, *Oxford history*, i. 340.
42  As in, for example, *Select cases from the ecclesiastical courts*, 361–2.
43  Donahue, *Law, marriage, and society*, 676 (*Texts and commentary*, n. 39).

had first-hand knowledge – the basic rule was also that two witnesses were required.[44]

If this law was applied strictly, as advocated by the eminent canonist Hostiensis, such questioning would be applied to every witness in every case touching upon kinship. Hostiensis took a hard line on kinship evidence.[45] To follow his rules would make kinship difficult to prove. There was a degree of rhetoric in Hostiensis's discussions, particularly in the faux naïve questions he raised and dismissed to advance his argument. For example, he posited as a straw man an objection to his rules for examining witnesses that if his 'formal' rules were maintained there might be no annulments on the grounds of consanguinity and affinity. Then he vehemently disagreed: 'No! Indeed, unless everything is proved with absolute rigour it is better to cast judgement in favour of the marriage.'[46] This has the flavour of an academic context.[47] It may be that a somewhat more pragmatic view held sway in practice and among other canonists (certainly Hostiensis was objecting to 'the judges of our time' who 'have kept this [canon 52] badly, caring little or nothing for such things').[48] Hostiensis was conscious that the kinship rules were a matter of human law and could be subject to cynical misuse.[49] He had been scandalised by an old man who had deliberately manipulated witnesses to allow 'divorces' on the grounds of consanguinity (or affinity). He had invented family relationships by talking about the fictitious relationships in the presence of ten or twelve people. He would then, according to Hostiensis's account, divide the potential witnesses into groups, causing them to spread the word to more people 'saying they had heard it from their elders'.[50] Hostiensis's list of questions that a judge should ask a witness echoed the detailed considerations set out in the canon, amounting to a difficult burden of proof.[51] He also set out a process for the count: the witness should give his account in the presence of the parties, and then the judge should interrogate him separately. The witness had to begin his account from the *stipes* or from full-blood brothers. He should be asked whether he had seen every degree, although it was not necessary that he had done so: the first, the second or the third would suffice for evidence.[52]

---

[44] Helmholz, *Oxford history*, i. 340.

[45] d'Avray, *Medieval marriage*, 105–12, 242–9.

[46] 'Diceret alius: si hec forma servetur, ob causam consanguinitatis vel affinitatis dabitur divortii sententia vix aut numquam: numquid tutius esset hanc formam omittere et sententiam divortii ferre, et si omittantur aliqua de predictis? Respondeo: Non! Imo melius est, nisi ad unguem probentur omnia, pro matrimonio iudicare': ibid. 245.

[47] Ibid. 109.

[48] Ibid. 108.

[49] Ibid. 110.

[50] 'dicentes quod ita audierant a maioribus suis': ibid. 244.

[51] Ibid. 107–8, 244–5.

[52] 'Judex ergo faciet testem iurare in presentia partium. Postea ipsum seorsum interrogabit quoniam scit parentelam. Si testis incipiat a stipite vel germanis considerabitur

There is evidence in English cases which demonstrate a similar, if not so exhaustive, detail when questioning witnesses. *Richard de Bosco c Johanna de Clapton* showed some questions around the extent of the witnesses' knowledge. *Alice la Marescal c Elias de Suffolk* included evidence that the witnesses knew that two alleged ancestors were sisters 'both by public report and by the way they greeted one another'.[53] The record of *Tangerton c Smelt* in 1294, however, included a whole series of questions. A witness was asked if he had seen all whom he had named; if he knew the degrees; if he was a consanguine or affine of either of the parties; how long had passed since he knew the degrees; whether his testimony arose from any contract with either party; whether he had been present at the banns; whether he had contradicted them; whether any others had; whether there was any scandal about the marriage; and whether he would prefer the parties to be married or separated.[54]

That it was not easy to prove kinship was not only because of the thoroughness with which witnesses were properly tested. Witnesses' evidence could be uncertain or contradictory.[55] Public knowledge was not always widespread. Sometimes even evidence that seemed good, as in *Richard de Bosco c Johanna de Clapton*, was not sufficient to succeed (although it is not clear why in that case).[56] If kinship was difficult to prove, it would also have been more difficult to pretend than when claiming a prior contract, given the more private nature of sexual relations as compared to familial connection. Collusive allegations of kinship probably occurred, but it was not the normal way to escape an unwanted marriage.

The system evidenced by practice in the courts reveals some interesting patterns which are not suggested by the discussions in contemporary books and treatises. In a sample of sixty-two instances from York, Ely, Lincoln, Wisbech and Canterbury that raised kinship in some manner, by far the

---

qualiter distinguet gradus ... Queritur etiam si viderit omnes gradus: si dicat sic, queritur si habebant se pro consanguineis, et tenebant: sufficit etiam si dicat quod viderit personas primi gradus, secundi vel tertii pro consanguinei se habere alias non valet': Hostiensis, *Summa*, fo. 212r.

[53] *Select cases from the ecclesiastical courts*, 359.

[54] 'Requisitus si vidit omnes quos nominavit, ... Requisitus a quibus didicit sic distinguere gradus, ... Requisitus si sit de consanguinitate vel affinitate partium predictarum, ... Requisitus quantum tempus est elapsum quod sic scivit distinguere gradus, ... Requisitus si iste testis interfuit alicui contractui inito inter dictos Henricum et Johannam, ... Requisitus si unquam fuit presens in editione bannorum inter eosdem Henricum et Johannam, ... Requisitus si dictis bannis tunc contradixerit ... Requisitus si aliqui alii tunc tempore dictis bannis contradixerunt ... Requisitus etiam si scandalum foret si dicti Henricus et Johanna matrimonialiter coniungerentur, ... Requisitus utrum mallet coniunctionem quam separationem inter dictos Henricum et Johannam': Helmholz, *Marriage litigation*, 216.

[55] Donahue, *Law, marriage, and society*, 106, 106–7, 114, 147–8, 709, 719 (*Texts and commentary*, nn. 188, 190, 283).

[56] *Select cases from the ecclesiastical courts*, 83.

## Table 1
### Types of kinship alleged in the canon law sample

| | Affinity | Consanguinity | Public honesty | Spiritual kinship | Unspecified 'incest' | TOTAL |
|---|---|---|---|---|---|---|
| **Thirteenth century** | | | | | | |
| Canterbury | 2 | 0 | 0 | 0 | 0 | 2 |
| **Fourteenth century** | | | | | | |
| York | 7 | 3 | 0 | 0 | 0 | 10 |
| Ely | 11 | 5 | 1 | 2 | 1 | 20 |
| Lincoln | 12 | 3 | 0 | 2 | 4 | 21 |
| **Fifteenth century** | | | | | | |
| York | 1 | 4 | 0 | 2 | 0 | 7 |
| Wisbech | 0 | 1 | 0 | 0 | 1 | 2 |
| **TOTAL** | 33 | 16 | 1 | 6 | 6 | |

*Sources:* a sample of canon law cases from the archbishop of York's consistory court in the fourteenth and fifteenth centuries and Ely consistory court in the fourteenth century (1374–81) as discussed by Donahue; the archbishop's court in Canterbury from the thirteenth century (using cases from after 1215 only); the court of the dean and chapter of Lincoln in the fourteenth century (1336–49); and the deanery of Wisbech in Ely in the fifteenth century (1458–84).

greater majority raised objections on grounds of affinity: thirty-three affinity and sixteen consanguinity (*see* table 1).[57] This reverses the relative amount of attention given in the treatises, which tended to devote more space to consanguinity. In one sense affinity implied consanguinity because the consanguinity rules underlay the application of affinity. The disparity is interesting, however, as it suggests that people were either more likely to obey the consanguinity rules than the affinity rules, or that people were more likely to falsely allege an affinial relationship. There is some evidence for the second suggestion arising from the number of cases (at least twenty-three) based on affinity through illicit intercourse, a less public relationship than a marriage or betrothal.[58] Yet the pattern was sustained in office cases where it can be supposed that there were fewer opportunities for collusion

[57] Details of this sample are set out at pp. 115–16 below.
[58] Donahue, *Law, marriage, and society,* 106, 106–7, 145, 238, 259, 286–7, 270–1, 282–3, 287–8, 571 572, 573–4, 709 (*Texts and commentary,* nn. 188, 190); *Lower ecclesiastical jurisdiction,* 11–12, 13, 37, 145, 170, 177, 195, 197, 213; *Select cases from the ecclesiastical courts,* 96–102, 350–65.

(thirteen out of eighteen cases alleging affinity of any type).[59] Therefore it is likely that a combination of both factors was at work. It is enough to note that consanguineous relationships seem to have been more scandalous than relationships with affines.

The other types of canon law kinship were comparatively rare in the sample of cases. There were, for example, only six allegations of spiritual kinship.[60] This may be because godparenthood was a public matter and because the relationships clearly banned by the rules were limited. The cases in the sample tended to involve relationships where the rules were less clear-cut. *Wistow c Cowper* and *Ask c Ask and Conyers* were both cases where spiritual fraternity was alleged: i.e. the parent of one party was godparent to the other. In the first case a papal dispensation was applied, while the other may have been collusive.[61] Public honesty was also rare, again probably due to the public nature of betrothals as opposed to affinity by illicit intercourse. Only one case occurred in the sample. In *Office and Andren and Edyng c Andren and Solsa*, in Ely in 1381, public honesty was alleged as one ground among many including affinity through illicit intercourse and crime.[62] This ground was extremely rare.[63]

The canon law kinship system was not merely learned and academic (although it was both). It was part of a successful and widespread system of marriage law and was used, applied and enforced in England. The law in books was inevitably less prone to compromise and manipulation than the law in practice, but the very degree of compromise and manipulation, combined with evidence of scandal when some of the laws were not obeyed, show that this was a living system. People may not have accepted the canon law kinship system in its entirety, but it is telling that they seem to have been more willing to accept the more intuitively obvious consanguinity rules.

## At common law

The parentelic structure of common law kinship can be seen in many types of cases, in almost any case, in fact, where a claim relied on an ancestor's right and seisin (although summaries of counts of descent were not recorded in all cases, kinship simply being stated).[64] An example is *Robert de Meringe*

---

[59] Donahue, *Law, marriage, and society*, 145, 286–7, 287–8, 573–4; *Lower ecclesiastical jurisdiction*, 11–12, 13, 37, 145, 170, 177, 195, 197, 213.

[60] Donahue, *Law, marriage, and society*, 202, 270–1, 293, 572; *Lower ecclesiastical jurisdiction*, 11–12, 59.

[61] As detailed in Donahue, *Law, marriage, and society*, 572, 202.

[62] As detailed ibid. 287–8.

[63] Ibid. 709 (*Texts and commentary*, n. 189); Helmholz, *Marriage litigation*, 78 n. 14.

[64] As in, for example, *Susanna Attelegh and others v Thomas of Shireford*, an entry case: *The roll of the Shropshire eyre of 1256*, ed. A. Harding (Selden Society lxxxvi, 1981), no. 333.

v. *Robert de Clifford*, a nuper obiit case from 1304.[65] The issue that eventually went to the jury was a proposed female ancestor's place in the family tree. The plaintiff, Robert de Meringe, claimed that he and the tenant, Robert de Clifford, were descendants of two sisters (Alice and Mabel, daughters of the *propositus*), and that the *propositus* (on whose tenancy the claim was founded) was their great-great-grandfather, meaning that they both should have a share of the inheritance. The tenant claimed that his female ancestor Mabel was the daughter of the *propositus'* younger son (that the *propositus* was her grandfather); this would mean that when the direct line of descendants from that younger son failed (with the death of the *propositus'* great-grandson, Ralph, with no heirs of his body), the whole of the inheritance ought to have resorted to Mabel or her representative. The case was not argued on relative closeness to the common ancestor, but on the parentelic pattern and on allegedly factual configurations of the family. Thus, the tenants' lawyer asked 'since he is issue of Mabel who is of the blood in a lower degree [*del saunk plus bas*], judgement, if he ought to be answered on his [the plaintiff's] resort which he has made to one of the blood higher up [*en le saunk plus amount ou plus haut*]'.[66] The resort to Mabel would have been a closer one than the resort to Alice, the plaintiff's ancestress.

Parentelic kinship was applied to, and by, thousands of Englishmen and women. Parentelic inheritance, as argued by lawyers at Westminster, could apply and be known across the country and across the divides of wealth and privilege (excepting villeins), although it was also possible to enforce recognised customary inheritance patterns, such as parage in the common law courts. Not only the very wealthy attended and used the king's courts; for example, when the eyre came to visit a county 'special arrangements' could sometimes be needed for the crowds.[67] It has been estimated that 2 per cent of the population were litigants at the Court of Common Pleas every four years in the fourteenth century, a total not including those called as witnesses or jurors.[68] Involvement with the common law did not occur without some mediation. Litigants were advised by senior Chancery clerks and also by lawyers.[69] Certainly by the late thirteenth century, with the pleading system in full swing, it would be a foolish litigant who attempted to proceed to pleading without representation. The litigant had to meet complex technical prerequisites over and above knowledge of kinship law, the merest of which was ensuring that the case was within the appropriate time limits.

---

[65] *Year books 32 & 33 Edward I*, 16–21.
[66] Ibid. 18–9. Horwood added the term degrees in his translation.
[67] Milsom, *Historical foundations*, 29.
[68] This was based on figures between 1327 and 1328 and 1331 and 1334: R. C. Palmer, *The Whilton dispute, 1264–1380: a social-legal study of dispute settlement in medieval England*, Princeton 1984, 5–9.
[69] Carpenter, 'The English royal chancery', 35.

Proof at common law was more opaque than at canon law. Instead of examinations of witnesses there was the spectacle of lawyers arguing about pleas and potential exceptions until they reached an issue that could be put to the jury. The count and exception process did not function as proof, but its role in relation to proof and kinship is interesting. Both plaintiff and defendant would want the issue that went to the jury to be set in a way as favourable to them as possible, but, in doing so neither could go beyond what the other side could challenge (except in cases where the exception was advanced at the wrong time or in the wrong procedural order, essentially losing ground on a technicality). A well-advised litigant would not make an entirely implausible count. If he did, the defendant might make an exception or the jury might find against him. This is not to imply that the system avoided lies; merely that lies and false claims were, to a degree, constrained by the format.

Indeed, in the area of kinship, it was not merely lies about the structure of a kindred on which a claim was founded that could lead to failure; naming the wrong kin member, or failing to name the right kin member could open a count to challenge. Potentially detailed knowledge of the family was needed. This can be seen in the discussion around whether to count an 'empty degree'. In the early thirteenth century this seems to have been a matter of some controversy. There were several voices in *Bracton*, of the author and of various interpolators. The author wrote that 'no mention' was to be made of an eldest brother who died in his father's lifetime; only people who survived the *propositus* (the last person seised and rightfully entitled) should be included in the count.[70] An interpolator disagreed: the count must go 'through all the degrees and those persons to whom seisin would have gone had they claimed in their lifetimes, or survived to a time at which they could have been heirs'. This was explained as 'where something descends to children, their ancestors being dead'.[71] The most inclusive version of the count, described in another interpolation, included an eldest son whether or not he died in his father's lifetime or had children 'because of the right which would have descended to him had he survived his ancestor's death'.[72] This internal discussion was repeated several times in the text.[73] It was essential to litigants that this be resolved. If a pleader made the wrong count before a justice they could open the case to exception. By the 1290s the author of *Britton* maintained that a count should go through all the 'occupied degrees' and 'sometimes through the vacant degrees; as in case where the eldest son, having issue, dies before his ancestor'. However, not all 'vacant degrees' needed to be mentioned: 'Sometimes in counting by descent the vacant degrees are passed over, as, where the eldest sons die without heirs of their

---

70  *Bracton*, ii. 198.
71  Ibid. ii. 196.
72  Ibid. ii. 198.
73  Ibid. ii. 367, 377; iii. 280, 306; iv. 173, 174.

bodies in the lifetime of their ancestors.'[74] The combination of right and seisin was the key: if it had not passed through a kinsman, or would not have, there was no need to mention him.[75] Even so, the person making a claim would need knowledge of the people involved, their relationships to each other, when they had died, whether they had had children and, most important, whether those children were legitimate (given the common law's attitude to the bastard).

Moreover, challenges based on the inclusion, or not, of kin members were relatively common. In a sample of cases from the roll of the Shropshire eyre in 1256 and from the four books in which Paul Brand has edited the *Earliest English law reports*, based only on those cases which were founded on a count of descent,[76] there were twenty-seven cases which contained challenges to the count based on a kinsman who had not been named (approximately 21 per cent of those on which there is information). These alleged lines or persons who had a greater right than the plaintiff. There were nine which alleged that the plaintiff had an older brother who had not been mentioned in the count;[77] three which alleged that the *propositus* had children who had not been mentioned;[78] ten which alleged that the *propositus* had a sibling and sometimes that a line descended from him or her;[79] and three involved more complex allegations.[80] The rate of challenge, at approximately one-fifth of cases, shows how important it was to make the right count (although, of course, not every such challenge was successful). Challenges were not as straightforward as they appear. A challenge of omission in the count could be a disguised way of challenging the legitimacy of one of the parties or one of their ancestors. Challenges to the descent were often 'a way of getting to the heart of the dispute'.[81]

The books of the common law closely reflect practice. The common law system was, however, open enough to function with several questions unanswered and points of view ongoing. For example, there were at least three views of the shape of the family (alongside the parentelic system) current during the course of the thirteenth and early fourteenth centuries. These were centred specifically around the definition of who was a cousin and who could use cosinage, an area where the law was unclear.

All three views of these shapes were explored in *Latimer v. Clendon*, a case in 1311 of *formedon in the reverter*. The plaintiffs, Alice and Thomas,

---

[74] *Britton*, ii. 322.

[75] In practice, however, they were mentioned sometimes.

[76] For the background to this sample see chapter 5 below.

[77] *Earliest English law reports*, ii. 185–7; iii. 283–4, 302–4; iv. 338–43, 389–90; *Roll of the Shropshire eyre*, nos 151, 168, 262, 326.

[78] *Earliest English law reports*, iv. 441–2; *Roll of the Shropshire eyre*, nos 99, 227.

[79] *Earliest English law reports*, i. 61–5, 179–80; ii. 231–42, 251, 290–5; iii. 97–9, 109–10, 291–3; iv. 329–32, 434–5, 441–2.

[80] Ibid. ii. 211–13; iv. 432–3, 574–7.

[81] Ibid. iv, p. cxxx.

counted that the donor of the gift, Henry, was Alice's great-grandfather, and Thomas's great-great-grandfather. The writ had called this ancestor *consanguineus* of 'Thomas' (there is a discrepancy between the names in the report and record). Three reports of this case survive and the pleas, and Chief Justice Bereford's replies, were slightly different in each. In the first report, according to the Chief Justice: 'Neither in Latin nor in French can a great-great-grandfather be made a cousin'. The second report elaborated: 'My great-great-grandfather will never be named cousin to me, for cosinage is always in the collateral line'. The justices would not apply the wider definition of cousin as any blood-kinsman. A cousin had to be a collateral relative, so there ought to be a resort in an action of cosinage. There was room for dispute, however, for Bereford was also reported to have said that 'the younger generation were strictly speaking "cousins" to their grandfathers, great-grandfathers and great-great-grandfathers', meaning that descendants were 'cousins' to their ancestors but not *vice versa*. Legally, named and specified ascendants for whom the common law had particular terms could not be called cousins to their descendants: 'the elders are grandfathers, great-grandfathers and great-great-grandfathers with respect to the younger generation'.[82] So cousins could be blood-kinsmen descending from a common ancestor. As an aside, this definition has an interesting parallel with that of the canon law. In his logical treatise Kilwardby had said that such a sense of cousin was a possible misreading of the canon law definition.[83] Returning to *Latimer v Clendon*, a third, competing definition was advanced for the plaintiff. Herle argued that the Chancery allowed no other writ for the *tresaiel* 'for the great-great-grandfather is always supposed to be cousin to him who demands'.[84] This reveals cousin as a catch-all term for kinsmen, a definition which is reminiscent of the fuller canon law sense. This was convenient for the plaintiff, as there was no other writ available.[85] In the end, the plaintiff failed because 'Great-great-grandfather is a term of the law of the land both in Latin and French'; therefore, since there was no writ available there was not meant to be one, and there was a discrepancy between the writ and the count.[86] From the 1290s to the 1340s the justices quashed attempts to call

---

[82] *Year books of 5 Edward II (1311)*, ed. G. J. Turner, completed with an introduction by T. F. T. Plucknett (Selden Society lxiii, 1947), 95–7 at pp. 96–7.

[83] See chapter 3 n. 121.

[84] *Year books 5 Edward II*, 96–7.

[85] Ibid. 96. There Herle, for the plaintiff, said that the Chancery did not use the term 'tresael', and that there was no other writ available there.

[86] Ibid. The term *abavus* is rare: it does occur in *Year books of the reign of King Edward the Third: year XV*, ed. and trans. L. O. Pike, London 1891, 373. Brand, 'Time out of mind', 45 n. 42, lists some (earlier) cases where plaintiffs based their claim on the seisin of their great-great-grandfather. However, they did not use the term *abavus*, but said that when x 'antecessor suus fuit seisitus'. In *Curia regis rolls, of the reign of Henry III*, London 1957, xii, no. 2036, Henry I was termed 'avus avi' of Henry III rather than *abavus*.

lineal ancestors cousins.[87] But lawyers kept repeating the arguments and litigants kept bringing claims that raised the issue. This gives cause to wonder
why these litigants were so persistent in the face of previous failures. Were
they all badly advised?

The answer was partly tactical. Who could call themselves a *cosin* was
important, as there was strong pressure from litigants to use the possessory
remedy, which was often tactically preferable to the writ of right, and, as the
time limits receded, more distant relatives tried to claim and lineal descendants called themselves cousins to try to gain access to the remedy not otherwise available (this can be seen in the frequent pleas that no other writ was
available from Chancery).[88] Mixed actions (joint claims by one parcener
who was within the scope of an action and one parcener who was more
distant) also raised interesting questions. *Bracton* envisaged a mixed action
of mort d'ancestor and aiel (although he called it cosinage) where a daughter
and her sister's son joined in a claim.[89] When more distant descendants tried
to claim they often called themselves cousins to the dead ancestor, but the
courts were not as forgiving as *Bracton*.

Why then were the common law courts so resistant to this wide definition of cousin? The justices' restraint seems to be linked to normal, practical,
lawyerly concerns about the boundaries between actions. They were reluctant to allow cosinage when other writs were available, as the writ of right
was.[90] If cosinage was allowed as widely as the author of *Bracton* envisaged
it could have swallowed other actions (even most writ of right actions were
within six degrees). The justices did not want cosinage to impinge upon the
actions which allowed claims of land based on dead direct ancestors (aiel
and later besaiel), and they were reluctant to extend cosinage beyond the

---

[87] *Year books of the reign of King Edward the first: years* XX *and* XXI, ed. and trans. A. J.
Horwood, London 1866, 154–7, 226–9; *Year books 30 & 31 Edward I*, 104–7; *Year books
32 & 33 Edward I*, 16–21; *Year books 5 Edward II* (SSlxiii), 95–7; *Year books of the eyre
of Kent, 6 and 7 Edward II (1313–14)*, ed. W. C. Bolland, F. W. Maitland and L. W. V.
Harcourt (Selden Society xxvii, 1912), ii. 8–9; *Year books of 10 Edward II (1316–1317)*,
ed. M. D. Legge and W. Holdsworth (Selden Society liv, 1935), 7–8; and *Year books of the
reign of King Edward the third: years* XII *and* XIII, ed. and trans. L. O. Pike, London 1885,
360–1.

[88] In *Year books 20 & 21 Edward I*, 154–7, the plaintiff's lawyer argued that he could
have no other writ and that as soon as the great-grandfather was passed 'he is a cousin'.
In *Year books 20 & 21 Edward I*, 226–9, the plaintiff's lawyers argued that this should be
allowed 'notwithstanding the descent be lineal and not collateral' since the Chancery
gave no writ except cosinage beyond the great-grandfather (at pp. 226–8). In *Year books
12 & 13 Edward III*, 360–1, two heirs claimed the land of their common ancestor, saying
that he was grandfather of one and cousin of the other, when actually he was the great-
grandfather of the other. Gayneford, for the plaintiffs, defended their count, because
there was no other, and that was the form of writ given by the Chancery (at p. 360). All
failed.

[89] *Bracton*, iii. 250 (actually mort d'ancestor and aiel).

[90] For example, *Year books 20 & 21 Edward I*, 154–7, where the plaintiff was driven to
his writ of right.

limits that those actions imposed.[91] Frequently, their rationale was based on the rules of pleading. They would not allow a difference between the writ that founded the claim and the count that stated it.[92]

The question of why litigants continued to bring writs that made lineal ascendants into cousins is complicated by the role of the Chancery. The Chancery issued, wrote and sealed the writs to begin the actions. Senior Chancery clerks advised the litigants on which writs to buy and a 1345 case stated that 'a great-great-grandfather is in Chancery made cousin according to their custom'.[93] But what exactly was the process when people brought their writs? Did they merely go into Chancery and demand a writ based on the seisin of their cousin? If so, it would seem that a wide definition of cousin (of cousin as kinsman generally, which seems analogous to the canon law definition) was current among non-legal circles. But it seems more likely that a litigant got some legal advice on which writ to choose before, or when, he went to the Chancery. At least once the Chancery knowingly issued a writ where a lineal ascendant was described as cousin.[94] This was a case of mort d'ancestor, where the land was claimed by two parceners, one of whom was the daughter of the *propositus* and the other was a great-great-grandson (who descended from the *propositus'* other daughter). Because of the structure of this mixed action, based on mort d'ancestor claiming on the 'father's' seisin, the Chancery clerks must have understood that they were issuing a writ that made this direct descendant out to be a cousin. Perhaps they were thinking along the same lines as *Britton* and Chief Justice Bereford – that direct descendants could be cousins – yet the plea roll entry says that the assize was to recognise whether the *propositus* was 'consanguineus Johannis de Burleye' (cousin of the second parcener), meaning that the case was framed as if the ascendant were the cousin, making it likely that the Chancery was following the wider definition. It seems at least possible that the Chancery may have been using the common currency canon law definition of cousin (*cosin/consanguineus*) – anyone related by blood. After all, a writ of cosinage was a *breve de consanguinitate*.

---

91 For example, *Year books of the eyre of Kent, 6 and 7 Edward II*, ii. 8–9, where the plaintiff claimed land on the death of Robert his great-grandfather. He brought a writ of cosinage, which supposed that the last ancestor seised was a cousin. Since he could have brought besaiel the tenant's lawyer prayed judgement on the writ. Justice Spigurnel abated the writ (so the plaintiff lost). *Year books 10 Edward II*, 7–8, was a case of aiel brought by parceners. They made the ancestor out to be cousin to one of them and the writ was abated because he was in fact great-grandfather to that parcener.

92 For example, 'you can not deny he is great-great-grandfather, whereas your writ supposes that he is cousin': *Year books 20 & 21 Edward I*, 226–9 at p. 228.

93 *Year books of the reign of King Edward the third: year XIX*, ed. and trans. L. O. Pike, London 1906, 332. See also 'the form of the writ is that given in Chancery': *Year books 12 & 13 Edward III*, 360.

94 *Year books 20 & 21 Edward I*, 154–7. The plea roll entry is JUST 1/303 (1292 Herefs eyre), m. 26. My thanks to Paul Brand for pointing this out and providing a transcript of the plea roll entry for this case.

Not until the 1340s did the justices bow to the Chancery definition and allow litigants to call their *tresaiels* cousins 'because there is no other form of writ, in as much as a great-great-grandfather is in Chancery made cousin according to their custom'.[95] Cousin at common law now meant blood-kinsman, like the canon law definition of consanguine, and the limit for possessory actions was effectively raised to the fourth degree. It seems that the ideas of the canon law had a certain common currency. This raises the question of how far the canon law dominance in general ideas about kinship as was reflected in common law books, was also reflected in practice.

## The canon law in the common law

Canon law kinship material did not have a substantial impact on the common laws' own system. However, case records and reports of pleading show that some elements of canon law thinking were drawn upon by common lawyers. The problems over the definition of cousin may be an example. The fact that four degrees was used as a limit for kinship when no natural common law limit was available, much as in *Britton*, was definitely an example of this. The four-degree limit was used in various cases. The limits on cosinage and possessory actions have already been discussed. Initially there was confusion; in the 1250s there was no possessory writ where the grandfather was passed; with the advent of besaiel the limit was the great-grandfather. There was a case from 1278 that put the limit at the great-great-grandfather.[96] In the 1340s the four-generation limit was confirmed when the *tresaiel* was accepted as a cousin.

The most famous limit on kinship related to *maritagia* and the like limited gifts where the first donee to do feudal services would be in the fourth degree – that was the point when a reversion (to the donor or his heirs) became unlikely, as a new family had been established coincident with the point at which kinsmen could marry.[97] Several cases mentioned this limit and a note attached to a plea in frankmarriage recorded in the year books linked the limit directly to the canon law rule: 'In such a case because there can be a marriage after the fourth degree the blood relationship is over and in case of naifty, if a stranger perform villein services from father to son, once they

---

[95] *Year books of the reign of King Edward the third: year XIV*, ed. and trans. L. O. Pike, London 1888, 370–3, and *Year books 19 Edward III*, 332–5.

[96] Brand, *Kings, barons and justices*, 54 n. 45.

[97] *Bracton*, ii. 77. See also Biancalana, *The fee tail*, 43–51. This is confirmed in, for example, *Year books michaelmas 33, 34 & 35 Edward I*, 28–37, where, according to Passeley the lord/donor would have an action to demand due services from the tenant 'after it has come to the fourth degree' (at p. 34). Bereford confirmed that a 'tenant in frank-marriage ought to be quit of all manner of services until the third degree be passed' (at p. 36).

have passed the fourth degree they will be villeins permanently'.[98] This is reminiscent of a note added to the text of *Britton*.[99]

An analogous limit was put on the entail in the famous case *Belyng v. Anon* (1312) where Chief Justice Bereford unilaterally extended (or corrected) the scope of *De donis*.[100] The 1285 statute meant to give effect to the donor's wishes and prevent heirs of the donee of a limited gift from alienating the land.[101] Briefly and simplistically, such a gift might be to a man, his wife and the heirs of their joint bodies. If this was interpreted as a conditional gift then, when heirs were born, the donee could alienate the land (which had not been the donor's intent). *De donis* was obscurely worded; it would have allowed the issue to alienate. In *Belyng v. Anon* Bereford prevented that: 'He that made the statute meant to bind the issue in fee tail as well as the feoffees until the tail had reached the fourth degree; and it was only through negligence that he omitted to insert express words to that effect in the statute.'[102] Bereford's assertion was not disputed. Notably, he expressed his limit in terms of degrees. Some common lawyers used generations instead, but the end result was the same.[103]

Battle or the grand assize were denied to competing kinsmen in writ of right cases and some common lawyers thought that four degrees also provided a limit to this bar. In 1280, in *William son of Henry of Gisleham and his wife Isabel v. Thomas and John sons of John Osbern*, a writ of right case, the plaintiffs tried to claim that a grand assize could not stand between them and the defendants because they were of the same stock. The defendants, according to the report, claimed that they were more distantly related. Their lawyer said that they 'have passed the fourth degree of consanguinity and so we are advised that the mise lies between us'.[104] The case became an argument over how many generations separated the two sides of the family, implying that the argument was worth exploring. This, however, was surely wrong. Battle and the grand assize were to be avoided because the decision could bar

---

[98]   *Earliest English law reports*, iii. 200–11 at p. 201.

[99]   *Britton*, i. 195, n. q.

[100]  *Year books of 5 Edward II (1311–1312)*, ed. W. C. Bolland (Selden Society xxxi, 1915), 76–7.

[101]  The changing interpretations of the limit on alienation in *De donis* (and the difference between this limit on alienation and the rules about the duration of the right of reversion) are discussed in Biancalana, *The fee tail*, 83–128. Commentators on *De donis* suggested limits at the fourth degree (at p. 89).

[102]  *Year books of 5 Edward II* (SS xxi), 177. Bereford set the limit on alienation at the fourth degree but would have allowed the entail (and thus the right of reversion) to continue 'after the fourth degree': *Year books of 5 Edward II (1312)*, ed. W. C. Bolland (Selden Society xxxiii, 1916), 226.

[103]  For example, in tail 'lineal issue in the second, third or fourth generations will have the same advantage as the first, and yet they are not begotten of the body of the first donee': *Year books of the reign of King Edward the third: years XVIII and XIX*, ed. and trans. L. O. Pike, London 1905, 194–207 at p. 202.

[104]  *Earliest English law reports*, iv. 574–7 at p. 574.

parties from a later reversion. In theory, under the parentelic system, such reversions could stretch infinitely far. This hints at the power of the canon law limit on kinship for shaping general thinking.

Parceners who shared the right to a piece of land through descent (for example a sister and her sister's son) could bring joint actions to claim their lands. Justice Brompton added a four-degree limit to clause 6 of the Statute of Gloucester, which had said only that the heirs who could claim by mort d'ancestor could draw parceners 'of a further Degree' into the action.[105] In *Robert de Lascelles and Others* v. *Thomas of Moulton and Others*, however, it was said that 'the fourth degree of lineal descent can and ought to attract the other degrees even though they are more remote'; so long as one of the parceners was within the scope of the action they could draw in the other parceners, who were of a distance that would normally prevent them using the action.[106]

When regulating how far land could resort (i.e. pass to or through an ascending collateral kinsman) and still be within possessory actions such as cosinage some common lawyers again chose a four-degree limit (the descent, and, presumably, the resort could be infinite in a claim via writ of right). In *Robert de Lascelles and Others* v. *Thomas of Moulton and Others* it was argued that 'In the ascent in making a resort it is only possible to count up to the fourth degree.'[107] Both the report and record revolved around the acknowledgement that there was a limit on the degrees land could ascend in making a resort in this action, and the question of whether there was any limit on the degrees that land could descend after that resort. The record confirmed this: 'In the ascent no resort is allowed beyond the fourth degree.'[108]

When common lawyers sought a limit for kinship in such actions, they often chose that of the canon law. This was because canon law kinship was common knowledge; it offered a convenient number when an arbitrary one might otherwise be needed. The canon law operated and people who wanted to get married, presumably some common lawyers among them, would have been made aware of the rules. It seems that the basics of the canon law system were fairly well known (if not always obeyed). Yet applied common knowledge of canon law kinship was not systematic; not everyone turned to canon law limits. Sometimes, for example, the fifth degree, was chosen instead.[109]

---

[105] It is difficult, however, to tell what type of degrees these were: *Year books 30 & 31 Edward I*, 104–7, cf. 6 Edward I, Statute of Gloucester, c.6.

[106] *Earliest English law reports*, ii. 264, 262.

[107] Ibid. ii. 262.

[108] Ibid. ii. 264.

[109] In *Robert de Lascelles and Others* v. *Thomas of Moulton and Others* the limit was twice set at the fourth degree: ibid. ii. 262, 264. However, Justice Brompton also said that 'one can only make resort to the fifth degree in ascending' (at p. 263). Other cases also chose the great-great-grandparent as a limit, for example *Year books of the reign of King Edward the third: years XIII and XIV*, ed. and trans. L. O. Pike, London 1886, 352–3. In another

Another area in which canon law influence can be glimpsed is in attempts to count in degrees of kinship. Degrees were mentioned in common law reports as a way of measuring kinship, particularly as a way of expressing limits or generations.[110] Common lawyers seem to have had their own usage equivalent to hands the land passed through – as with the degrees of entry – or generations, rather than a comparative measure of distance in the sense that canon lawyers used.[111] Indeed, there would be no need for learned style degrees in the common law system. In fact, because of representation (i.e. the fact that a child could be taken to represent their deceased parent in the family structure), either the canon law or the civil law system of counting in degrees would have caused confusion. The common law usage of degree fitted with the general sense of the word; it is likely, however, that the learned laws were an inspiration for the continued flourish of using degrees in relation to kinship.

This evidence shows once again the reach of the canon law conception of kinship into secular thinking. In some senses its application in common law cases is even more telling than its inclusion in books since it was outside that textual setting, although these common lawyers and justices (and clerks) were educated men. It is revealing that there was no reciprocal influence of common law kinship on canon law. There was less scope for it (because of the type of rule and system the canon law applied); there were few prominent English canonists; the civil law had taken the role of secular law for formal comparison with the canon law; and, overall, the canon law was part of a Europe-wide legal system. Although the canon law might make fine distinctions to accommodate English practice (for example, by and large not resisting the common law's claimed jurisdiction over some forms of bastardy decisions following the Council of Merton), it did not change course for one single *ius proprium*.[112]

Both kinship systems worked in practice, although not always in the way that the law in books might imply. It is interesting, for a sense of canon law primacy in the field of general ideas about kinship, that the canon law in common law books was echoed, differently and less directly, in common law cases. That there was a gap between the kinship structures written about in books and applied in practice should not be surprising, nor should the fact that this gap appears narrower between the books and cases of the common

---

case Justice Hengam said that 'I have not learned how far parcenary endures in the blood': *Year books 32 & 33 Edward I*, 300.

[110] S. Worby, 'Consanguinity and the common law: 'idle ingenuities' in *Bracton?*', in A. Lewis, P. Brand and P. Mitchell (eds), *Law in the city: proceedings of the seventeenth British legal history conference, London 2005*, Dublin 2007, 24–41 at p. 37.

[111] Ibid. 36–7, and 'Kinship in thirteenth-century England', 214–16.

[112] R. H. Helmholz, 'Bastardy litigation in medieval England', *American Journal of Legal History* xiii (1969), 360–83.

law than between those of the canon law. People did not behave like ideal-ised models, they did not necessarily know their whole family, nor did they necessarily want to follow the rules or the paths that the systems would dictate. People used and manipulated the rules as part of a set of tactics available to them.

The application of both kinship systems as they appear from court records are in some sense negative. If all worked ideally then no one would have married, or have tried to marry, incestuously, and the right heir would always have been in his or her inheritance. The very statement is preposterous. In both systems litigants pursued their goals as best they could with the tools available: kinship could be one way to defend against an unwanted marriage as it could be a way to avoid battle or grand assize. Lawyers (common lawyers were particularly visible) used arguments based around structures of kinship to achieve the outcome that they wanted for their clients. Officials and judges applied the law, for example, in canon law office cases, although the story of the judge Richard de Clyve shows that they did not always apply it as officiously as they might. There was room at all these points for the laws to be a filter through which people had to force their claims. They did this by creating a narrative that would fit with the legal structures, if they wanted the best guarantee of success. Given the potential rewards from inheritance and the implications of an unwanted marriage, if the litigant involved had money, advice and a reasonable case they had every incen-tive to make a claim. The officials of the courts may have been swayed by sympathy or personal beliefs, but as emerging professionals they also had a duty to the systems that they upheld (if only in the Weberian sense of maintaining a monopoly of their own special knowledge). The structures of both kinship systems were set, although both were to a degree fluid at the edges, for example, in the definition of cousin, or the types of relation-ship that gave rise to an impediment of spiritual kinship. Their operation in practice was more varied and contingent than legal books could always capture. Both systems operated and were used and applied by litigants who constituted a respectable portion of the population. These kinship systems were known. Yet the contingency of real kinship meant that the relation-ship between structures, rules and practice was not straightforward, and, for example, canon law kinship concepts could affect common law decisions.

# 5

# Trends Underlying Legal Kinship Structures

Kinship is and was multifarious. In the Middle Ages, as now, it extended far beyond learned or legal culture into everyday actions, norms and vernacular practices (each of which represent layers in people's understanding of it). Because legal kinship interacted with practice and knowledge in these areas in a non-straightforward manner it is possible to explore patterns of kinship in society through the filter of the legal structures. It is also possible to glimpse what uses of the formal kinship systems reveal about knowledge and understanding of kinship among non-experts. Beyond legal kinship were patterns of behaviour that suggest a general sense of kinship focused on blood kin and often the three-generation family. The dominance of legal kinship, however, particularly canon law kinship, left little space for any more formal non-legal kinship system.

## Canon law patterns

To look beyond legal kinship it is necessary to get a sense of the behaviour underlying interaction with the law. In this case it is illuminating to explore the patterns of behaviour indicated through a sample of litigation records. The sample of cases used here are from the archbishop of York's consistory court in the fourteenth and fifteenth centuries and Ely consistory court in the fourteenth century (1374–81) as discussed by Donahue; the archbishop's court in Canterbury from the thirteenth century (using cases from after 1215 only); the court of the dean and chapter of Lincoln in the fourteenth century (1336–49); and the deanery of Wisbech in Ely in the fifteenth century (1458–84).[1] They amount to fifty-nine cases including sixty-two instances where some form of 'incest' was raised as an issue (not that all these allegations can be believed); twenty-seven of these occurred in litigation between parties (seventeen from York, eight from Ely, two from Canterbury),[2] and

---

[1]  Donahue, *Law, marriage, and society*, 106, 106–7, 107, 114, 145, 146, 147–8, 175–6, 202, 210, 236, 290, 238, 252–4, 259, 263–4, 270–1, 276, 277–8, 282–3, 286–7, 287–8, 290, 293, 293–4, 295, 571, 571–2, 572, 574–5, 709, 744 (*Texts and commentary*, nn. 188, 190, 191, 487); *Lower ecclesiastical jurisdiction*, 11–12, 13, 32, 33, 37, 59, 63, 64, 68, 108, 135, 145, 170, 177, 195, 197, 213, 220, 232, 381, 475; *Select cases from the ecclesiastical courts*, 96–102, 350–65.

[2]  Donahue, *Law, marriage, and society*, 106, 106–7, 107, 114, 145, 146, 147–8, 175–6, 202, 210, 238, 252–4, 259, 263–4, 270–1, 276, 277–8, 571, 571–2, 572, 574–5; *Select cases from the ecclesiastical courts*, 96–102, 350–65.

thirty-three in office cases, where the courts were exercising their quasi-criminal jurisdiction (one from York, ten from Ely, twenty from Lincoln and two from Wisbech).[3] Within the sample, kinship was one of the grounds for 'divorce' in seven cases;[4] a defence against a case trying to enforce a marriage sixteen times;[5] and one of the grounds for prosecutions twenty-eight times.[6] There was also one citation against a priest for solemnising an incestuous marriage,[7] and one citation against a priest for refusing to.[8] Finally there were several cases that raised incest in a less straightforward manner.[9] Incest as a defence was more common than incest as a ground for divorce, and, naturally, lower courts entertained a higher proportion of office cases.

Records from the canon law courts show a revealing nexus between the canon law kinship rules and practice. They indicate that there was less acceptance of the affinity rules and that such relationships – especially those created through sex rather than marriage – were regarded as less scandalous. There were more occasions where affinity was an issue in court cases than consanguinity (see table 1: of the total of sixty-two occasions where kinship was an issue, more than half concerned alleged affinity). An analysis of the sample by date and type of kinship alleged reveals a specific pattern. In the fourteenth century affinity was alleged almost three times as frequently as consanguinity. Interestingly, although the numbers were small, there appears to have been a shift in the fifteenth century as allegations of consanguinity become more common. Within these totals the types of kinship claimed in office and instance cases (for example in prosecutions and litigation) were very similar, although consanguinity was somewhat more commonly alleged in instance cases.[10] The number of times affinity was raised in office cases (for example its relative frequency compared to consanguinity cases in the court in Lincoln) suggests that some people were more likely to participate in relationships (of marriage or fornication) with affines than they were with consanguines. Particularly in the fourteenth century people were either less

[3] Donahue, *Law, marriage, and society*, 145, 236, 282–3, 286–7, 287–8, 290, 293, 293–4, 295, 573–4; *Lower ecclesiastical jurisdiction*, 11–12, 13, 32, 33, 37, 59, 63, 64, 68, 108, 135, 145, 170, 177, 195, 197, 213, 220, 232, 381, 475.

[4] Donahue, *Law, marriage, and society*, 145 (including one office divorce case), 259, 571, 572.

[5] Ibid. 106, 106–7, 114, 146, 175–6, 202, 263–4, 571 (probably also 210, 238 though these are not certain), 252–4 and 270–1 share elements with office cases; *Select cases from the ecclesiastical courts*, 96–102, 350–65.

[6] Donahue, *Law, marriage, and society*, 236, 290, 282–3, 286–7, 293, 293–4, 295; *Lower ecclesiastical jurisdiction*, 11–12, 13, 32, 33, 37, 59, 63, 64, 68, 135, 145, 170, 177, 195, 197, 213, 220, 232, 381, 475.

[7] Donahue, *Law, marriage, and society*, 573–4.

[8] Ibid. 290.

[9] Ibid. 107, 147–8, 276, 574–5, 709, 719, 744 (*Texts and commentary*, nn. 191, 283, 487); *Lower ecclesiastical jurisdiction*, 108.

[10] Affinity made up 53% of the sample in office cases, 56% in instance; consanguinity 18% in office cases, 33% in instance; spiritual kinship 9% in office cases, 11% in instance.

## Table 2
### Degrees of kinship alleged in the canon law sample

|  | Affinity | Consanguinity |
|---|---|---|
| First degree | 6 | 1 |
| Second degree | 2 | 0 |
| Third degree | 9 | 1 |
| Fourth degree | 3 | 10 |
| **TOTAL** | 20 | 12 |

*Sources*: as table 1. Sorted according to the degree of relationship, where this is known, stated in the longer line.

likely to obey the affinity rules than the consanguinity rules, or more likely to fabricate an allegation of affinity.

There are also patterns in the closeness of relationship alleged in the cases in this sample. Of cases where consanguinity and affinity was alleged there are a total of thirty-two alleged relationships where the purported degree is known (remembering that this information may not be accurate).[11] Within these the degree of relationship has been classified according to the canon law rule that when there were two lines of different lengths the longest was chosen to measure whether the parties could marry. In one sense this over-estimates the distance of relationships between people (as there were always two different lines to the *stipes* and only the longer is shown here).[12] This, however, was the way the rules were supposed to work. Affinity was significantly more common than consanguinity in all degrees but the fourth (*see* table 2). Allegations of consanguinity were unusual below the fourth degree. Both types of incest were less common in the second degree.

People were more likely to obey the rules about not marrying a blood kinsman in the closer degrees (up to the third degree). In the third and fourth degrees it was possible to purchase a dispensation which suggests that relationships in those degrees were regarded as less problematic. Increasing distance of generations would also have made people less likely to know of any pre-existing relatedness. The low number of cases for both affinity and consanguinity in the second degree compared to the first degree is intriguing. It seems likely that kinship in the second degree was recognised and the rules

[11] Donahue, *Law, marriage, and society*, 106, 107, 114, 145, 146, 147–8, 175–6, 239–40, 259, 277–8, 282, 290, 293–4, 571, 572, 573, 574, 709 (*Texts and commentary*, n.188) (where there is ambiguity in Donahue's account the stated relationship has been used as a basis where possible); *Lower ecclesiastical jurisdiction*, 13, 32, 37, 50–1, 64, 68, 74, 80, 87, 108, 111, 135, 145, 148–9, 162, 163, 197, 213, 220, 381; *Select cases from the ecclesiastical courts*, 96–102, 350–65.
[12] Where there is doubt (as in Donahue, *Law, marriage, and society*, 114, 571), the lesser of the two alternatives has been used.

### Table 3a
### Degrees of kinship: thirteenth century (post-1215)

|  | Affinity | Consanguinity |
|---|---|---|
| First degree | 0 | 0 |
| Second degree | 0 | 0 |
| Third degree | 1 | 0 |
| Fourth degree | 1 | 0 |
| **TOTAL** | 2 | 0 |

### Table 3b
### Degrees of kinship: fourteenth century

|  | Affinity | Consanguinity |
|---|---|---|
| First degree | 6 | 1 |
| Second degree | 2 | 0 |
| Third degree | 7 | 0 |
| Fourth degree | 2 | 7* |
| **TOTAL** | 17 | 8 |

### Table 3c
### Degrees of kinship: fifteenth century

|  | Affinity | Consanguinity |
|---|---|---|
| First degree | 0 | 0 |
| Second degree | 0 | 0 |
| Third degree | 1 | 1 |
| Fourth degree | 0 | 3 |
| **TOTAL** | 1 | 4 |

* In *Blakden c Butre* witnesses testified variously to the fourth or fifth degree (the fourth has been counted here): Donahue, *Law, marriage, and society*, 114, 571.

Source: as table 1. Allegations of consanguinity and affinity are sorted according to the degree of relationship, where this is known, stated in the longer line.

were obeyed. Incest in the first degree would have been a worse infringement of the rules, considering the close family members involved and the fact that such close relationships were explicitly prohibited under divine law.[13] However, incest in the first degree may appear more frequently in the sample because it was more scandalous, and also because people lived in closer association with nearer kin, so that there would have been more opportunities for sexual encounters with close affines.[14] This pattern of scandal is confirmed by the fact that office cases were more likely to be prosecuted in the nearer degrees.[15]

The rules concerning affines were not so well accepted as those concerning blood-kinsmen (possibly due to the un-intuitive possibility of affinity arising through sex). Tables 3a, b and c show the degree of relationship alleged in consanguinity and affinity cases in the sample broken down by century. An allegation of consanguinity below the fourth degree was rare.[16] There seems, however, to have been a shift of behaviour in the fifteenth century, although the sample that indicates this is small. In the fifteenth century, affinity was less likely to be raised as an issue. This may reflect a change in the underlying pattern of, or attitude toward, kinship in the fifteenth century, although the absolute numbers are too small to say this with certainty. Donahue saw a shift to 'greater social control over marriage', i.e. more arranged marriages, in the fifteenth as compared to the fourteenth centuries.[17] Perhaps some families were consolidating wealth through marriage where they would not have done so before.

The underlying patterns revealed by the sample of canon law cases suggest that people were more likely to obey the rules concerning consanguinity and not marry or have sex with blood-kinsmen up to a relatively distant degree (people related by a great-grandfather), particularly in the fourteenth century. The higher numbers of cases in the distant degrees reflect both the possibility of purchasing dispensations (while the rules were regarded as important in the aggregate, the system of dispensations allowed them to be measured against necessity in individual cases) and the fact that people may not have felt that these rules were so intrinsic and acceptable. The pattern revealed suggests that the general population's underlying conception of kindred was less wide than that of the canon law system: it might not have been natural for some people to have regarded people related in the fourth degree as kinsmen. The fact that there were more affinity cases

---

[13] Leviticus xviii.6–18.

[14] For example, a man was cited for sleeping with his wife's daughter: *Lower ecclesiastical jurisdiction*, 37, 50–1, 74, 80, 220.

[15] In office cases based on allegations of consanguinity and affinity where the degree is known 44% were prosecuted in the first and second degrees; in instance cases in contrast 14% were in the same degrees.

[16] *Lower ecclesiastical jurisdiction*, 64; Donahue, *Law, marriage, and society*, 572.

[17] Donahue, *Law, marriage, and society*, 201.

raised by illicit intercourse than marriage probably reflects both the fact that more people regarded marriage as creating a genuine bond, and the fact that affinity through illicit intercourse was easier to allege collusively. The overall lack of spiritual kinship cases seems to reflect both a genuine sense of some sort of kinship where the rules were settled (baptism was a public and spiritual act after all) and the generational scope of the rules, i.e. people did not tend to want to marry their godparents, whereas they might more often want to marry their godparent's children. The lack of public honesty cases probably reflects relatively large numbers of informal marriages (rather than arranged betrothals) and also that straightforward affinity, or affinity by illicit intercourse, would have been better known and easier to allege. Overall there was a level of obedience to the canon law rules, but also several disjunctions between the formal system and the patterns of behaviour as revealed in the cases.

## Common law patterns

A similar analysis of cases in the common law courts reveals a pattern between blood-kinsmen that echoes that seen through canon law cases: kinship through the great-grandparent seems to have been widely recognised. The sample of common law cases used to reach this result is based on an analysis of cases from the *Earliest English law reports* and the *Roll of the 1256 Shropshire eyre*. The *Earliest English law reports* provide a selection of interesting cases from the common bench and various eyres (in sixteen counties) across England between 1268 and 1289.[18] Since it is likely that such collections of reports underestimate the number of legally uninteresting cases and because they may not therefore provide an accurate reflection of the wider business of the courts, the records of a single eyre have been used to offset this. Eyre records may overestimate some categories of case (for example it might have been more cost effective to wait for an eyre for regular business or disputes over small parcels of land than go to the more expensive central courts). The use of the two types of collection allows a sufficiently random sample. This sample includes only those cases in the *Earliest English law reports* for which Brand was able to find a record in the plea rolls (the official record of the case). Plea rolls were not unfailingly accurate, but they were more reliable than the reports produced by common lawyers recorded in the year books for these particular purposes: while the record usually contained only a summary of the count, the year book reporters sometimes changed facts to fit a memorable legal point.[19] For the purposes of this sample, it is the alleged facts that matter. The sample consists only of those cases that were

---

[18] Seventeen if Westmorland and Cumberland are counted separately.
[19] *Earliest English law reports*, iv, p. cxxii. For an example of changed facts see ii. 262–4.

## Table 4
### Main actions involving kinship at common law, second half of thirteenth century

|  | EELR | Shropshire | TOTAL |
|---|---|---|---|
| Writs of right (including rationabili parte) | 18 | 6 | 24 |
| Mort d'ancestor | 31 | 41 | 72 |
| Mort d'ancestor mixed with another possessory action | 1 | 1 | 2 |
| Aiel | 3 | 0 | 3 |
| Besaiel | 1 | 0 | 1 |
| Cosinage | 9 | 0 | 9 |
| Other | 16 | 1 | 17 |

Source: Sample of cases where a count of descent founded the claim: Brand, *Earliest English law reports*; 1256 Shropshire eyre.

founded on a pedigree (for example they began with a count of descent), plus cases of mort d'ancestor. This gives a total of 130 cases, although there were more pedigrees as some cases involved multiple plaintiffs.[20] Common law cases generally included many more potential pedigrees (for example, pedigrees given in defence), but limiting the sample to those cases that were founded on a pedigree, plus mort d'ancestor, allows consistency. These reveal a pattern of family memory and, to some extent, interaction, in the second half of the thirteenth century.

A substantial part of business in the common law courts was actions founded on the right or seisin of a kinsman and, among these, the majority were based on the seisin of the limited circle of close kin allowed by the action of mort d'ancestor (father, mother, uncle, aunt, brother and sister, though, of course, within the allowed limits of mort d'ancestor some kin were cited far more frequently than others). Table 4 shows the relative prominence of mort d'ancestor in the sample (three times as common as any other type of case), and how comparatively rare were even the other actions of limited descent, such as cosinage, aiel and besaiel.

[20] Ibid. i. 2–3, 33–5, 40–3, 44–7, 54–9, 61–5, 74–8, 78–80, 110–13, 118–20, 124–5, 128–32, 177–8, 179–80; ii. 185–7, 211–13, 220–8, 262–4, 228–31, 231–42, 251, 282–7, 290–5, 296–7, 301–2, 302–3; iii. 2–3, 3–4, 6–8, 10–16, 46–7, 52–3, 53–6, 60–1, 73–6, 83–6, 97–9, 102–5, 109–10, 144–6, 147–8, 148–50, 150–2, 133–4, 136–41, 155–6, 160–3, 164–5, 170–2, 212–17, 224–8, 228–32, 235–44, 245–9, 249–51, 257–61, 270–5, 277–82, 283–4, 284–6, 291–3, 297–9, 299–301, 302–4, 307–9; iv. 324–7, 329–32, 335–6, 338–43, 381, 346–51, 386–7, 389–90, 425, 426–9, 432–3, 434–5, 436–9, 439–40, 441–2, 574–7; *Roll of the Shropshire eyre*, nos 14, 16, 23, 26, 30, 33, 36, 42, 52, 55, 64, 77, 82, 99, 101, 106, 120, 126, 129, 137, 151, 160, 161, 164, 168, 209, 213, 214, 227, 228, 239, 240, 241, 242, 256, 260, 262, 273, 284, 292, 299, 304, 306, 309, 326, 332, 334, 340, 428.

## Table 5
## Kinsmen named as *propositus* in the common law sample

| Propositus | EELR | Shropshire | TOTAL |
|---|---|---|---|
| father | 29 | 31 | 60 |
| uncle | 8 | 14 | 22 |
| great-grandfather | 7 | 6 | 13 |
| brother | 7 | 4 | 11 |
| grandfather | 6 | 1 | 7 |
| mother | 4 | 3 | 7 |
| great uncle | 5 | 1 | 6 |
| great-great-grandfather | 5 | 0 | 5 |
| first cousin twice removed (female) | 3 | 0 | 3 |
| first cousin thrice removed (male) | 3 | 0 | 3 |
| first cousin twice removed (male) | 2 | 0 | 2 |
| second cousin (male) | 2 | 0 | 2 |
| first cousin (male) | 1 | 0 | 1 |
| first cousin once removed (male) | 1 | 0 | 1 |
| first cousin four times removed (male) | 1 | 0 | 1 |
| great-great-great-great-grandfather | 1 | 0 | 1 |
| grandmother | 1 | 0 | 1 |
| nephew | 1 | 0 | 1 |
| neice | 1 | 0 | 1 |
| sister | 0 | 1 | 1 |
| great-great uncle | 1 | 0 | 1 |

*Source*: as table 4. Frequency of kin members on whose rightful seisin or right claims were based.

The pattern of kinsmen on whose right or seisin the claims were founded (in relation to the claimant) reflects both the high proportion of mort d'ancestor claims within the sample, and also the pattern of relatives most likely to have held land (i.e. males). Table 5, which shows the relative frequency of each type of kinsman named as *propositus* (arranged in order of frequency), does not reveal the straightforward pattern that might be expected, i.e. it does not quite reveal concentric circles of kin with claims from more distant ancestors becoming progressively less frequent. Two points are of particular interest. The first is that claims based on the seisin of a great-grandfather

### Table 6
### Distance in canon law degrees between the plaintiff
### and *propositus* in common law cases

| Canon law degrees between plaintiff and *propositus* | Percentage of claims % |
|:---:|:---:|
| 1 | 53 |
| 2 | 22 |
| 3 | 15 |
| 4 | 7 |
| 5 | 2 |
| 6 | 1 |

*Source*: as table 4.

were more frequent than those based on a grandfather; the second is that claims based on the right and seisin of a first cousin twice removed occur so often. The second point is most easily explained. It reflects the way in which the claims have been counted. Since there were occasionally several plaintiffs claiming together at different distances from the *propositus*, each line has been counted as a claim (thus there are 150 claims in this sample of 130 cases). One case included three claims on the seisin of the same person who was a first cousin twice removed to all the claimants, leading to a higher total of claims based on this figure than would seem reasonable.[21] Still this was a relatively distant kinsman being cited as *propositus* and shows the potential width of family memory.

The frequency of claims based on the seisin of a great-grandfather compared to the grandfather hints that the great-grandfather could sometimes have been regarded as head of the family, and that three generations may have been a regular extent for family memory. Although it might have been thought that disputes would be less likely to arise for closer kinsmen as the descent would be better known, the high number of claims based on fathers and uncles and other close kinsmen argues against this. In fact, the pattern becomes more peculiar when claims of mort d'ancestor are discounted, as then the great-grandfather occurs as frequently as the father (thirteen each out of sixty-nine claims). The great-grandfather was also the most distant kinsman to found a claim in the Shropshire sample. Table 6 shows the distances between plaintiffs and *propositi* in canon law degrees: 97 per cent of cases were within the canon law limit, but nearly 90 per cent were based on a *propositus* within the three-generation family. Table 7 shows the relatives named in counts of descent (i.e. those between the plaintiff and the *propositus*) according to their distance from the plaintiff in canon law

---

[21] *Earliest English law reports*, ii. 296–7.

## Table 7
### Distance in canon law degrees between the plaintiff and any kinsman mentioned in the count of descent

| Canon law degrees of person mentioned in count | Frequency (overall) | Persons cited | Frequency (overall) | Frequency (within degree) |
|---|---|---|---|---|
| 1 | 83 (37%) | Father | 53 (23%) | (64%) |
|   |          | Brother | 20 (9%) | (24%) |
|   |          | Mother | 7 (3%) | (8%) |
|   |          | Sister | 3 (1%) | (4%) |
| 2 | 62 (27%) | Grandfather | 36 (16%) | (58%) |
|   |          | Uncle | 13 (6%) | (21%) |
|   |          | Grandmother | 7 (3%) | (11%) |
|   |          | Nephew | 2 (1%) | (3%) |
|   |          | Aunt* | 2 (1%) | (3%) |
|   |          | First cousin | 1 (0%) | (2%) |
|   |          | Niece | 1 (0%) | (2%) |
| 3 | 51 (23%) | Great-grandfather | 24 (11%) | (47%) |
|   |          | Great-uncle | 11 (5%) | (22%) |
|   |          | Great-grandmother | 6 (3%) | (12%) |
|   |          | Great aunt | 2 (1%) | (4%) |
|   |          | Second cousin | 2 (1%) | (4%) |
|   |          | First cousin once removed | 1 (0%) | (2%) |
| 4 | 19 (8%) | Great-great-grandfather | 7 (3%) | (37%) |
|   |          | Great-great-uncle | 4 (2%) | (21%) |
|   |          | First cousin twice removed | 5 (2%) | (26%) |
|   |          | Great-great-grandmother | 3 (1%) | (16%) |
| 5 | 7 (3%) | First cousin thrice removed | 3 (1%) | (43%) |
|   |          | Great-great-great uncle | 2 (1%) | (14%) |
|   |          | Great-great-great-grandfather | 1 (0%) | (14%) |
|   |          | Great-great-great-grandmother | 1 (0%) | (14%) |

| | | | | |
|---|---|---|---|---|
| 6 | 4 (2%) | Great-great-great-great- uncle | 2 (1%) | (50%) |
| | | First cousin four times removed | 1 (0%) | (25%) |
| | | Great-great-great-great-grandfather | 1 (0%) | (25%) |

*Some relationships are underrepresented because only individual lines of descent have been counted when two kinsmen claim together (i.e. the kinsmen in each individual's more or less direct path to the *propositus* have been counted).

*Source*: as table 4 (excluding cases of mort d'ancestor).

degrees. Once again, there was a distinct change in frequency beyond the third degree: 87 per cent of people cited were within the three-generation family.

A three-generation sense of family fits with what can be seen in the legal literature of the common law. *Bracton's* author explicitly favoured six degrees as the extent of the kindred based on a civil law exemplar.[22] Yet he anticipated patterns of action that show families to have been much more limited. He listed a warranty descending from: the father, mother, brother, sister, uncle, aunt, grandfather, grandmother, great-grandfather, or great-grandmother of the complainant, 'though he who complains is a very remote heir'.[23] This may be rhetoric, but it is interesting, in the light of his six-degree preference, that he considered a great-grandson to be very remote. In the writs and examples of claims to an ancestor's land in *Bracton* the author often elaborated a list of possible ancestors (although the writs were usually not restricted to these ancestors). Frequently the author merely used the general term 'ancestor', but where he did cite relationships the most distant was the great-grandparents, perhaps in an unconscious echo of the pattern in practice.[24]

Combining the evidence from both the canon and common law cases it is apparent that people in late medieval England could recognise and remember potentially wide family groups, including examples of people related as distantly as the sixth degree, but the greatest sense of family was with people related within three-generations, i.e. sharing a common great-grandparent. Three generations is a common knowledge extent for family memory.[25] The evidence in this sample shows that this three-generation family extended horizontally as well as vertically. Although the male ancestors were more likely to die leaving land, knowledge of kin, as reflected by

[22] *Bracton*, ii. 196.
[23] Ibid. iv. 243.
[24] Ibid. iii. 159–60, 184, 250, 251, 319, 324, 326; iv. 30, 34, 38, 49, 243.
[25] E. van Houts, *Memory and gender in medieval Europe, 900–1200*, Basingstoke 1999, 6.

those people named in counts of descent was not restricted to the direct line. Blood kinship was more strongly identified with family than kinship through marriage, and kinship through a sexual encounter was probably only tentatively accepted (although it would have been easier to allege falsely and this was undoubtedly recognised by some).

## Family memory

Family memory could extend widely. The mean number of people included in a common law count of descent (in all non mort d'ancestor cases, since these did not record a count of descent) was five, including both the *propositus* and the plaintiff. The mean number of canon law degrees in these cases was 2.6. Thus counts often involved other relatives collateral to the right line (an uncle who died without heirs of his body would be a typical example). Overall, people were more likely to be cited in the direct line, but family memory could encompass a wide range of kinsmen, all of whom ought to be named in a count.

Sometimes family groups acted together and were thus more than merely a reflection of a kind of kin memory. Such groups could include people who were distantly related, particularly where the law gave them an incentive. The case of *Robert de Lascelles and Others v. Thomas of Moulton and Others* shows four distant cousins acting together to claim the land of another (then deceased).[26] They were related through a common ancestor who was the great-great-grandfather of one, the great-great-great-grandfather of two and the great-great-great-great-grandfather of the other. Together they claimed the land of one of the grandsons of that distant common ancestor. All were descendants of daughters of the common ancestor and one of the plaintiffs was the aunt of another (she was third cousin once removed to one of the other plaintiffs and fourth cousin to the last). The family acting together in this case was unusually wide. It is instructive to consider how such distantly related kinsmen would have known of their relationship and their link to the *propositus*.

Clearly there were incentives to remember. The possibility of inheriting or claiming land was powerfully attractive. There was also an incentive for people to know who they could or could not marry, particularly if marriage involved property (in case dower or inheritance was threatened by an illegitimate marriage). If this seems to suggest that knowledge of wider family would be more likely among the landed and wealthy this should not be surprising. Certainly there was more evidence of family involvement in marriage, although probably only involvement of a limited range of close kin, where wealth was at stake.[27]

---

[26] *Earliest English law reports*, ii. 263–4.
[27] Donahue, *Law, marriage, and society*, 205.

There were several routes for family memory. The most obvious was from the family themselves. Women were particularly important for maintaining and sharing family memories.[28] A conventional demographic pattern, at least among the nobility, was for women to reproduce young and survive into old age. Theoretically it was even possible that a woman who survived to the age of seventy-one might live to see her great-great-great-grandchildren's marriage negotiations.[29] If each generation reproduced at the age of sixteen such a woman could become a great-grandparent at forty-eight, a very respectable age and one that makes the three-generation family pattern seem plausible. Canon lawyers believed that memory of family shared across the generations might be a reliable way of passing knowledge about family. Another route for family memory was documents and written evidence, particularly where land was involved. There were numerous examples of cases at common law where people produced writs or deeds or fines of agreements made in court. People could have access to a wide range of legal and official documents, and a level of practical literacy was relatively common in society.[30] Such routes for memory could be reinforced by public rituals and family gatherings such as baptisms, marriages, funerals and feasts.

Memory of kinship was not restricted just to the kindred involved. The community was expected to know about kinship up to quite distant reaches. They were expected to make consanguinity or affinity known at the banns, or, as a jury, to decide who had better right to land. Witnesses could be required to have detailed knowledge of other people's kinship. Personal observation and knowledge would have been an important element in understanding someone else's kinship. Again, canon lawyers acknowledged this. One way that canon lawyers looked for evidence of familial connections was to rely on evidence of how putative kinsmen had been seen to address one another.[31] A certain level of widespread hearsay knowledge about other people's relationships was expected.

Public recitations and reinforcement of other people's relatedness would surely have been an important route for spreading knowledge about other people's kinship through the community. The banns and marriage ceremonies at the church door are a prime example. Shared rituals, such as marriage and endowerment at the church door, would fix family relationships in people's memory, as per the witness who recalled that one of the reasons he knew the relationship between two people in a marriage enforcement case was that he had passed through the town where one party's grandmother had married. Though it was not through the marriage that he evidenced the relationship, the event of the marriage was clearly memorable.[32] The business of

---

[28] van Houts, *Memory and gender*, ch. iv.
[29] d'Avray, *Medieval marriage*, 106.
[30] M. Clanchy, *From memory to written record: England, 1066–1307*, Oxford 1993.
[31] *Select cases from the ecclesiastical courts*, 359.
[32] Ibid.

the courts would have been another public source of knowledge about other people's kinship. Eyres were busy communal events. Though the language of the pleaders at common law (law French) might have been a barrier to understanding the legal cases, the occasion itself would have generated discussion and gossip. The church courts may have played a prominent role too, and cases involving kinsmen would have been a source of scandal or speculation.[33] If a person was punished for adultery and incest they could have been flogged (though people often paid fines to avoid this); a repeat offender could be excommunicated.[34] Such occasions would surely have been remarkable, perhaps causes for pity or cruel entertainment. They would not have been the usual manner in which people learned about another's kinship – there is evidence that English office cases may have been less organised than other jurisdictions – but they would have fixed kinship in the community memory.[35]

Family membership would not only be revealed in disputes. Outside the formal structures of the common law (governing inheritance and ability to bring particular actions), kin had many prominent sub-legal roles which would have been seen publicly. They could have been important as proof: determining a villein's status (if a man's close kin were villeins then it was likely he was)[36] and they could determine nationality for Englishry (to avoid paying the *murdrum* fine).[37] It was the closest male kin member, or a lord, or a wife if her husband died in her arms, who were supposed to appeal a man's murder.[38] Kin could stand in for a man when he was too ill to come to court and sue.[39] Kin could be expected to look after the interests of an heir: to complain if the heir's land held in wardship was being wasted, or if the lord proposed a marriage that disparaged an heir under fourteen years old.[40] There is also evidence of family members purchasing the wardship and marriages of relatives.[41] These legal expectations represent a whole range of informal and cooperative roles for kin members.

Relatively settled communities might be likely to have a soap-opera style knowledge of other people's families and pedigrees (this may have changed in the fifteenth century). Though the normally co-resident kin group in late medieval England was rather small (often the nuclear family), people could sometimes have wide knowledge and three generations was common. It is difficult to see how far such knowledge extended among the less wealthy, and

---

[33] Potentially 'magnum scandalum': *Lower ecclesiastical jurisdiction*, 157.
[34] For example, ibid. 13, 50. See also Helmholz, *Oxford history*, i. 618–20.
[35] Donahue, *Law, marriage, and society*, 599.
[36] *Bracton*, ii. 411.
[37] Ibid. ii. 379.
[38] Ibid. ii. 295. When there were several appellors the nearer kinsman was preferred, ibid. ii. 352. This is an interesting parallel to the system given in the *Mirror of justices*.
[39] *Bracton*, ii. 353.
[40] Ibid. ii. 264; iii. 36, 153.
[41] Holt, 'The heiress and the alien', 264.

it is possible, even somewhat likely, that people below the level of wealthy landowners did not have such great knowledge of their extended kin.[42] People did not always know their own relatedness, nor did other members of the community always know about alleged relationships.[43] A great mass of relatedness was probably unmentioned or unknown. But a great deal could also be known and made memorable.

## Ideas about kinship

People's casual understanding of their own kindred and their place in it did not wholly fit with that of the legal systems under which they operated. For the common law the differences between the parentelic pattern and the people who sometimes attempted to gain seisin (i.e. younger brothers *versus* grandchildren) may reflect cynical attempts to gain land, but they also indicate a sense of entitlement between brothers within the same generation that primogeniture and the parentelic system did not allow. Parental settlements of land on younger children occurred commonly enough to show that there was some discomfort with the winner-takes-all system to which the strict application of inheritance rules could lead. For the canon law there was less acceptance of kinship created through affinity, and, it seems, less weight placed on family connections beyond the third degree. This is especially interesting as the evidence of canon law ideas in a common law context suggests that the four-degree limit was one of the factors of canon law kinship most easily understood and applied elsewhere.

There were layers of kinship beyond the formal legal rules. People would have had their own sense of values in relation to kinship and their kindred, which could be varied and were sometimes very negative. One cynical interpolator in *Bracton* repeated the commonplace that a younger sister should not be put in wardship to an elder 'that the sheep be saved from the jaws of the wolves, because of the expectation and possibility of succession, which might occur if they should die within age through some machination'.[44] Another interpolation explained the customs of London. There a wife with dower could claim no extra unless her husband bequeathed it, and, 'according to some', the same rule applied to children: 'for a citizen could scarcely be found who would undertake a great enterprise in his lifetime if, at his death, he was compelled against his will to leave his estate to ignorant and extravagant children and undeserving wives'. The interpolator went on to state that it was necessary to give a man freedom of action 'for thereby he will curb misconduct, encourage virtue, and put in the way of both wives and children

---

[42] Brand, 'Family and inheritance', 58–9.
[43] For example, Donahue, *Law, marriage and society*, 146–9, where proof was slow or doubtful, or *Select cases from the ecclesiastical courts*, 355, 358.
[44] *Bracton*, ii. 227.

an occasion for good behaviour, which indeed might not come about if they knew without doubt that they would obtain a certain share irrespective of the testator's wishes'.[45] He expected family to be rebellious and greedy, only willing to obey the father if he bribed them with his will. This jaundiced picture seems a stereotype of a small, bad family, at odds with the duties that the author of the text elsewhere expected of kin. Ideas about kinship and family could be as varied as there were people and families.

Some such expectations can also be seen in contemporary tales and literature. One example where family was both important and pervading is the romance Fouke Fitz Waryn, which survives in one manuscript and can be dated to about 1330.[46] Family was a prominent presence. Fouke was supported by a band of his four brothers and two cousins and other men who frequently acted together.[47] It is not unexpected that brothers should be close and, at two points, Fouke's relationship with his brothers was especially vital to the story. Once, his brother William was wounded so severely that he was on the point of death and Fouke had to leave him behind to be captured: 'No one has ever seen greater sorrow than that shared between these two brothers.'[48] And another time, in a traditional trope, Fouke acted as champion for a foreign king and almost fought his brother Philip who did not recognise him until Fouke showed a sign.[49] Elsewhere Fouke sheltered with his aunt and mourned the death of his mother, praying 'compassionately for her soul'.[50] This was in contrast to his reaction to his father's death which was noted briefly with the remark that Fouke took fealty from his father's men.[51] This hints that some family dynamics, such as the generational desire for lordship and power, could lead to tension.

Family was also an important source of alliance and loyalty and of connections across society. In Fouke woman were identified through male relatives and the men they had or would marry.[52] Ties of affinity were expected to form bonds of alliance between people.[53] Men were occasionally identified by their tie to the king.[54] The king initially welcomed Fouke because of their kinship ('Fair son, ... you are welcome to me, for you are of my blood, and I will help you'), although the later part of the tale consisted of Fouke's adventures in opposition to the king.[55]

---

[45] Ibid. ii. 180–1
[46] 'Fouke Fitz Warin', ed. T. E. Kelley, in T. H Ohlgren (ed.), A book of medieval outlaws: ten tales in modern English, Stroud 2000, 106–67 at p. 106.
[47] Ibid. 131–2, 135, 143, 145–6, 163.
[48] Ibid. 157.
[49] Ibid. 161.
[50] Ibid. 132
[51] Ibid. 126
[52] Ibid. for example 140, 165.
[53] Ibid. 137.
[54] Ibid. 156.
[55] Ibid. 128.

Ties of kinship were viewed in the tale as sources of obligation. For example, the king's cousin asked to be vanguard in an attack against Fouke as he claimed that the English in the king's party were all Fouke's cousins and probably therefore traitors. The English lords were stung and replied that 'the king will see for himself who might be holding back for reasons of family ties'.[56] The expectation of cooperation between kinsmen was only partially fulfilled by the events portrayed in the text. One of the English lords, Randolph of Chester, had a somewhat piteous encounter with Fouke where Fouke called Randolph 'cousin' and begged him help for his brother William who was lying near to death. He told Randolph to 'go back to your lord the king, and do his service without hesitation or regard for us who are related to you by blood', which the earl did sadly.[57] The author expected 'cousins' to have had ties of obligation; in the story Randolph did capture William and take pity on him and send him to be nursed, to the king's wrath. Other unspecified relatives were a source of support or succour.[58] The author expected this world of wealthy men to be a web of kinship connections and loyalties.

It is notable that the author's understanding of kinship also seems to have been influenced by the canon law. When Fouke met a mariner he said ' "yours is a very perilous trade. Tell me, brother Mador, of what death did your father die?" Mador answered that he had drowned at sea. "How did your grandfather go?" "In the same way." "How about your great-grandfather?" "In like manner, as did all my relations, to the fourth generation, as far as I know." '[59] It is suggestive that the third generation was included for specifics, and the fourth as a suitable extent of Mador's mariner family.

Understanding of kinship would have been a kind of situational toolkit of ideas, to be applied depending on the circumstances. There is good evidence that people, particularly the elite or the educated, knew and applied the canon law and the common law kinship systems as part of this toolkit. There is also good evidence that the canon law structures were the foremost general way of thinking about kinship structures (although they did not affect some practical matters such as inheritance or access to land).

## The dominance of canon law

The ideas of the canon law held the field. There are several reasons for this. The most important was its reach into people's lives. The parentelic system of the common law applied to anyone inheriting under the auspices of feudal tenures and non-customary socage (unless, for example, a different pattern

[56] Ibid. 156.
[57] Ibid. 158.
[58] Ibid. 125, 163.
[59] Ibid. 148.

was deliberately specified, such as fee tail in the male line). The common law courts, however, also enforced local customary patterns of inheritance where they were recognised. In addition there was a great mass of villein kinship. The canon law applied to everyone wanting to marry.

The canon law had enforcement mechanisms that would foreground kinship structures at vital moments, largely in the shape of the banns. There was also *ex officio* jurisdiction of local canon law courts (though *ex officio* jurisdiction was not always exercised routinely).[60] Under the common law, the lord ought to have employed the parentelic system when putting a tenant into their inheritance, but the rules carried no sanction not driven by a positive choice. People could settle their way out of the system if they chose to, and the later history of the common law is full of collusive actions. Some cases that reached court were settled before judgement and this need not have been according to the conventional pattern of common law inheritance (though that pattern, affecting which way the decision would ultimately be likely to go would have influenced the relative strength of the parties' negotiating positions). People had an incentive to press their claims, since land was so valuable, but without external sanction (and social and honourable pressures on non-systematic decisions would have supplied some element of this) it relied on the vigilance of the parties involved. In practice the difference in enforcement may have been slight as neither legal system was wholly consistent, but the difference would have had theoretical implications for people's understanding of the nature of the two kinship systems.

The kinship rules of the canon law were also simpler, more comprehensively framed and more closely articulated. Its essence was the relatively simple negative rule that forbade marriage to anyone defined as a kinsman. Knowing this, it was just a matter of understanding the definition of who counted as a kinsman. This was supported by a framework of potentially elaborate detail. However, it could be summarised effectively: you could not marry anyone within four generations of a common great-great-grandparent, or anyone related to that extent to someone you had married or had had sex with. In contrast, common law kinship was a matter of reckoning the nearest heir among numerous potential options and applying a suite of considerations such as legitimacy, age, gender and all the other issues for deciding priority as discussed in *Britton* (though this should not imply that the common law system was uncertain by the thirteenth century, except at its edges).The common law rules were developing and demand-led. While there was uncertainty around some parts of the canon law, for example in the lack of clarity around spiritual fraternity, the canon law system may have seemed clearer.

This clarity came in part from the education system that underpinned

---

[60] The court at York, for example, was predominantly a dispute resolution forum: Donahue, *Law, marriage and society*, 215. Other, lower, courts would have done this work.

it. The canon law was taught in universities from big, authoritative books which, together with the existence on the continent of specialist canon law teachers, encouraged systemisation. The whole purpose of Gratian's *Decretum* was to bring harmony to discordant canons. The university system encouraged experts and intellectuals who argued, and wrote treatises about, their arguments and opinions. The universities also encouraged introductory texts that simplified and captured the basics of canon law kinship, building upon such important learning devices as the gloss. In contrast, there was less drive towards systematisation in the common law. The author of *Bracton* attempted it, possibly as part of a school of synthesis; *Fleta*, Gilbert de Thornton and *Britton* followed in this tradition with their attempts to write big books encompassing the common law. Some of these books were widely read. Yet they were not ultimately very successful.[61] At common law, learning on the case was important. Apprentices watched pleading from the crib and attended occasional lectures which leaned towards practical points about types of action and procedures rather than systematic explorations of the rules. Such explorations of kinship belonged to the big books of the common law, not to practice, so ultimately were not pursued in the same way as canon law kinship. In the common law the very process in the courts and the rules of pleading directed attention elsewhere. It was necessary to get the count right, which needed knowledge of the underlying structures, but circumstances were more important than systems. In intellectual terms canonists and common lawyers probably knew their own kinship systems equally well, but the one system articulated this while the other did not. The sheer number of canon law treatises and discussions on kinship probably also played a role in the relative prominence of the canon law kinship systems.

Canon law was also dominant, specifically in the legal literature, because its rules were part of a long tradition and were systematised in 1215 as part of an influential body of reforms. The parentelic rules may have been less obviously settled at this point: for example, the *casus regis* injected uncertainty into one part of the system in the early thirteenth century. The canon law tradition of writing about kinship was well established by the time that *Bracton* was in general circulation and during the late thirteenth and early fourteenth centuries when most manuscripts of *Bracton* and *Britton* were copied.

Finally, images were important. They fixed concepts in people's minds. Stephen Jay Gould has written on the importance of images in modern culture, on 'the central role of pictures, graphs, and other forms of visual representation in channelling and constraining our thought' and 'the power of pictures, as epitomes or encapsulators of central concepts in our culture'.[62]

---

[61] 'The obsolescence of *Bracton* ... left the common law without systematic exposition for the next five hundred years': Baker, *Introduction*, 176–7.
[62] S. J. Gould, 'Evolution by walking', in his *Dinosaur in a haystack: reflections in natural history*, London 1996, 248–59 at p. 249.

His insight is reminiscent of that quotation from Horace so popular with medieval canon lawyers and specifically used to refer to the image of the tree: 'Less vividly is the mind stirred by what finds entrance through the ears than by what is brought before the trusty eyes.'[63] Or of the promise in *Bracton* of a figure that would make the lines of descent 'appear more clearly to the eye'.[64] The canon law had the powerful image of the *arbor consanguinitatis* and the less clear *arbor affinitatis* (*see* figures 1 and 2). Such trees were copied in hundreds of contexts. The common law had no kinship image to compare. There were, it is true, occasional attempts to draw and adapt trees, but these began firmly from the influential canon law model which was not quite suitable to their needs.[65] Some reporters drew pedigrees and kin connections: simple horizontal lists like flow diagrams.[66] Some common law lectures used handouts and visual images.[67] The fact that a tree based on the canon law model survives in a manuscript that was probably a teacher's or student's collection is at least suggestive of the use of these images in a pedagogic context.[68] Common law kinship, however, was not pictured schematically. Without a regular image or pattern, it may have been more difficult to visualise when divorced from the practical world of its own application.

Why, however, was there any space at all for the dominance of formal legal kinship systems? In late medieval England there was an unusual degree of individualism; and there was little in the way of a widespread corporate or clannish kinship system. Although there is a sense of the three-generation family, this pattern is not strong enough to suggest that a corporate kinship system operated comparable to the type of exogamous clans found in Italy.[69] That system, of effective and cooperative clans, was not in any way comparable to the situation in England.

Yet there is some evidence that it had been once. The Anglo-Saxons had a more corporate kinship system, evidence for which is particularly tied in with the evidence for feuds. Kindred can be glimpsed in Anglo-Saxon

---

[63] 'Segnius irritant animos demissa per aurem quam que sunt oculis subiecta fidelibus': Horace, 'Ars poetica', *Satires, epistles and ars poetica*, 180–1.

[64] *Bracton*, ii. 200.

[65] As discussed at pp. 79–80 above.

[66] For example, *Emma Daughter of Hugh de la Grene v. Richard Fitzwaryn (or John de Ifeld)*, in *Year books of 14 Edward II (michaelmas 1320)*, ed. S. J. Stoljar and L. J. Downer (Selden Society civ, 1988), 123. This pedigree occurs in six manuscripts: CUL, MS Ff.3.12, fo. 119r; MS Gg.5.20, fo. 125v; BL, MS Add. 35094, fo. 209r; MS Add. 25183, fo. 63v; MS Add. 37658, fo. 263r; MS Harley 3639, fo. 112v. The image probably occurred in the source text.

[67] Brand, 'Courtroom and schoolroom', 62 n. 21. There are figures in BL, MS Lansdowne 467, fos 156r, 158rv. The figure on fo. 158r, for example, pictured three lines extending horizontally from a common ancestor.

[68] BL, MS Harley 493a, fo. 11r.

[69] Heers, *Family clans*; d'Avray 'Lay kinship solidarity', 198–9.

law codes claiming bodies,[70] supporting feuding parties,[71] standing surety,[72] shielding wrongdoers[73] and claiming or paying compensation or wergild.[74] The kindred, as a positive, negative or neutral force seems to have been a prominent presence in Anglo-Saxon society, an image confirmed by its role in the literature and reported feuds.[75]

The kind of active quasi-corporate kin-group that is implied by the practice of feud is not easy to reconstruct from the scant evidence. The anonymous tract *Wer* said that a man paying wergild would need kinsmen as sureties: eight from his paternal kin, and four from his maternal kin. This is a potentially wide group, it implies a more active and co-operative kinship group than is often found in the later Middle Ages, but it is not specific. Only the closest family group, the first to receive payment, were specified: the victim's children, his brothers and his father – a small, close family group.[76] Strategies of recruitment would have been important in feuds to enlist the help of friends and kinsmen.[77] This, combined with amorphous group of sureties in *Wer*, suggest that Anglo-Saxon kinship groups were not monolithic.

Kin terminology in Anglo-Saxon was well defined upwards but less so sideways and downwards. There were specific names for male ascendants up to the *sixta fæder* (the great-great-great-great-grandfather) and for female ascendants up to the *fifte modor* (the great-great-great-grandmother), for the uncles and aunts on both sides and the male cousins on both sides, the son and daughter and male descendants, but a dearth of specific names for cousins.[78] This pattern is in some ways similar to that in later medieval England, where, for example, there was among common lawyers, less use of collateral

---

[70] III Ethelred 7:1; II Cnut 56: *English historical documents, c. 500–1042*, ed. D. Whitelock, 2nd edn, London 1979, 441, 463. For a discussion of how to translate this difficult passage see S. Jurasinski, '*Reddatur parentibus*: the vengeance of the family in Cnut's homicide legislation', *Law and History Review* xx/1 (2002), 157–80.

[71] II Edmund 1:3; VIII Ethelred 23–24: *English historical documents*, 428, 450.

[72] II Athelstan 1:3–4, 2, 6:1; VI Athelstan 12:2: ibid. 417–18, 427.

[73] VI Athelstan 8:2; II Edmund 1:1–2: ibid. 425, 428.

[74] Laws of Alfred 30; II Athelstan 11; II Edmund 7; and VIII Ethelred 25: ibid. 413, 419, 428–9, 450.

[75] See, for example, S. D. White, 'Kinship and lordship in early medieval England: the story of Sigeberht, Cynewulf, and Cyneheard', *Viator* xx (1989), 1–18. See also T. Charles-Edwards, 'Anglo-Saxon kinship revisited', in J. Hines (ed.), *The Anglo-Saxons from the migration period to the eighth century: an ethnographic perspective*, Woodbridge 1997, 171–204 at pp. 174–6.

[76] P. Wormald, *The making of English law: King Alfred to the twelfth century*, I: *Legislation and its limits*, Oxford 1999, 376–7. H. R. Loyn gives this (the *healsfang* group) as the victim's children, his brothers and his father's brothers: 'Kinship in Anglo-Saxon England', *Anglo-Saxon England* iii (1974), 197–209 at p. 204. Wormald's translation is to be preferred.

[77] P. Hyams, *Rancor and reconciliation in medieval England*, Ithaca–London 2003, 21–32.

[78] L. Lancaster, 'Kinship in Anglo-Saxon society', *British Journal of Sociology* ix (1958), 230–50, 359–77 at pp. 235–7.

kin terms. It is also interesting to see the contrast between terms for ascendants and descendants, a pattern which fits with the model of Anglo-Saxon royal genealogies which stretched back to mythical male founders. This suggests a system where kinship was reckoned by links to known male ancestors. Such a system, with a sort of *stipes* at the head, fits with the mention in the law codes of 'knees' of kinsmen. However, any detail is difficult to reconstruct without borrowing the system of joints from the fourteenth-century German text *Sachsenspiegel*.[79] The Anglo-Saxon evidence gives less detail.

The surviving evidence of Anglo-Saxon inheritance does not allow the reconstruction of family structure in any great detail. Inheritance was probably largely customary, although a law of Cnut states that, in intestate succession, the lord should ensure a fair division between the widow, children and close kin.[80] This open statement leaves much unclear, particularly who were the close kin, and this is without turning attention to the vexed question of bookland and folkland and what kind of inheritance was customary, whether alienation was allowed, or whether kin members had a residual claim, and what this might mean in practice.[81] The patterns of landholding from the Domesday Book suggest inheritance of land by co-heirs who then held in *parage*.[82] A kind of generational kinship pattern seems a safe assumption, but even this goes beyond what the evidence baldly states. That the Anglo-Saxons had a stronger and wider sense of kinship than existed in post-Conquest England seems clear: the pattern of gifts in wills suggests that there were conventions that encouraged testamentary gifts across a range of horizontal kin, in real contrast with post-Conquest England, where testament of land was not allowed.[83]

Evidence for quasi-corporate kin groups tied to the feud system seems to shine more strongly in the earlier Anglo-Saxon period, yet, even then, the feuding kindred appeared in royal laws which may reflect a gradual decline of the kindred, as kings attempted to promote their own role in criminal justice. The traditional argument is that the increasing importance of lordship and royal power replaced kinship as the primary social bond.[84] This

---

[79] *The Saxon mirror: a sachsenspiegel of the fourteenth century*, trans. M. Dobozy, Philadelphia 1999, 69. In Norway later lawyers talked about wergild in terms of knees: Loyn, 'Kinship', 197. For an example of Anglo-Saxon usage see Wormald, *Making of English law*, i. 376.

[80] II Cnut 70:1: *English historical documents*, 465.

[81] For two sensible discussions of this difficult subject see S. Reynolds, 'Bookland, folkland and fiefs', *Anglo-Norman Studies* xiv (1991), 211–27, and E. John, *Reassessing Anglo-Saxon England*, Manchester 1996, p. viii.

[82] Maitland, *Domesday book and beyond*, 182.

[83] Holt, 'The revolution of 1066', 165.

[84] II Athelstan 2 suggests that the role of the lord in justice was prior to that of the kin; VI Athelstan 8:2–3 provides details on how to deal with a kindred so strong that they 'stand up for a thief'; II Edmund Prol. 2 laments 'The illegal and manifold conflicts which take place among us'; and II Edmund 1 provides a mechanism for kindred to exempt

may be so, yet some traces of feuds and of active, if vague, kindreds can be seen in late Anglo-Saxon England.[85] Kinship patterns were also changing in other parts of Europe in the tenth and eleventh centuries; on the continent the vertical *lignage* was emerging from more horizontal (clannish?) kinship patterns.[86]

The sufficient conclusion may be drawn that there appears to have been a more corporate and active kindred in England in the period before the Conquest, though the outlines are vague. By the early twelfth-century, however, one of the best post-Conquest legal writers on Anglo-Saxon law could not reconstruct or find material on the customs or norms that governed Anglo-Saxon inheritance.[87] The author of *Leges Henrici Primi* (written 1116–18) clearly thought that he ought to include a section on kinship and inheritance. Instead of Anglo-Saxon law, however, he used the seventh-century *Lex Ribuaria*: allowing parents to succeed, then brothers or sisters, then the father's or mother's sister, then relatives up to the fifth 'joint'.[88] Other collections of Anglo-Saxon law were made during the early twelfth century, some probably from antiquarian impulses.[89] It seems that these laws, with what little kinship they contained, were not applied. Kinship, particularly around inheritance, had become a customary matter. Something had changed between 1066 and 1215 which allowed the canon law to become the main general way of thinking about kinship.

The Conquest clearly had a disruptive effect, but there were longer term elements in this change. The first is tied to the absence of the feud, but not only this. More broadly, it was the absence of recognised patterns of behaviour or rights that would have given a quasi-corporate kindred an arena within which to act, and would have reinforced both personal connections and the pattern of any kinship system. The second was a symbolic change in the way that ideal kinship was portrayed.

In the later Middle Ages the kin did not share rights to land and they did not have a recognised arena in which to act together. This would have made it difficult to maintain more corporate kindreds in the putative Anglo-Saxon model. Where land was shared between family members there is evidence of wider and more actively cooperative kin groups. This can be

---

themselves from the feud: *English historical documents*, 417, 425, 428. Such a kin exemption may have been customary anyway: Hyams, *Rancor and reconciliation*, 82.

[85]  R. Fletcher, *Bloodfeud: murder and revenge in Anglo-Saxon England*, London 2002.

[86]  G. Duby, *The chivalrous society*, trans. C. Postan, London 1977.

[87]  On the quality and ambitious programme behind the *Leges Henrici Primi* and *Quardipartitus* see P. Wormald, 'Quadripartitus', in Garnett and Hudson, *Law and government*, 111–47.

[88]  'geniculum': *Leges Henrici Primi*, ed. and trans. L. J. Downer, Oxford 1972, 70, 20a at p. 225.

[89]  On post-Conquest manuscripts of Anglo-Saxon law see Wormald, *The making of English law*, 224–53. For some of the key texts see F. Liebermann, *Die Gesetze Der Angelsachsen: Heraus gegeben im Auftrage der Savigny-Stiftung*, Halle S. A. 1903, i. 492–670.

seen in a small way from the sample of common law cases discussed above. Where sisters inherited land they took in parts, a structure that encouraged cooperation. The sample contains fifty-five cases where it is possible to tell whether the line of descent went through a woman (excluding cases of mort d'ancestor). In the eighteen counts where this happened there was a mean of two plaintiffs,[90] as opposed to one in cases where it did not.[91] Not only were kinsmen more likely to need to act together, but more distant kinsmen were likely to be involved if a line went through a woman. Where a count went through a woman there was a mean of seven people in the count related by an average of three canon law degrees, as opposed to a mean of four people and an average of two degrees when a line did not. Since women held less land, opportunities to make claims through them were less frequent and were likely to involve longer memory and greater cooperation if the land had descended to several lines of kinsmen. The *Lascelles* case shows how widely such cooperation could reach.[92] The evidence of descent through women suggests that shared rights to land reinforced family bonds and cooperation. Under the common law shared rights to land were not the norm, although customary partible inheritance did survive in places. In addition, cooperative kin had few recognised arenas in which to act. Feuds had been replaced by the king's criminal law so that where kin and neighbours were seen to be acting together it seems more often to have been in disputes over claims to have access to or management of land, for example in dissesins, than in any accepted manner.[93]

The combination of primogeniture and parentelic kinship may have done much to limit any corporate kinship that had survived the upheaval (and replacement of the land-owning class) of the Conquest by reducing accepted areas for cooperation between kin. The primacy of primogeniture was also symbolically important. In some ways the attitude towards kin between the tenth and thirteenth centuries shows fundamental similarities. Kinship was a source of closeness and bonds, but it was never the only such source. Excepting the prominence of the feud there is not such a great leap between

---

[90] *Earliest English law reports*, i. 33–5, 40–3, 124–5, 179–80; ii. 211–13, 262–4, 296–7; iii. 53–6, 83–6 144–6, 164–5, 224–8; iv. 434–5, 574–7; *Roll of the Shropshire eyre*, nos 16, 30, 64, 332.

[91] *Earliest English law reports*, i. 2–3, 61–5, 74–8, 78–80, 110–13, 118–20, 128–32, 177–8; ii. 220–8, 228–31, 251, 282–7, 290–5, 302–3; iii. 6–8, 10–16, 37, 46–7, 73–6, 102–5, 160–3, 170–2, 212–17, 245–9, 249–51, 277–82, 283–4, 284–6, 291–3, 297–9, 299–301, 307–9; iv. 324–7, 432–3; *Roll of the Shropshire eyre*, nos 151, 161, 227, 428.

[92] *Earliest English law reports*, ii. 262–4.

[93] In cases of novel disseisin family members, particularly brothers, were often accused together. For example in *Rolls of the justices in eyre: being the rolls of pleas and assizes for Lincolnshire, 1218–9, and Worcestershire, 1221*, ed. D. M. Stenton (Selden Society liii, 1934) groups of (accused) disseisors included brothers: nos 42, 74, 102, 119, 157, 203, 205, 796, 820, 830, 916, 928, 946; father and son(s): nos 42, 80, 187, 721, 821, 928, 930, 1057; mother and son(s): nos 54, 78, 344, 816, 831, 991, 1018; father and daughters: nos 429, 786; mother and daughter: no. 787; brothers and sisters: no. 119; and sisters: no. 998.

Ælfwine in the *Poem of the Battle of Maldon* who feared to shame his kin and suffered 'no common grief' on the death of a man who 'was both my kinsman and my lord',[94] and the accusation of and reply to Sir James of Normandy in *Fouke fitz Warin* that 'the English, at least all the nobles, were cousins of Sir Fouke, hence they were most probably traitors to the king, and would not help take these felons'. The English nobles' response in *Fouke* may be read to reflect the dominance of lordship: 'the king will see for himself who might be holding back for reasons of family ties'.[95] Yet a man engaged in feud in the Anglo-Saxon period would still have needed to recruit aid from kinsmen influenced by myriad ties and it was possible for kinsmen to opt out of a feud, so the differences need not be vast.[96] Still, something interesting had changed about the underlying ideal which was reflected in the story. Anthropologists have reflected on how, in representations of kinship systems, 'people's conceptions are linked to an ideal form'.[97] Under common law kinship the ideal was not one of cooperation or a wide kindred. Of course, people did not necessarily follow ideals, but nor would a widespread sense of corporate kinship have been able to survive without reinforcement in some ideal manner.

Common law kinship patterns idealised a model of the family that did not encourage wide or cooperative kinship. The Conquest marked a break of personnel (most 'noble' landowners changed), custom and, eventually, law. The Normans in England showed more of a sense of *lignage* (part of a change in pattern of family perception across Europe) than the Anglo-Saxons had.[98] Common law kinship did not emerge fully formed. In the early post-Conquest period actual behaviour (compromise with lordship, focus on close family) met idealised form (inheritance within the family).[99] By the time of *Bracton* common law kinship had reached an idealised form (excepting the civil law patina) of pattern and structure without such compromises. This symbolically important system was individualistic, focused on a single inheriting heir, and allowed little generational equality and no residual rights for the kin group not created by special arrangement. This firming up of common law kinship happened before the canon law system became widespread and before the drive to apply the canon law more broadly, reflected in the development of a system of consistory courts in the mid-thirteenth century. Thus, the developing common law kinship structures would have played a role in removing any widespread residual clannish or corporate kinship system. Of course, such a claim is limited to a rather elevated segment of society.

---

94 'Poem of the Battle of Maldon': *English historical documents*, 319–24 at p. 323.

95 'Fouke Fitz Warin', 156.

96 II Edmund 1: *English historical documents*, 428, discussed in Hyams, *Rancor and reconciliation*, 82.

97 Dumont, *Introduction to two theories*, 93.

98 Holt, 'The revolution of 1066', and 'Politics and property'.

99 Hudson, *Land, law, and lordship*, especially chs iii, iv.

Yet there was no residual peasant clan, and it is not clear that the peasant kinship structures seen in court records were not a factor of the courts themselves trying to impose order.[100] In this it is difficult to go much further, yet accepting that common law kinship reduced the likelihood of any corporate kin, the eventual priority of canon law kinship may seem slightly ironic.

Each individual would have had concentric rings of kin, some they lived with, some they associated closely with, some they merely knew. They would have applied different kinship concepts in different circumstances as appropriate. It seems that there was a tendency for people to regard three generations as the normal practical reach of kin; and this may be a factor of the normal reach of memory. Yet many people did know and apply or try to obey (or manipulate) the existing legal kinship systems, both of which encompassed kinship more widely. It is also likely that, if such people thought about kinship structures and the extent of kinship, particularly if they were educated, it was the system of the canon law that would most generally have come into their minds. Legal kinship was never the whole of medieval English kinship, but there was no other formal system to rival the legal ideas, particularly those of the canon law which would apply whenever a couple wanted to marry legitimately. Such legal kinship structures were a more or less formal and artificial way of ordering relationships, but they are both interesting and important because people used and learned and lived under them and, at vital life events such as inheritance or marriage, had to fit their own lives to their structures and concepts.

---

[100] P. Hyams, *King, lords and peasants in medieval England: the common law of villeinage in the twelfth and thirteenth centuries*, Oxford 1980, 181.

# Conclusion

The kinship system of the canon law was the foremost general model for thinking about kinship structures in late medieval England. Even common lawyers, specialists in their own system of kinship, turned to the canon law where they perceived that there was a gap their own literature, or no inherent answer in their rules. On a wider level, the structures of canon law kinship were also understood, by theologians such as Kilwardby, as part of the way in which the social world was ordered. In practice, there was no clan or quasi-corporate kinship system. There were locally recognised variations and patterns of kinship, but only hints of structured kinship survived outside the law (more indicative of patterns of practice than a system).

Both canon and common law applied in their specific contexts. The dominance of the canon law can be seen through the canon law kinship treatises, pictures and ideas that appeared in common law contexts, in particular ideas about the limit of kinship (at four degrees or generations) and about the underlying structures (rather than marriage rules themselves). Such borrowed ideas were not always very sophisticated, and they had very specific impacts on common law practice, such as providing a limit on kinship where one was not inherent. The canon law kinship system, particularly in relation to blood kinship, was dominant because it had a simple negative rule, was easily summarised and, in literate contexts, clearly expressed and because the system was applied to anyone wanting to marry legitimately and supported by public enforcement mechanisms such as the banns. The system was live and widespread, unlike that of the civil law which was, in England at that time, a relic studied in universities. The author of *Bracton* had attempted to summarise common law kinship borrowing civil law concepts, but this had not been successful. Later common lawyers instead incorporated canon law kinship treatises into their texts.

The system of the canon law was also intellectual and taxonomic, studied and discussed by expert lawyers in the universities. Beyond the law faculties, the theologian Kilwardby used canon law kinship as part of a scheme for ordering the social world. Kinship was, after all, one of the more important social bonds. There were layers of kinship in medieval England (and on the continent), which ranged from academic game playing, to a formal and sometimes abstracted system thought and argued about by specialist lawyers, to structures applied in courts and understood as common knowledge in everyday life.

These formal legal kinship structures were known, used and followed by many people across thirteenth- and fourteenth-century English society, particularly among the more wealthy. There is suggestive evidence that the structures did not uniformly fit with people's normal recognition of kinship.

141

At common law, the systemisation of structure that, in limited circumstances, gave preference to the direct female heir was not easily accepted even by some common lawyers (such as the author of *Britton*). At canon law, the wide application of the affinity rules and the four-degree limit on kinship do not seem to fit with the patterns of kinship recognised in society. For example, blood-kinship seems more regularly to have extended to the kinsmen linked through a common great-grandfather than to kinsmen linked through a common great-great-grandfather, and the affinity rules were accepted less easily than those on consanguinity. None the less, non-active kinship knowledge could be wide, and could be applied and utilised in both legal kinship structures. The formal legal structures did not operate in competition with any quasi-corporate or clannish kinship system. A more corporate kinship system had been a factor in Anglo-Saxon society, although, by the later Anglo-Saxon period it was likely in decline, but was not a feature of post-Conquest society where the winner-takes-all common law inheritance patterns and criminal law would have done much to undermine any remaining arena for the wide and active kin. Through the detail of legal kinship systems it is possible to see certain broad features of high and later medieval English kinship, particularly for those wealthy enough to be revealed in the records of the Church's and king's courts or those learned enough to write about the rules.

The canon law kinship system forbade marriage to kinsmen and, after 1215, defined kinsman as people related by blood within four generations of a common great-great-grandfather; relatives of a spouse up to that extent; relatives of a betrothed or sexual partner up to that extent; and spiritual kinsmen, most clearly godparents to their godchildren, or the parents of their godchildren. Such a system may seem wide, yet it applied in practice to a significant degree (although not perfectly of course, as some people may have ignored it or only obeyed as far as their limited knowledge extended). The system was made public and policable through the mechanism of the banns and nuanced by the possibility of papal dispensations. Divorce on grounds of kinship was rare, but kinship was used as a defence against marriage and incestuous sexual relationships were prosecuted. The affinity rules seem to have been less accepted and more readily used for creating false evidence of relatedness, than the rules concerning blood-kinship.

The kinship system of the common law was directed at finding the right heir. Common law inheritance involved the application of a number of rules, best encapsulated by Maitland: a living descendant excluded his own descendants; a dead descendant was represented by his own descendants; males excluded females of equal degree; among males of equal degree only the eldest inherited; females of equal degree inherited together; and the rule of representation overrode the preference for the male sex.[1] Under the

[1]  Pollock and Maitland, *History of English law*, ii. 260.

parentelic system each person's descendants were called in order, following the rules up the generations. This system was a powerful set of social as well as legal norms and was applied at the point of inheritance. It could be enforced in the courts, most fundamentally through a claim via the writ of right, but also (in the arena of kinship) in a series of actions related to the possessory assize of mort d'ancestor, including aiel, besaiel and cosinage. The common law also allowed for the enforcement of customary systems such as parage or ultimogeniture where they were accepted practice.

Certain structural features were shared; these were basic building blocks to a common conception of kinship. Both the canon and common law kinship systems were bilateral in that they recognised kinship through men and women. The canon law had an equal regard for kinship traced through both genders under its broad prohibition on marriage to kinsmen. In contrast, while the common law traced kinship through both men and women it clearly privileged the paternal line and descent through the male (a sense of lineage that was strong in noble society). Both systems shared a concern for ancestors as mediators of kinship that took effect in their present day. Both systems regarded collateral blood-kinship as less strong than direct kinship. Canon lawyers expressed discomfort about theoretical marriages in the direct line rather than between two collateral lines and common lawyers privileged the direct, 'right' line of descent.[2] Both systems encompassed several senses of kinship including blood kinship and ties through marriage, though the canon law focussed on affines more widely while the common law had a formal focus on blood-kinship and descent, and a strong demand for legitimacy, but acknowledged affinial relationships through devices such as dower and curtesy (the latter tempered by the rule that the qualifying marriages ought to have born a live child).

Other features, such as a sense of generations as steps, were widely understood, but did not always sit easily with the systematic structures of either legal kinship system. Among canon lawyers there was tension between their sense of nearness being dependent on distance of generations and the way that the possibility of marriage was measured according to the longer line (meaning that people in a closer generation were labelled with a degree that did not reflect their nearness to the common ancestor: see figure 1). Among common lawyers the sense of generations as steps was in tension with the hierarchy imposed by primogeniture, and with the underlying preference for male heirs (as expressed in problems with representation such as the *casus regis* and in the occasional discomfort with direct female heirs taking in preference over collateral males).

Experts in both legal systems were conscious that their rules did not encompass all senses of kinship. Common lawyers were explicitly conscious of the canon and civil law kinship systems, and of local customary systems

---

[2] 'lineam rectam': *Bracton*, ii. 197.

such as gavelkind. Canon lawyers were less clearly aware of other practical, operating kinship systems. Although they acknowledged legal kinship for purposes of succession, their attention in this was upon the civil law of the universities. Canon lawyers were also conscious of different types of kinship within their own system. They acknowledged the difference between divine (biblical) kinship, human legal kinship and natural kinship. The idea of underlying natural kinship was shared by common lawyers, as shown by comments that marked how the bastard was legally a stranger to his family.

An important feature that was not shared was the canon laws' limit on kinship (for the purposes of marriage; they recognised that kinship could extend more widely for inheritance). Common law kinship was potentially infinite, but included some *ad hoc* limits in particular circumstances (most commonly, for example, in limiting the heirs who could use an action, such as mort d'ancestor). Thus the canon law's four-degree limit was the feature that appeared most strongly borrowed in secular, common law contexts, even though it did not fit with the three-generational pattern that appears to have been common in society.

Finally, some prominent elements of kinship were not a factor in the canon law system, such as the importance of the nuclear and close family, a pattern reflected by the popularity of mort d'ancestor at common law which allowed claims based on the seisin of a restricted range of close relatives (father, mother, uncle, aunt, brother, sister). Other relationships were also marked through common law actions, such as aiel (grandparents) and besaiel (great-grandparents). The role of ancestors as vehicles for wealth and inheritance was important.

Kinship systems beyond the strictures of legal structures could vary from person to person, depending on locality and context. The struggle over the definition of who was a cousin (and thus whose land could be claimed with the action of cosinage) suggests this, although it cannot fully reflect the variety of senses of kin that would have existed. There were several senses of the shape of the kindred: one that included all blood-relatives (essentially similar to that of the canon law); one that contrasted descendants with ancestors (for example descendants were 'cousins' to named ancestors, who were not, in technical legal terms, 'cousins' back); finally, a strictly common law and case specific sense that marked collaterals as different from direct kin.

Alan MacFarlane was mistaken when he said that the English had in the twentieth century 'roughly the same family system as they had in about 1250'.[3] In medieval England structured, formal, legal kinship was recognised and applied; the canon law after 1215 defined blood kinsmen as people within four generations of a common great-great-grandparent, and included kinsmen of a spouse or sexual partner up to that extent, as well as spiritual

---

[3]  MacFarlane, *Origins*, 158.

kinsmen (certain relationships mediated via baptism); the common law sorted kinsmen into an infinite hierarchy. Yet the pattern of interaction, with an everyday focus on the nuclear family and a three-generation normal family memory, is not unfamiliar. The difference is that these patterns were overlaid and interwoven with other, wider, more hierarchical kinship structures that mattered in practice at vital milestones such as at marriage, divorce or inheritance.

# APPENDICES

These texts are not claimed as editions; rather they are intended to be critical transcriptions, based on manuscripts that are good enough to allow an adequate rendering.

Spelling has, by and large, been regularised, although certain medieval traits are retained (such as -e for -ae); -ci- has been replaced by -ti-; occasionally, where called for, an -i- has been replaced by -e-. Numbers have been regularised. Certain common spelling variants or consistent, if peculiar, abbreviations have not been recorded in the footnotes, such as set for sed, or seu for sive, michi for mihi. Words in square brackets [ ] in the main text have been added for better sense.

## Manuscripts and sigla

| | |
|---|---|
| BL, MS Additional 41258 | A |
| BL, MS Harley 653 | H |
| BL, MS Royal 6 E VI | RA |
| BL, MS Royal 10 D VII | RB |
| Bodl. Lib., MS Rawlinson C 160 | R |
| Winchester Cathedral Library, MS 18 | W1 |
| Worcester Cathedral Library, MS F 87 | W |

# APPENDIX 1

# *Quia Tractare Intendimus*

This is the most popular of the thirteenth-century short canon law kinship treatises. It was written by Raymón de Penyafort, probably about 1235. The base manuscript used here is a typical set of fourteenth-century decretals, BL, MS Royal 10 D VII, fos 257v–258v (*RB*). For the section of the treatise dealing with consanguinity this is compared against BL, MS Royal 6 E VI, fos 382v–384r (*RA*), an extract from a mid fourteenth-century *Omne Bonum* collection. For the section dealing with affinity it is compared to Winchester Cathedral Library, MS 18, fos 193v–194v (*W1*), a fourteenth-century common law statute book. This last has not been used throughout because it has several omissions, although it is reasonably consistent with the base.

It should be acknowledged that the combination of these manuscripts do not necessarily offer an edition of the original; however, they do provide an adequate view of the treatise as it circulated in the fourteenth century.

There is reportedly an edition of *Quia tractare intendimus*. However, it was not possible to access it,[a] and it has been heavily criticised.[b]


1   Quia tractare intendimus de consanguinitate et eius gradibus et de arboris consanguinitatis expositione, ad eius evidentiam pleniorem videndum est primo et prenotandum quid sit [1]consanguinitas, unde dicatur, quid sit linea consanguinitatis et [2]quot sunt linee, quid sit gradus et qualiter [3]computetur usque ad quem gradum prohibeatur matrimonium.

---

[a]   X. Ochoa and A. Díez, *Summula de consanguinitate et affinitate* (Universa Bibliotheeca Iuris 1-C, 1978).   [b] The edition is 'a mutilation': S. Kuttner, 'On the method of editing medieval authors', *The Jurist* xxxvii (1977), 385–6 at p. 385. Or 'something quite different from accurate and reliable editions by modern standards': J. A. Brundage, 'Book review of 'Summa de paenitentia; Summa de matrimonio by Raymond of Peñafort: edited by Xavier Ochoa and Aloisius Diez', *The Jurist* xlix (1979), 514–17 at p. 514. For further criticism see García y García, 'La canonística Ibérica', 44.

[1]   consanguinitas] consanguinitas et *RA*
[2]   quot] quo *RA*
[3]   computetur] computetur et *RA*

**2**  Consanguinitas vero est vinculum personarum ab eodem stipite [4]descendentium carnali propagatione [5]contractura. Stipitem autem dico illam personam [6]a qua aliqui duxerunt originem sicut Adam fuit stipes Caym et Abel et filiorum qui ab eis processerunt. Dicitur autem consanguinitas a communi sanguine quasi communem sanguinem habentes vel de uno sanguine procedentes.

**3**  Linea est ordinata collectio personarum consanguinitate coniunctarum ab eodem stipite descendentium, diversos gradus continens et eos ab unitate [7]stipitis secundum numeros distinguens. Linearum tres sunt species: ascendentes, [8]descendentes, transversales, sicut triplex est diversitas consanguineorum vel [9]propinquiorum. Linea ascendentium est que continet illos a quibus originem traximus, sicut pater mater, avus avia et deinceps. Descendentium est illa que continet illos qui duxerunt originem a nobis sicut filius filia, nepos neptis [10]et deinceps. Transversalium sive a latere venientium est illa que continet illos qui non a nobis duxerunt originem nec nos ab ipsis ut est frater et soror et eorum progenies. xxxv.[11]q.v. *primo gradu.*[c]

**4**  Et nota quod due linee descendentes unam faciunt transveralem ut apparet in hoc exemplo: filii duorum fratrum, vel etiam duo fratres, attinent sibi in linea transversali, et quilibet eorum recta linea descendit ab avo eorum communi, qui est communis stipes a quo traxerunt originem.

**5**  Gradus est quedam habitudo sive distantia personarum facta adinvicem collatione ad communem parentem qua cognoscitur quota generationis distantia due persone inter se differant. Qualiter gradus computentur infra dicetur.

**6**  [12]Prohibetur matrimonium hodie usque ad quartum gradum: Extra de consanguinitate et [13]affinitate *non debet.*[d]

---

[c]  C.35 q.5 c.6 [reference to *Decretum Gratiani*, Causa 35, quaestio 5, canon 6].   [d] X 4.14.8 [reference to *Decretales Gregory IX*, Liber 4, titulus 14, capitulum 8].

4   descendentium] descendentium ~~stipite~~ RB
5   contractura] contractrum *RA*
6   a qua] *in the margin.* RB
7   stipitis] stipite *RA*
8   descendentes] descendentes et *RA*
9   propinquiorum] propinquorum *RA*
10  et deinceps] *omitted* [hereinafter *om.*] RA
11  q.] q.capitulo *RA*
12  Prohibetur] Prohibetur autem *RA*
13  affinitate] affinitate capitulo *RA*

**7** Hiis premissis ad lectionem arboris [14]descendendum est sic hoc modo legas arborem, primo constituas eam, secundo legas regulas tam canonicas quam legales et earum artificio [15]invenias gradus tam canonicos quam legales in qualibet linea, tertio [16]querere de quibusdam dubitabilibus. Ut sic ternario numero lectio nostra sit completa.

**8** Prius tamen quam ad [17]hoc tria descendas, notabis quare arbor fuit inventa, rationem habes Instituta, de gradibus cognationis .ss. [18]*agnationis*,[e] alias incipit .ss. *sed cum magis* [19]*oculata*,[f] et Oracius: [20]'Segnius irritant animum demissa per aurem. Quam que sunt oculis subiecta fidelibus.'[g]

**9** Est autem [21]authentica pictura [22]arboris .xxxv.q.v. *primo gradu*,[h] [23]et capitulo *ad sedem* circa [24]finem.[i]

**10** Item in medio arboris debet poni quedam cellula que dicitur Truncus .xxxv.q.v. *series*.[j] Hec cellula dicitur esse vacua. Nam cum tam ascendentes quam descendentes [25]quam transversales exceptis hiis qui determinantur per [26]genitiuum respectu eius nomina sortiuntur, ut patet in figura arboris, ipse truncus [27]respectus diversorum diversa debet habere nomina, et sic uno nomine non poterit designari, nec omnia nomina que respectu diversorum sortitur, poterant in una cellula comprehendi.

**11** Item truncus non potest contrahere cum aliquo qui in arbore ponitur. Illi tamen qui sunt ex una parte [28]possunt contrahere cum illis qui sunt ex altera, exceptis hiis qui ponuntur in tribus lineis inferioribus Sed inter se qui

---

[e] *Institutes* 3.6.8.  [f] *Institutes* 3.6.9.  [g] 'Segnius irritant animos demissa per aurem quam que sunt oculis subiecta fidelibus': Horace, 'Ars poetica', *Satires, epistles and ars poetica*, 180–1.  [h] C.35 q.5 c.6.  [i] C.35 q.5 c.2 ss 7.  [j] C.35 q.5 c.1.

[14] descendendum est] est descendendum *RA*
[15] invenias] invenies *RA*
[16] querere] quere *RA*
[17] hoc] hec *RA*
[18] agnationis] agnitionis *RA*
[19] oculata] occulta *RA*
[20] Segnius] Segniuiie(?) *RA*
[21] authentica] *om. RA*
[22] arboris] arboris ut notatur *RA*
[23] et . . . finem] *om. RA*
[24] finem] finem, forme calumpnia videlicet non et si non ipse *RB* (this addition may be a reference, possibly to C.2 q.3.c.2, though this is not an entirely good fit).
[25] quam] quam et *RA*
[26] genitiuum] genitum *RB*
[27] respectus] respectu *RA*
[28] possunt] possint *RA*

sunt ex una parte non possunt contrahere excepto abnepote trunci et sorore [29]abneptis trunci, qui possunt contrahere cum fratre et sorore trunci et cum sua posteritate cum sint eis in quinto gradu.

**12** Item nota quod non ponitur in arbore tota [30]consanguinitas trunci. Nam truncus habet quatuor avos, avum et aviam paternos, [31]avum et aviam maternos, et octo proavos, et sedecim abavos et sic semper duplicantur ascendendo.

**13** Item licet hodie quatuor gradus sint distincti tantum. Dico tamen quod adhuc consanguinitas extenditur ultra hos [32]gradus quia civilis racio non potest naturalia iura tollere .ff. de capite *minutis eas*,[k] et institutio *de legi[tima] agnatii* ss. ultra [*recte. de successione cognatorum*],[l] non obstat. xxxv. [33]q.v. *ad sedem*,[m] quod enim dicitur circa finem [34]ibi quod ultra hos gradus [35]vero est consanguinitas intellige quantum ad impedimentum matromonii [36]tantum.

**14** Si aliquis cognoscit consanguineam suam in v. gradu non committit incestum quia potius [37]a constitutione ecclesie. Quam a iure nature dicitur quis committere incestum unde ipsa consanguinitas ex sui natura, non est impedimentum matrimonii sed sola constitutio impedit .xxxv. [38]q.i. *cum igitur*.[n]

**15** Item licet [39]artati sint gradus quantam ad matrimonium non tamen quantum ad successionem quia usque ad .x. gradum legalem fit successio: .xxxv. [40]q.v. *ad sedem*,[o] cum enim post istos gradus, usque ad .x. gradum succedatur ergo est ibi consanguinitas: .xxxv.q.iii.c.i.[p]

**16** Item nota quod avus et avia et alii superiores non sunt vir et uxor sicut pater et mater quia tunc pater et mater essent fratres nisi dicas avum et aviam bigamos fuisse. Puta avus scilicet paternus genuit patrem ex alia et avia scilicet materna matrem ex alio et sic de aliis ascendentibus.

---

[k]  *Digest* 4.5.8.  [l] *Insitutes* 3.5.5.  [m] C.35 q.5 c.2.  [n] C.35 q.1 c.1.  [o] C.35 q.5 c.2.  [p] C.35 q.2 & 3. c.1.

---

[29]  abneptis] abnepotis *RA*
[30]  consanguinitas] consanguiniitas *RB*
[31]  avum] avium *RA*
[32]  gradus] gradus sint *RA*
[33]  q.] q.capitulo *RA*
[34]  ibi] ibi cura *RA*
[35]  vero] *om. RA*
[36]  tantum] tamen *RB*
[37]  a] *om. RA*
[38]  q.] q.capitulo *RA*
[39]  artati] arctati *RB*
[40]  q.] q.capitulo *RA*

**17** Arborem consanguinitatis hoc modo [41]describas: protende a vertice prothei sursum lineam ascendentem continentem quatuor cellulas in quorum prima ponitur pater et mater, in secunda [42]avus [43]avia, in tertia proavus proavia, in quarta abavus [44]abavia.

**18** Similiter [45]describe descendentem lineam a protheo continentem quatuor cellulas in quarum prima ponitur filius filia, in secunda nepos neptis, in tertia pronepos proneptis, in quarta abnepos abneptis.

**19** Restat videre de lineis transversalibus quarum due oriuntur ex protheo, et a quolibet suo [46]superiori oritur una tam ex patre quam ex matre. Ab inferiori nulla oritur quia omnes qui ab inferioribus descendunt, recta linea descendunt a protheo. Pone ergo tam iuxta protheum quam iuxta quemlibet superiorem fratrem et sororem, designans eos illis nominibus relativis quibus referuntur ad protheum. Deinde singulis eorum designa filios et nepotes usque ad quartum gradum respectu prothei et sic includes consanguinitatem prothei usque ad quartum gradum.

**20** Et quidam consanginitatis sufficeret medietas arboris ad doctrinam tradendam, ut staret ad modum vexilli, sed alia medietas fuit posita ad decorem vel [47]ut scirentur nomina consanguinitatis ex parte masculini quam feminini sexus.

**21** Nunc assignemus computationem graduum. Primo canonicam et legalem in linea ascendenti et descendenti quia eadem est computatio, secundo canonicam in linea transversali, tertio legalem.

**22** Gradus est [48]quedam habitudo sive distantia personarum adinvicem facta collatione ad communem parentem.

**23** In linea ascendenti et descendenti quelibet persona adiecta superiori vel inferiori gradum adicit .xxxv. [49]q.v. *ad sedem*.q

---

q   C.35 q.5 c.2.

[41]   describas] prescribas *RA*
[42]   avus] avis *RB* avus et *RA*
[43]   avia] aviam *RB*
[44]   abavia] abvia *RA*
[45]   describe] discribe *RA*
[46]   superiori] superori *RA*
[47]   ut] non *RA*
[48]   quedam] quidam *RA*
[49]   q.] q.capitulo *RA*

**24** Sic protheus non facit gradum; sed est truncus et est pater in linea descendenti, in ascendenti filius.

**25** A protheo ergo distat filius primo gradu, nepos in secundo, [50]et sic usque [51]ad adnepotem qui distat in quarto. Similiter in superiori linea; pater distat primo gradu a protheo, avus secundo et sic usque ad abavum qui distat quarto.

**26** Et nota quod gradus legales designantur nigris [52]punctis inferiori parte cuiuslibet cellule canonici [53]vero rubeis et in superiori parte ad designandam excellenciam canonice scientiae ad legalem.

**27** Item persone que distant equaliter a communi parente dicuntur esse in gradu et facere gradum que inequaliter dicuntur distare gradu ut .xxxv. [54]q.v. porro, parentele.[r]

**28** Canonicam computationem in linea transversali facias per istam regulam: quoto gradu distat quis ab aliquo superiori, eodem [55]distari a quolibet descendenti ab eo per aliam lineam, usque ad lineam equalitatis. Postea pro numero personarum gradus [56]opponitur, hanc regulam habes: Extra de consanguinitate et affinitate *quod dilectio.*[s]

**29** Incipiamus ergo secundum predictam regulam a superiori cellula: sic abavus distat a trunco [57]quarto gradu. Ergo propatruus qui descendit ab [58][ab] avo per aliam lineam, similiter [59]avi, et propatrui et filius similiter avus, et sic de aliis. Quod totum sic probo: propatruus et proavus sunt duo fratres, ergo sunt in primo gradu .xxxv.q.v. *ad sedem,*[t] ergo avus filius proavi distat secundo a propatruo, pater tertio, truncus quarto. Similiter filius propatrui distat quarto a trunco. Probatio: filius propatrui et avus sunt duo nepotes, ergo in secundo gradu quia sunt filii duorum fratrum, qui sunt in primo gradu ergo pater distat a filio [60]propatrui tertio gradu., truncus quarto. Similiter nepos [61]propatrui distat quarto a trunco. Probatio: nepos propatrui et pater

---

[r]   C.35 q.5 c.3 & 4.   [s]  X 4.14.3.   [t]  C.35 q.5 c.2.

[50]  et sic usque] *om. RB*
[51]  ad adnepotem qui distat] *repeated RB*
[52]  punctis] punctis in *RA*
[53]  vero] non *RA*
[54]  q.] q.capitulo *RA*
[55]  distari] distat *RA*
[56]  opponitur] apponitur *RA*
[57]  quarto] quo(?) .iiii. *RB*
[58]  abavo] avuo *RA*, avo *RB*
[59]  avi] qui *RB*
[60]  propatrui] propatruum *RB*
[61]  propatrui] propatruum *RB*

sunt pronepotes, quia sunt tertio gradu, [62]quia filii duorum nepotum qui sunt in secundo gradu. Ergo truncus distat quarto, similiter pronepos propatrui est in quarto gradu cum trunco, et in linea equalitatis que continet omnes personas equaliter cum descendentes. Probatio: sunt duo abnepotes, ergo sunt in quarto, quia sunt filii duorum pronepotum qui sunt in quarto.

**30** Item ascende ad proavum, ipse distat a trunco tertio gradu, ergo patruus magnus qui descendit ab eo per aliam lineam similiter tertio distat, proprior sobrinus tertio, filius eius secum est in tertio in linea equali. Deinde pro numero personarum [63]adicitur gradus. In probatione ista procede ut prius, quia patruus magnus et avus sunt duo fratres, ergo in primo gradu, ergo pater distat secundo, truncus tertio a patruo magno, et ita de aliis. Hec probatio colligitur: .xxxv.q.v. *ad sedem.*[u]

**31** Sequitur de legali computatione in linea transversali, que sit iuxta hanc regulam: quot persone connumerantur hinc inde a communi parente descendentes, praeter ipsum stipitem, toto gradu distant ultime persone de [64]quarum distantia queritur.

**32** Verbi gratia: si una persona de qua queritur distat a communi parente per quartum et altera per duos. Omnes ille persone cum communi parente sunt septimo. Ergo remoto communi parente sexto [65]remanent persone, toto ergo gradu distant inter se [66]scilicet sexto.

**33** Et sic patet quod legales quandoque duplicant gradus [67]canonicos, quandoque non duplicant [68]nisi linea equalitatis sed supra, et infra non. Hic [69]est recolligende [70]de regule prius tradite ut [71]facilius possit [72]de regule haberi doctrina.

**34** Prima regula est talis: linea est ordinata collectio personarum consanguinitate coniunctarum diversos gradus continens, et eos ab unitate distinguens communiter secundum leges et canones in linea ascendenti et discendenti,

---

[u]   C.35 q.5 c.2.

[62]  quia] quia sunt *RA*
[63]  adicitur] adicit *RA*
[64]  quarum] quartum *RB*
[65]  remanent] remanet *RB*
[66]  scilicet] sed *RA*
[67]  canonicos] canonicos gradus *RA*
[68]  nisi linea equalitatis ] *om. RA*
[69]  est] sunt *RA*
[70]  de] *om. RA*
[71]  facilius] facilior *RA*
[72]  de regule] *om. RA*

quelibet persona adiuncta superiori et inferiori gradum adicit: .xxxv.q.v. *ad sedem.*[v]

**35** Gradus est quedam habitudo sive distantia personarum facta adinvicem collatione ad communem parentem qua cognoscitur quota generationis distantia [73]due persone inter se differant.

**36** Item quoto gradu distat quis ad aliquo superiori toto distat a quolibet descendenti ab eo per aliam lineam, usque ad lineam [74]equalitatis postea pro numero personarum, gradus apponitur: Extra de consanguinitate et [75]affini-tate *quod dilectio.*[w]

**37** Item quot persone [76]connumerantur hinc inde et in linea ascendenti et collateralia a communi parente descendentes, praeter ipsum stipitem, [77]toto gradu distant ultime persone de quarum distantia queritur et ita exponitur secundum leges. Secundum canones expone hinc id est linea ascendenti.

**38** Si vis constituere arborem in manu; potes hoc modo: singulos digitos habes distinctos per quartum articulos; cum ergo quoto gradu vis invenire aliqui distent numera articulos duorum [78]collateralium, medium superiorem partem medii digiti habeas pro stipite sive [79]communi parente et procede secundum has regulas.

**39** Si vis scire quoto gradu una persona distat ab alia, in linea ascendenti vel descendenti, numera omnes personas et una dempta, quot persone remanent toto gradu distant.

**40** Si vis scire quoto gradu una persona distat ab alia in linea transversali secundum canones, vide si equaliter descendunt et quot persone sunt ab una ad communem [80]stipitem et toto gradu distant inter se. Si inequaliter, quoto gradu distat remotior persona a [81]communi parente, toto distant inter se et hoc dicitur: Extra de consanguinitate et affinitate in decreto nona, [82]decreto *vir qui a stipite.*[x]

---

[v]  C.35 q.5 c.2.  [w] X 4.14.3.  [x] X 4.14.9.

[73]  due] que *RA*
[74]  equalitatis] equalitatis et *RA*
[75]  affinitate] affinitate capitulo *RA*
[76]  connumerantur] conumerantur *RA*
[77]  toto] tota *RB*
[78]  collateralium] collateralium digitorum *RA*
[79]  communi] comuni *RA*
[80]  stipitem] stipite *RB*
[81]  communi] comuni *RA*
[82]  decreto] *om. RA*

**41** Sequitur videre de quibusdam dubitabilibus. Et nota quod non valet hec [83]argumentato: P[etrus] et Martinus [84]et consanguinei. P[etrus] potest accipere in uxorem filiam Martini. Ergo et Martinus filiam P[etri].

**42** Nam propatruus et truncus sunt consanguinei. Propatruus potest ducere filiam trunci, quia est sibi in v. gradu. Non tamen truncus potest ducere [85]filiam [86]propatrui, quia est sibi in quarto. Sed hoc [87]ideo est quia filius trunci adicit gradum respectu propatrui cum sit sub linea equalitatis, sed filia propatrui non adicit gradum respectu trunci cum sit supra lineam equalitatis.

**43** Item nota quod licet propatruus et eiusdem pronepos in eodem gradu attineant trunco, tamen [88]maior consanguinitas est inter truncum et [89]propatruum quam inter truncum et [90]pronepotem propatrui: Extra de consanguinitate et [91]affinitate, *quod dilectio.*[y]

**44** Item queritur quare protheus ab avo distet quarto gradu, et non distet a propatruo quinto, tamen persona addita persone per carnis propagationem adiciat gradum.

**45** Ad hoc dicunt quidam quod propter predictam racionem debent distare quinto, sed propter [92]aliam debent [93]distare tertio, scilicet [94]quia est in eodem gradu tamen proavo qui distat tertio. Et propter istarum [95]repugnantiam racionum electa fuit media via, ubi distat quarto.

**46** Item cum fit computatio ab inferiori ad superiorem, [96]descendente a latere, non ascenditur usque ad superiorem illius de cuius queritur attinentia, sed usque ad collateralem. Ideo cum proavus sit in tertio, eius collaterales erunt trunco in tertio. Item cum proavus et propatruus sint in eodem [97]gradu,

---

[y]  X 4.14.3.

[83]  argumentato] argumenta *RA*
[84]  et] ~~filiam~~ et *RB* etiam *RA*
[85]  filiam] filiam Marti *RA*
[86]  propatrui] patrui *RB*
[87]  ideo] ido *RB*
[88]  maior] maigor *RB*
[89]  propatrum ... et] *om. RB*
[90]  pronepotem] pronepotem et *RA*
[91]  affinitate] affinitate capitulo *RA*
[92]  aliam] aliam racionem *RA*
[93]  distare] distat *RA*
[94]  quia ... proavo] *om.RB*
[95]  repugnantiam] repungnantiam *RA*
[96]  descendente] descendentem *RB*
[97]  gradu] gradum *RB*

videtur quod quoto gradu distat [98]proavus a trunco eodem debet distare, propatruus et econverso.

**47** Ad [99]hoc dicas: quod illi dicuntur esse in eodem gradu respectu communis parentis scilicet [100]abavia quo descendunt equaliter, non respectu prothei cuius [101]respectus uno gradu plus distinguitur propatruus quam proavus.

**48** Item pone quod duo volunt contrahere: quorum alter distat a communi parente tertio vel quarto gradu, [102]alius quinto: poteruntne contrahere? Videtur quod non, argumentum Extra de consanguinitate et [103]affinitate *quod dilectio*.[z] Sed contrarium, verum est, cum hodie de iure communi possint contrahere in quinto gradu et isti distent quinto gradu. Illa vero decreta loquitur in dispensatione in qua strictius procedendum est.

**49** Item numquid committitur incestus cum sanguinea in v gradu? Non, quia constitutione videtur committi incestus: .xxxv.[104] *q.i. cum igitur.*[aa] Constitutione autem ecclesiae non committebatur incestus olim ultra septimo gradum, argumentum .xxxv.q.v.c°. *ad sedem.*[bb] Verbi illa quoque, ergo eadem racione, non committitur hodie ultra quartum gradum. Quasdam alias omitto quia non sunt dubie vel quia inutiles: .ff. *de in integrum restitutionibus* l.i.,[cc] vi.q.[105]i. sed omni.[dd]

**50** Affinitas est proximitas personarum ex carnali [106]commixtione proveniens omni carens parentela. Ex carnali [107]commixtione [108]ideo dico quod contrahitur tam [109]per legitimum quam fornicarium [110]coitum: [111].xxxv.q.iii. *nec eam,*[ee] Extra de eo qui [112]cognovit consanguineam [113]*discretionem,*[ff] Extra eodem capituli *tue fraternitatis.*[gg]

---

[z] X 4.14.3.   [aa] C.35 q.1 c.1.   [bb] C.35 q.5 c.2.   [cc] *Digest* 4.1, possibly 4.1.1 (?).   [dd] This may refer to C.6 q.1.c.7, but the subject matter is not immediately relevant.   [ee] C.35 q.3 c.10.   [ff] X 4.12.6.   [gg] X 4.12.10.

[98]   proavus] proavis *RB*
[99]   hoc] hos *RA*
[100]   abavia] abvia *RA*
[101]   respectus] respectu *RA*
[102]   alius] illius *RA*
[103]   affinitate] affinitate capitulo *RA*
[104]   q.] q.capitulo *RA*
[105]   i.] i.capitulo *RA*
[106]   commixtione] coniunctione *W1*
[107]   commixtione] coniunctione *W1*
[108]   ideo dico] dico ideo *W1*
[109]   per] *om. W1*
[110]   coitum] *om. W1*
[111]   q.] q.v. *W1*
[112]   cognovit] congno(?) *W1*
[113]   discretionem] distinctionem *RB*

**51** Circa arborem affinitatis hunc modum vel ordinem servabimus: primo conponemus eam, secundo ostendemus [114]qualiter genus affinitatis inveniatur, tertio qualiter [115]computentur gradus affinitatis.

**52** In medio arboris ponitur quedam linea continens quatuor gradus, sine nominibus personarum. Et ponitur ideo in medio ut ostendat gradus affinitatis, in utroque [116]latere arboris, [117]computandos.

**53** Item in utroque latere istius linee ponitur una linea consanguinitatis continens similiter quatuor cellulas, quod [118]fit duplici de causa: prima ut ostendatur [119]quia omnis affinitas habet ortum a consanguinitate, secunda ut ostendatur gradus affinitatis esse computandos ex parte consanguinitatis tantum et non ex parte [120]appositionis.

**54** Item quia tam per matres quam per feminas [121]contrahitur affinitas. Et ideo ex una parte describitur linea continens fratrem cum sua successione usque ad pronepotem, ex alia parte linea continens sororem cum sua successione usque ad quartum gradum. Iuxta lineam fratris ponitur alia linea continens [122]similiter quatuor cellulas in quarum prima [123]ponitur fratris uxor, in secunda uxor filii fratris, in tertia uxor nepotis fratris, in quarta uxor pronepotis fratris.

**55** Et sic appellatur uxor que olim appellabatur relicta ad [124]designandum quod per istarum [125]copulam [126]debeatur trahi secundum genus affinitatis.

**56** Item ex alio latere iuxta lineam sororis, [127]describere aliam lineam cum quatuor cellulis in quarum prima ponitur vir sororis, in secunda vir filie sororis, in tertia vir neptis sororis, in quarta vir proneptis sororis.

**57** Et sic habes v lineas [128]quarum quelibet continet quatuor cellulas ad ostendendam quod prohibitio non extenditur ultra quartum gradum consanguinitatis vel affinitatis.

---

[114] qualiter] equaliter *RB*
[115] computentur] computetur *W1*
[116] latere] latere istius *W1*
[117] computandos] computando *W1*
[118] fit] sit *W1*
[119] quia] quod *W1*
[120] appositionis] appositionis xxxv.q.v. c. *porro* [C.35 q.5 c.3] *W1*
[121] contrahitur] ochitur *RB*
[122] similiter] *om. W1*
[123] ponitur] peius *RB*
[124] designandum] resignandum *RB*
[125] copulam] copula *W1*
[126] debeatur] deberat *W1*
[127] describere] describe *W1*
[128] quarum] quare *W1*

**58** Item ex utraque parte ponitur una auricula tantum ad decorem.

**59** Genus affinitatis invenitur iuxta hanc [129]regulam: persona addita persone per carnis [130]commixtionem [131]facit genus affinitatis, et [132]non gradum.

**60** Verbi gratia, frater ducit uxorem [133]cui commiscetur carnaliter. Per [134]hanc carnalem [135]copulam oritur primum genus affinitatis inter uxorem fratris et sororem fratris que est ex alio latere. Item da [136]uxorem istis tribus qui descendunt ex fratre quibus carnaliter coniungantur. Per istas copulas oritur [137]primum genus affinitatis inter eas et sororem fratris.

**61** Et ideo quidam habent quandam ymaginem [138]frater [139]super cellulam sororis tenentem in manu quandam lineam [140]protensam usque ad [141]uxorem fratris que dicat: 'soror venite ad me omnes [142]qui estis in illa linea quia estis michi affines in primo [143]genere'. [144]Eodem modo ex alia parte arboris soror nubit viro, [145]coniugitur carnaliter. Per hanc carnis copulam oritur primum genus affinitatis inter virum sororis et fratrem sororis et ita [146]ut prius.

**62** Unde habent quidam aliam [147]ymaginem super [148]cellulam fratris tenentem in manu quandam lineam protensam ad lineam viri sororis qui dicat [149]'frater venite etcetera' ut supra.

**63** Ad huc habetis duas lineas reflexas quarum una oritur in cellula uxoris fratris et [150]terminantur in cellula sororis et est [151]scriptum in utraque 'primum

---

129  regulam] rubricam *W1*
130  commixtionem] coniunctionem *W1*
131  facit] facit vel(?) copulam *W1*
132  non] nondum *W1*
133  cui] *om. W1*
134  hanc] *om. W1*
135  copulam] copulam hunc *W1*
136  uxorem] uxores *W1*
137  primum] primu *RB*
138  frater] mulieris *W1*
139  super] *om. RB*
140  protensam] pertensam *RB*
141  uxorem] sororem *W1*
142  qui] que *W1*
143  genere] genere scilicet affinitatis *W1*
144  Eodem] Eadem *W1*
145  coniugitur] coniugitur alias commiscetur *W1*
146  ut] non *W1*
147  ymaginem] ymaginem hominis *W1*
148  cellulam fratris] fratris cellulam *W1*
149  frater] fratres *W1*
150  terminantur] terminatur *W1*
151  scriptum] scriptus *RB*

genus affinitatis', [152]inter viri, alia oritur in cellula viri sororis et [153]terminatur in [154]cellulam fratris.

**64** Secundo generi et tertio inveniendo [155]nec insisto quia hodie sublata sunt [156]verum. Si quas alias [157]lineas vel cellulas habes [158]supervacue nisi ad decorem.

**65** Gradus [159]invenies per hanc regulam: persona addita persone per carnis propagationem mutat [160]gradum et non genus.

**66** Verbi gratia: frater ducit uxorem. Illa est affinis [161]sorori fratris in primo [162]genere et in eodem gradu in quo frater consanguineus, [163]scilicet non est mutatus gradus. Adde sorori personam per carnis propagationem, scilicet filiam, ista mutat gradum ergo attinebit uxori fratris in secundo gradu genere non mutato, quia in primo est [164]cum illud non [165]mutetur per carnis propagationem. Adde aliam personam per carnis propagationem, scilicet [166]neptem. [167]Illa mutat gradum et non genus, ergo [168]erit in tertio gradu, genere non [169]mutato. Adde aliam, scilicet proneptam. [170]Similiter illa mutat gradum et non genus, ergo erit uxori fratris in quarto gradu et primo genere affinitatis.

**67** Eodem modo computabis [171]gradus ex alio latere, quia vir sororis est [172]affinis fratri et sue successioni in primo genere et in diversis gradibus [173]ut supra.

---

[152]  inter viri] *om. W1*
[153]  terminatur] terminantur *RB*
[154]  cellulam] cellula *W1*
[155]  nec] non *W1*
[156]  verum] *om. W1*
[157]  lineas] habeas *RB*
[158]  supervacue] supervacue sunt *W1*
[159]  invenies] inveniens *W1*
[160]  gradum] *om. W1*
[161]  sorori] sororis *W1*
[162]  genere] genere affinitatis *W1*
[163]  scilicet] scilicet in primo quia tum non fuit hic carnis propagatio *W1*
[164]  cum] tum *W1*
[165]  mutetur] muture *RB*
[166]  neptem] nepotem *W1*
[167]  Illa] Illa similiter *W1*
[168]  erit] erit uxori fratris *W1*
[169]  mutato] mutato quia in primo *W1*
[170]  Similiter] Sibi *W1*
[171]  gradus] gradum *W1*
[172]  affinis] affinus *W1*
[173]  ut supra] *om. W1*

**68** Et [174]nota quod hac regula, scilicet persona addita persone etcetera sicut diximus in consanguinitate, non habet locum in superioribus respectu inferiorum sed econtra sicut in linea transversali. Unde uxor pronepotis fratris distat a fratre tertio gradu quia toto distat vir eius, a filio fratris secundo, quia toto etcetera, a nepote primo a sorore fratris distat quarto, a filia sororis quarto, a nepte sororis quarto, a pronepote non [175]distat sed est cum ea in quarto gradu et in linea [176]equalitatis.

**69** [177]Habes duas regulas de inventionis generis affinitatis et gradum unde versus: mutat nupta genus sed generata [178]gradum.

**70** In summa breviter, [179]notabis fructum arboris: omnes [180]consanguinei uxoris sunt [181]affines viro in primo genere affinitatis et in eodem gradu in [182]quo [183]consanguinei uxoris, et, econverso, [184]omnes [185]consanguinei viri sunt affines [186]uxori in primo genere affinitatis et in eodem gradu in quo sunt consanguinei.

**71** Viro consanguinei vero viri et consanguinei uxoris, inter se non sunt [187]affines.

**72** Item omnes mariti [188]consanguineorum mearum sunt michi affines in primo genere affinitatis et in eodem gradu in quo uxores eorum sunt michi consanguinee. Item per omnia [189]intelligens de uxoribus consanguineorum meorum. Hec omnia probantur: .xxxv.q.iii. *equaliter*,[hh] Extra de consanguinitate et affinitate *quod super hiis*,[ii] et .xxxv.q.v. *porro*.[ji]

---

[hh] C.35 q.2 & 3 c.13.   [ii] X 4.14.5.   [ji] C.35 q.5 c.3.

[174] nota] non *RB*
[175] distat] *om. W1*
[176] equalitatis] equalitatis et sic *W1*
[177] Habes] *repeated RB*
[178] gradum] gradus *W1*
[179] notabis] nobis *W1*
[180] consanguinei] consanguines *W1*
[181] affines] affinies *W1*
[182] quo] quo sunt *W1*
[183] consanguinei] consanguines *W1*
[184] omnes] *om. W1*
[185] consanguinei] consanguines *W1*
[186] uxori] uxori viri *W1*
[187] affines] affines, Extra de consanguinitate et affinnitate *super hiis* [X 4.14.5] *W1*
[188] consanguineorum] consanguinearum *W1*
[189] intelligens] omnia *W1*

**73** [190]Autem patet per hac quod uxores duorum [191]fratrum vel aliorum consanguineorum non sunt affines, quia olim attinebant sibi in secundo genere affinitatis quod hodie est [192]sublatum. Quero ergo utrum [193]mortuis [194]maritis earum [195]alius possit ambas [196]ducere in uxores [197]successive? Potest dici quod [198]non, quia impediat affinitas cum nulla sit sed propter publice honestatis [199]iustitiarum que [200]sibi [201]erat olim: .xxxv.q.iii. *porro*.[kk] Nec est revocata per [202]constitutionem nisi illa publice honestatis iustitia que oritur ex secundis nuptis. Ergo [203]remanet quod [204]enim non mutatur quare stare prohibetur: [205].c. de testiamentis [206]vel sanctimus.[ll]

**74** Vel [207]melius dicas [208]quia nulla publica honestas impedit [209]nisi que oritur ex sponsalibus de futuro, quia illa causam habet ex [210]divina lege, illud vero capitulo *porro*,[mm] loquitur de [211]primo genere affinitatis et de publica honestate [212]quo oritur ex sponsalibus sicut aperte [213]minuit finis eiusdem capituli [214]*porro*.[nn]

[kk] C.35 q.2 & 3 c. 22.   [ll] It has not been possible to find the text or section to which this refers.   [mm] C.35 q.2 & 3 c. 22.   [nn] C.35 q.2 & 3 c. 22.

[190] Autem patet] *illegible RB*
[191] fratrum] fratruum *W1*
[192] sublatum] sublatio *RB*
[193] mortuis] mortuus *W1*
[194] maritis] maritus *W1*
[195] alius] alius vel(?) aliquis *W1*
[196] ducere in uxores] in uxores ducere *W1*
[197] successive] successione *W1*
[198] non] non que vero *RB*
[199] iusticiarum] iusticiam *W1*
[200] sibi] ibi *W1*
[201] erat] erant *RB*
[202] constitutionem ] constitutionum *RB*; constitutionem ecclesie *W1*
[203] remanet] remanet alia *W1*
[204] enim] *om. W1*
[205] .c.] *om. W1*
[206] vel sanctimus] *om. W1*
[207] melius] metius *RB*
[208] quia] quod *RB*
[209] nisi] nisi illa *W1*
[210] divina] dura *W1*
[211] primo] primis *W1*
[212] quo] que *W1*
[213] minuit] *or* innuit(?)
[214] porro] porro etc *W1*

# *The Historical Introduction to Sciendum Est*

This transcription presents the historical section at the start of the anonymous treatise *Sciendum est*. It is to be found in the *Bracton* manuscript, BL, MS Add. 41258, fo. 38r (A); only the very end of it is also in Bodl. Lib., MS Rawlinson C 160, fo. 36v (R).

**1** Sciendum est quod circa personas matrimonio copulandas et super gradibus consanguinitatis matrimonio prohibitis secundum varia tempora emanaverunt iura diversa divina pariter et humana.

**2** Omnis enim constitutio hominum a iure divino sumere debet initium, alioquin quod statuetur erit iniquum, dicente sapiente primo proverbio ¹8 capitulo: 'per me conditores legum iusta decernunt',ᵃ unde et quidam ²verborum venditores et grandiloquiorum trutinatores, qui, divina lege concepta, †³instanter glosantur ⁴tanquam humanis in eis ecclesiastici regimus sufficientiam contineatur blasphemii sunt, essentque ipsorum ora velud iniqua loquentium, hec de hiis.†⁵

**3** Notandum autem quod in ipso mundi principio contrahere licuit in primo gradu, cogente necessitate ex paucitate hominum: cum ⁶qua filius Ade contraheret nisi cum sorore sua? Immo et licuit quia et oportuit patrem ducere quasi filiam; nam et Adam duxerat Evam, quam eius dico ⁷filiam fuisse, non simpliciter, ⁸sed quasi filiam, cum prestiterit ei formalem materiam eam, que constet de particula corporis Ade fuisse formatam.

---

ᵃ 'Per me reges regnant, et legum conditores iusta decernunt': Proverbs viii.15. All biblical quotes are taken from: *Biblia sacra: vulgatae editionis sixti v Pontificis Maximi iussu recognita et Clementis VIII auctoritate edita*, Turin 1883.

¹ 8] 4 A
² verborum] virorum A
³ instanter] instatur A
⁴ tanquam] ħ tanquam A
⁵ This section within †† is corrupt.
⁶ qua] qua Xe A
⁷ filiam] written above A
⁸ sed] written above. A

**4** Postmodum hac causa cessante et multiplicato humano genere, prohibitus est gradus primus pariter et secundus et consanguinitatis et affinitatis, [9]Leviticus .xviii. capitulo: 'Omnis homo ad proximam sanguinis sui non [10]accedet ut revelet turpitudinem eius. Ego dominus'.[b]

**5** Hic ponit generale; postea specificat, dicens: 'Turpitudinem patris tui [11]et turpitudinem matris tuae non discooperies mater tua est; non [12]revelabis turpitudinem eius'[c] Et prohibetur hic primus gradus consanguinitatis in linea descendente.

**6** 'Turpitudinem uxoris patris tui non discooperies: turpitudo enim patris tui est':[d] primus gradus affinitatis.

**7** 'Turpitudinem sororis tue ex patre, sive ex matre, que domi vel foris est genita, non revelabis':[e] primus gradus affinitatis in linea transversa.

**8** 'Domi' dicit, glosa nutritur, id est ex patre; 'foris' glosa id est ex matre si de priori viro suscepta cum matre in domum venit.

**9** 'Turpitudinem filii tui vel filie tue': primus gradus consanguinitatis in linea descendente; 'vel neptis ex filia': secundus gradus consanguinitatis; 'non revelabis: quia turpitudo tua est.'[f]

**10** 'Turpitudinem filie [13]uxoris patris tui, quam peperit patri tuo, et est [14]soror, tua non revelabis':[g] primus gradus consanguinitatis tantum ex uno parente.

**11** 'Turpitudinem [15]sororis patris tui non discooperies quia: caro est patris tui':[h] secundus gradus consanguinitatis.

---

[b] 'Omnis homo ad proximam sanguinis sui non accedet ut revelet turpitudinem eius. Ego Dominus Deus vester': Leviticus xviii.6.   [c] 'Turpitudinem patris tui et turpitudinem matris tuae non discooperies mater tua est; non revelabis turpitudinem eius': Leviticus xviii.7.   [d] 'Turpitudinem uxoris patris tui non discooperies: turpitudo enim patris tui est.': Leviticus xviii.8   [e] 'Turpitudinem sororis tuae ex patre, sive ex matre, quae domi vel foris genita est, non revelabis': Leviticus xviii.9   [f] 'Turpitudinem filiae filii tui vel neptis ex filia non revelabis: quia turpitudo tua est': Leviticus xviii.10   [g] 'Turpitudinem filiae uxoris patris tui, quam peperit patri tuo, et est soror tua, non revelabis': Leviticus xviii.11   [h] 'Turpitudinem sororis patris tui non discooperies quia: caro est patris tui': Leviticus xviii.12.

[9]   Leviticus xviii] Ierem xiiii A
[10]  accedet] *after correction from* attendet A
[11]  et turpitudinem matris tuae] *om.* A
[12]  revelabis] *after correction* A
[13]  uxoris] uxor A
[14]  soror, tua] socer tuus A
[15]  sororis] soris A

**12** 'Turpitudinem sororis matris tue non discooperies, eo quod caro matris tue sit':[i] secundus gradus consanguinitatis.

**13** 'Turpitudinem [16]patrui tui non revelabis, ne [17]accedes ad uxorem eius, que tibi affinitate [18]coniungitur':[j] secundus gradus consanguinitatis.

**14** Et est differentia ad precedens in textu vel glosa hoc persequens, scilicet 'ne accedes' etcetera: item secundus gradus affinitatis et hinc patet quod tot gradus prohibentur in affinitate quot in consanguinitate.

**15** 'Turpitudinem nurus tue non revelabis, quia uxor filii tui est, nec discooperies ignominiam eius:'[k] primus gradus affinitatis.

**16** 'Turpitudinem uxoris tue et filii eius non revelabis' glossa: 'Ne putes tibi licere ambas habere'[l] et prohibetur hic primus gradus afffinitatis. 'Filiam filii eius, et filiam filie eius non sumes, ut reveles turpitudinem eius vel ignominiam eius: quia caro illius sunt et talis coitus incestus est':[m] secundus gradus consanguinitatis, unde glossa dicit neptem uxoris de filio vel de filia prohibet duci uxorem.

**17** 'Sororem uxoris tue [19]in pellicatum illius non accipies, nec revelabis turpitudinem eius adhuc illa vivente:'[n] primus gradus affinitatis.

**18** Post matrimonium humana [20]prohibitio usque ad septimum gradum se extendit, unde dicitur Sententiaram Libro iiii, distinctione xxxiiii, capitulo [21]i[a] 'alie parte legitime ante legem, alie sub lege alie in tempore gratie'.[o] Hec autem extensio dilatam de caritatis causa facta est, ut fieret connubium

---

[i] 'Turpitudinem sororis matris tuae non revelabis, eo quod caro sit matris tuae': Leviticus xviii.13.   [j] 'Turpitudinem patrui tui non revelabis, nec accedes ad uxorem eius, quae tibi adfinitate coniungitur': Leviticus xviii.14.   [k] 'Turpitudinem nurus tuae non revelabis, quia uxor filii tui est, nec discooperies ignominiam eius': Leviticus xviii.15.   [l] No source has been found for these glosses.   [m] 'Turpitudinem uxoris tuae et filiae eius non revelabis. Filiam filii eius, et filiam filiae illius non sumes, ut reveles ignominiam eius: quia caro illius sunt et talis coitus incestus est': Leviticus xviii.17. Note that Leviticus xviii.16 ('Turpitudinem uxoris fratris tui non revelabis: quia turpitudo fratris tui est.') has been omitted.   [n] 'Sororem uxoris tuae in pellicatum illius non accipies, nec revelabis turpitudinem eius adhuc illa vivente': Leviticus xviii.18.   [o] Magistri Petri Lombardi, *Sententiae*, ii.Lib 4, Dist. 34, c.1.

[16]  patrui] fratris A
[17]  accedes] acedes A
[18]  coniungitur] auditur (*before correction*). A. There is a marginal correction, but the start is missing '[-]iungitur'.
[19]  in pellicatum] implicatum A
[20]  prohibitio] prohibutio A
[21]  i[a]] i[a].a. A

165

'quoddam caritatis [22]seminarum',[p] ut docet [23]Augustinus in libro de civitate dei et scribitur .xxxv°.q. i[a] cum igitur.[q]

**19** Deinde restringitur vel restricta est hec extensio [24]prohibitionis usque ad gradum .iiii., et hoc pape dispendium quod inde [25]contingeret, ut Extra de consanguinitate et affinitate *non debet*.[r] [26]Ut ibidem scribitur: 'quaternarius [vero] numerus bene [27]congruit [28]prohibitioni coniugii corporalis, de quo dicit [29]Apostolus, quod vir non habet potestatem sui corporis, sed mulier, nec[que] mulier habet potestatem sui corporis, sed vir,[s] quia iiii[or] sunt humores in corpore, [30]qui [31]constant ex quatuor elementis.'[t]

---

[p] 'quoddam seminarum est karitatis;': C.35 q.1 c.1, which is from Augustine's *City of God* [xv. c.16]. However, the quote there is 'quoddam seminarum est civitatis': *City of God against the pagans*, London 1966, iv. 508.   [q] C.35 q.1 c.1   [r] X 4.14.8   [s] 'Mulier sui corporis potestatem non habet, sed vir. Similiter autem et vir sui corporis potestatem non habet, sed mulier': 1 Corinthians vii.4.   [t] X 4.14.8.

[22] seminarum] serminarum A
[23] Augustinus] aliquo (*before correction*) A, with 'Augustinus' in the margin
[24] prohibitionis] prohibutionis A
[25] R starts here.
[26] Ut] et ut R
[27] congruit] competit A R
[28] prohibitioni] prohibutioni A
[29] Apostolus] Apostolus, .io. ad corinthios vii a A R
[30] qui] quod et A R
[31] constant] constat A R

# APPENDIX 3

# *Quibus Modis*

This is a transcription of *Quibus modis*, an adaptation of Johannes Egitaniensis's *Lectura* on the trees of consanguinity and affinity which was made by common lawyers probably around the end of the thirteenth century. The adapted treatise occurs in two *Bracton* manuscripts, BL, MS Harley 653, fos 40v–41r, and Worcester Cathedral Library, MS F 87, fos 28v–29r. This transcription is based on the Harley manuscript (*H*), compared against the Worcester manuscript (*W*) and an edition (*E*) of the full original treatise by Johannes Egitaniensis: 'Lectura arborum consanguinitatis et affinitatis Magistri Ioannis Egitaniensis', ed. I. da Rosa Pereira, *Studia Gratiana* xiv, Collectanea Stephan Kuttner iv (1967), 155–82.

1 [1]'Quibus modis arbor de consanguinitate debet fieri'

2 [2]In medio videlicet arboris fiat quedam cellula, que truncus vel protheus appellatur.

3 [3]Protende [4]ergo a vertice prothei sive trunci sursum lineam ascendentem continentem quatuor cellulas, in [5]quarum prima [6]pater et mater ponantur; in secunda avus [7]et avia; in tertia proavus [8]et proavia; in quarta [9]abavus, abavia.

4 Similiter describe lineam descendentem a protheo [10]continentem quatuor

---

[1] 'Aliter arbor consanguinitatis secundum I. Hispaniensem discribitur hoc modo' is the rubric of *W*; 'Incipit Summa Magistri Iohannis Ispanii super arborem de consanguinitate' is the title of *E*.
[2] In medio . . . appellatur] *om. E*. The nearest parallel in *E* is lines 49–51: 'In medio arboris debet poni quedam cellula que dicitur truncus, ut .XXXV.q.V Series (C.35 q.5 c.1), vel Protheus vel Ioahcim'.
[3] Protende] This is line 73 of *E*.
[4] ergo] *om. E*
[5] quarum] qua *W*
[6] pater et mater ponantur] ponitur pater et mater *E*
[7] et] *om. E*
[8] et] *om. E*
[9] abavus] abavus et *W*
[10] continentem] continente *W*

167

cellulas, in quarum prima [11]ponantur filius [12]et filia; in secunda [13]nepos, neptis; in tertia pronepos, proneptis; in quarta [14]abnepos, [15]abneptis.

**5** Restat [16]igitur videre de lineis transversalibus, quarum due [17]linee [18]oriuntur [19]a protheo, [20]immo [21]a patre prothei, et a quolibet suo [22]superiori; oritur una linea tam ex patre quam ex matre.

**6** [23]Ex inferioribus, scilicet ab inferiori linea [24]directa [25]descendenti, [26]nulla oritur [27]transversalis, [28]quia omnes [29]qui ab inferioribus [30]descendunt [31]recta via [32]descendunt a protheo.

**7** Pone ergo tam iuxta protheum [33]quam quemlibet [34]superiorem fratrem et sororem, designans eos illis nominibus relativis quibus referuntur ad protheum, et [35]illos [36]liga [37]cum incausto ad designandum [38]quod faciunt unum gradum.

**8** Deinde singulis eorum assigna [39]filios et nepotes usque ad quartum gradum respectu prothei, et sic includes consanguinitatem usque ad quartum gradum.

[11] ponantur] ponitur *E*
[12] et] *om. E*
[13] nepos] nepos et *W*
[14] abnepos] abnepos et *W*
[15] abneptis] neptis. Jo<hannes> *E*. However these identifiers are omitted in all but one of the five manuscripts that da Rosa Pereira used.
[16] igitur] etiam *W*; *om. E*
[17] linee] line *W*; *om. E*
[18] oriuntur] oriantur *H*
[19] a] ex *E*
[20] immo] in uno *H*; uno *E*
[21] a] ex *E*
[22] superiori] superori *H*
[23] Ex] Ab *E*
[24] directa] recte *W*
[25] descendenti] ascendenter et *H*; *om. E*
[26] nulla] ulla *W*
[27] transversalis] transversali *W*
[28] quia] Johannes yspanus, quia *E*
[29] qui] que *H*
[30] descendunt] descenderunt *E*
[31] recta via] recta linea *W*; linea recta *E*
[32] descendunt] dependent *W*
[33] quam] quam iuxta *E*
[34] superiorem fratrem] fratrem superiorem *W*
[35] illos] eos *E*
[36] liga] ligare *W*
[37] cum] *om. W*; cum minio vel cum *E*
[38] quod] que *W*
[39] filios] scl' *H*, a scribal error for fil'?

**9**  Et [40]medietas arboris [41]sufficeret in doctrina tradenda, ut staret ad modum vexilli; sed alia medietas [42]vel [43]fuit posita ad decorem vel ut scirentur nomina consanguinitatis tam ex parte [44]masculini quam ex parte [45]feminina.

**10**  Et nota ex [46]precedentibus quod quinque sunt linee: prima est [47]descendens directa; secunda [48]est [49]ascendens directa; tertia [50]est linea equalitatis; quarta transversalis [51]superequalis; quinta [52]transversalis [53]subequalis.

**11**  [54]Assignemus [55]ergo [56]graduum computationem: [57]canonicam et [58]legalem in linea ascendente et descendente, que vel [59]quasi eadem est; secundo canonicam in linea transversali; tertio legalem.

**12**  Et primo videndum est [60]quare truncus appellatur et quare protheus, et postea quid sit linea et quid [61]sit [62]gradus.

**13**  [63] [64]Truncus vero dicitur quia ad [65]modum arboris se habet, cuius existencia [66]consistit in [67]trunco.

---

[40]  medietas arboris sufficeret] quidem sufficeret medietas arboris *E*
[41]  sufficeret] sufficere *H*
[42]  vel] alia *W*
[43]  fuit] sicut *H*
[44]  masculini] masculina *H*
[45]   feminina] femine *W*; feminini sexus. Raymundus *E*
[46]  precedentibus] precendenter *H*
[47]  descendens] ascendens *H E*
[48]  est] *om. W E*
[49]  ascendens] descendens *E*
[50]  est] *om. E*
[51]  superequalis] subequalis *after correction W*; *om. E*
[52]  transversalis] *om. E.*
[53]  subequalis] subequalis. Johannes yspanus. *E*
[54]  Assignemus] Tunc assignemus *E*
[55]  ergo] *om. E*
[56]  graduum computationem] computationem graduum *W E*
[57]  canonicam] canonicos *E*
[58]  legalem] legales *E*
[59]  quasi] qualis *H*; quia *W*
[60]  quare . . . postea] *om. E*
[61]  sit] *om. W E*
[62]  gradus] gradus Johannes yspanus *E*
[63]  truncus . . . vultus]. This section comes from another part of *E*, lines 51-6
[64]  truncus vero dicitur] et dicitur truncus *E* (line 51)
[65]  modum] *after correction from* mordum *H*
[66]  consistit] *om. E*
[67]  trunco] trunco ut .XXXV. q. V. Series (C. 35, q. 5, c. 1), unde versus << Truncus ponitur hic cum ramis ut decet arbor >>. *E*

**14** [68]Protheus vero dicitur propter diversos respectus quos habet [69]ad personas que sunt in arbore, [70]et ad [71]quemlibet [72]mutat vultum, unde [73]Oratius: 'quo teneam [74]nodo [75]mutantem [76]prothea [77]vultus'.[a]

**15** [78]Linea est [79]inordinata collatio personarum consanguinitate [80]iunctarum, diversos [81]gradus continens, et eos ab unitate stipitis secundum numeros [82]distinguemus.

**16** Gradus est quedam habitudo [83]vel [84]personarum distantia [85]adinvicem facta collatione ad communem parentem.

**17** In linea ascendenti [86]et descendenti [87]inveniuntur gradus tam [88]canonicos quam legales iuxta hanc regulam communem, [89]vel communiter secundum leges et canones in linea ascendenti et descendenti: [90]qualibet persona addita superiori persone vel inferiori gradum [91]adicit.

[a]  'quo teneam voltus mutantem Protea nodo?': Horace, 'Epistles', *Satires, epistles and ars poetica*, 1.1.90.

[68]  Protheus vero dicitur] Item dicitur Protheus *E*
[69]  ad] ad diversas *E*
[70]  et] et sic *E*
[71]  quemlibet] quamlibet *E*
[72]  mutat vultum] mittit vultum suum sicut Protheus *E*
[73]  Oratius] versus *H.*
[74]  nodo] nodum *W*
[75]  mutantem] mutante *W*
[76]  prothea] protheo *W*
[77]  vultus] vultum *W*
[78]  Linea] Return here to line 100 of *E*
[79]  inordinata] ordinata *E*
[80]  iunctarum] inventarum *W*
[81]  gradus] casus *E*
[82]  distinguemus] distinguens. Raymundus *E*
[83]  vel] sive *E*
[84]  personarum distantia] distantia personarum *W E*
[85]  adinvicem] abinvicem *W*; ad invicem *E*
[86]  et] vel *E*
[87]  inveniuntur ... descendenti] *om. W*
[88]  canonicos] canonici *H*; (*om. W*)
[89]  vel] alias *E*; (*om. W*)
[90]  qualibet] quelibet *E*
[91]  adicit] addicit, ut .XXXII. (*sic*) q. V. Ad sedem (C.35 q. 5, c. 2). *E*

**18** Si vis scire [92]quoto gradu una persona distat [93]ab alia in linea ascendenti [94]et descendenti: numera omnes personas et una dempta, [95]scilicet trunco, [96]quot persone remanent, [97]toto gradu distant.

**19** Et sic protheus non facit gradum, sed [98]est truncus, et est pater in linea descendenti [99]et ascendenti filius.

**20** A protheo [100]sic distat filius primo gradu, [101]nepos secundo, et sic usque ad [102]abnepotem [103]qui distat quarto.

**21** Similiter in superiori linea pater distat [104]primo gradu a protheo, [105]avus secundo, et sic usque ad abavum qui distat [106]quarto.

**22** Et nota quod gradus [107]legales designantur [108]nigris [109]punctis in [110]yma parte [111]cuiuslibet cellule; canonici vero [112]in [113]superiori parte [114]rubeis [115]punctis ad [116]designandum excellenciam canonice scientie [117]ad [118]legalem.

**23** Item persone que distant [119]equaliter a communi parente dicuntur esse in gradu et facere gradum; [120]que inequaliter dicuntur distare [121]gradu.

[92]  quoto] quanto *W*
[93]  ab] ad *E*
[94]  et] vel *W E*
[95]  scilicet trunco] *om. E*
[96]  quot persone] quo tempore *W*; quod [*sic*] persone *E*
[97]  toto] quarto *H W*
[98]  est] *om. W*
[99]  et] in *W E*
[100]  sic] ergo *W E*
[101]  nepos secundo] *om. W*
[102]  abnepotem] nepotem *W*; neptem *E*
[103]  qui] quod *W*
[104]  primo] a primo *W*
[105]  avus] *om. W*
[106]  quarto] quarto gradu *W E*
[107]  legales] legalis *H W*
[108]  nigris] in genere *W*
[109]  punctis] puncti *W*
[110]  yma] inferiori *E*
[111]  cuiuslibet] cuilibet *W*; quolibet [*sic*] *E*
[112]  in superiori parte rubeis] rubeis in superiori parte *E*
[113]  superiori] superori *H*
[114]  rubeis] rubris *H*
[115]  punctis] *om. E*
[116]  designandum] desingnandum *W*
[117]  ad] et *H W*
[118]  legalem] legalis *H W*
[119]  equaliter] *om. H W*
[120]  que] quando *E*
[121]  gradu] gradu ut .XXXV. q. V. Porro <et> Parentele (C. 35 q. 5, c. 3 et 4). Raymundus. *E*. Then six lines (122–7) are omitted.

**24** Si vis scire quoto gradu [122]una persona distat ab alia in linea transversali secundum canones: [123]vide si equaliter descendunt, et quot [124]sunt persone ab una parte ad communem [125]parentem, [126]toto [127]gradu distant inter [128]se.

**25** [129]Si inequaliter descendunt: quoto gradu distat [130]remotior a communi parente, [131]quoto gradu distant inter se.

**26** Incipiamus [132]igitur secundum predictam regulam a superiori cellula, scilicet ab abavo. [133]Abavus distat a trunco quarto gradu, ergo [134]propatruus qui descendit ab abavo per lineam [135]aliam similiter quarto gradu, propatrui filius [136]similiter quarto [137]gradu, et sic de aliis.

**27** Quod totum [138]probo sic: [139]propatruus et [140]proavus sunt duo fratres, ergo sunt in [141]gradu primo; ergo avus, filius proavi, [142]distabit secundo gradu a [143]propatruo; pater tertio; truncus ergo quarto.

**28** Similiter filius [144]propatrui distat quarto gradu a trunco. Probatio: filius [145]propatrui et avus [146]sunt duo nepotes abavi, ergo sunt in secundo gradu, quia sunt filii duorum fratrum, [147]qui [148]fratres sunt in primo gradu; ergo pater distat a filio propatrui [149]tertio gradu; truncus quarto.

[122] una persona distat] distat una persona W
[123] vide] *after correction* W
[124] sunt persone] persone sint W; persone sunt E
[125] parentem] stipitem E
[126] toto] quoto H
[127] gradu] *om.* E
[128] se] se Raymundus E
[129] si inequaliter . . . inter se] *om.* E
[130] remotior] a trunco remotior (*before correction*) W; (*om.* E)
[131] quoto] toto W; (*om.* E)
[132] igitur] ergo W E
[133] Abavus] Abavus autem W
[134] propatruus] proavus E
[135] aliam] suam H W
[136] similiter] *om.* W E
[137] gradu] *om.* E
[138] probo sic] sic probo E
[139] propatruus et proavus] patrui W
[140] proavus] propatruus H corrected to 'proavus' above the line by the later hand that drew the half tree of consanguinity
[141] gradu primo] primo gradu W; primo gradu, ut .XXXV. q. V. Ad sedem (C. 35, q. 5, c. 2). E
[142] distabit] distat E
[143] propatruo] patruo H W
[144] propatrui] patrui H W
[145] propatrui] patrui W
[146] sunt duo] *repeated* W
[147] qui] quia H
[148] fratres] fratrem H corrected above the line by the later hand
[149] tertio gradu] gradu tertio E

**29** Similiter nepos propatrui distat quarto gradu a trunco. Probatio: nepos propatrui et pater sunt duo pronepotes abavi, [150]sunt ergo in tertio gradu, quia sunt filii duorum nepotum, qui nepotes sunt in secundo [151]gradu; ergo truncus distat quarto.

**30** Similiter [152]pronepotes propatrui sunt in quarto gradu cum trunco et in linea equali que continet omnes personas equaliter cum eo descendentes. [153]Probatio: [154]pronepos propatrui et truncus sunt duo abnepotes abavi, ergo sunt in quarto gradu quia sunt filii duorum pronepotum.

**31** Item, ascende ad proavum. Ipse distat a trunco tertio gradu; ergo patruus magnus, qui descendit ab eo per aliam lineam, similiter est in tertio [155]gradu ; [156]proprior [157]sobrinus [158]in [159]tertio; filius eius est secum, [160]id est cum trunco in tertio et [161]linea [162]equali.

**32** Deinde pro [163]numero [164]personarum, [165]adiciatur gradus in probatione ista, [166]scilicet patrui magni et descendentium ab eo, et [167]tunc procede ut prius, quia patruus magnus et avus sunt duo fratres, ergo pater distat secundo gradu; [168]truncus tertio a patruo magno; et [169]ita [170]de [171]aliis.

---

[150] sunt ergo] ergo sunt *W E*

[151] gradu] *om. E*

[152] pronepotes ... Probatio] *om. H*

[153] Probatio] Probatio pronepotes propatrui est in tercio gradu cum trunco et in linea equlitatis, que continet omnes personas equaliter cum eo descendentes. *E*

[154] pronepos] pronepotes *W*

[155] gradu] *om. E*

[156] proprior] propinquior *W*

[157] sobrinus] consobrinus *W*

[158] in] *om. E*

[159] tertio] tertio gradu *W*

[160] id est] primo *E*

[161] linea] in linea *W E*

[162] equali] equaliter *W*; equalitatis *E*

[163] numero] *after correction H*

[164] personarum] personam *W*

[165] adiciatur] adicitur *H*; addiciatur *E*

[166] scilicet] sicud *W*

[167] tunc] trunci *H*; trunci et *W*

[168] truncus] truncus in *W*

[169] ita] sic *E*

[170] de] ab *H W*

[171] aliis] aliis. Hec probatio colligitur .XXXV. q. quinta, Ad sedem (C. 35, q. 5, c. 2). Raymundus. *E*. Here *H* and *W* cease to follow *E* (at line 154). *E* continues until line 233, when the affinity treatise begins.

**33** [172]Nota quod eadem linea dicitur ascendens et descendens, [173]superior et [174]inferior facta relatione ad diversam computationem.

**34** [175]Set si tantum una linea poneretur in arbore, que esset ascendens propter mutationem nominum personarum, esset ibi defectus, nec posset dici ascendens et descendens respectu trunci.

**35** Posite [176]ergo sunt [177]due linee ibi, ut [178]vitaretur defectus et ut diceretur [iste] ascendens, et [179]ille descendens, respectu trunci.

**36** Sed illud nota quod plures linee [180]sunt quam due in arbore ascendentes et descendentes. Nam a qualibet persona ascendente due emanant linee descendentes ex obliquo, sed non respectu trunci, et eedem dicuntur ascendentes [181]si computatio incipiat [182]ab inferiori.

**37** Item linea [183]equalitatis oritur [184]ex utraque [185]parte trunci et [186]proceditur ex transverso usque ad quartam et ultimam cellulam.

**38** Item linea directa [187]proceditur a qualibet cellula [188]linee [189]ascendentis usque ad proximam cellulam [190]et non ultra.

[172]  Nota] non *H*
[173]  superior] superiori *H*
[174]  inferior] inferiori *H*
[175]  Set] *om. W*
[176]  ergo sunt] sunt ergo *W*
[177]  due linee ibi] ibi due linee *W*
[178]  vitaretur] evitaretur *W*
[179]  ille] illi *W*
[180]  sunt quam due] quam due sunt *W*
[181]  si] sed *W*
[182]  ab] sub *W*
[183]  equalitatis] equaliter *W*
[184]  ex] ab *W*
[185]  parte] *om. W*
[186]  proceditur] protenditur *W*
[187]  proceditur] protenditur *W*
[188]  linee] linea *H*
[189]  ascendentis] ascendenter *H*
[190]  et] a *W*

# *Triplex Est*

This is a transcription of *Triplex est*, an adaptation of the section 'De cognatione carnali' from Raymón de Penyafort's *Summa de matrimonio*, made by common lawyers probably around the end of the thirteenth century. This adapted treatise is paired with *Quibus modis* in BL, MS Harley 653, fos 41r–v (H) and Worcester Cathedral Library, MS F 87, fo. 29r (W). The transcription is based on the two manuscripts, compared with the 1603 edition of Raymón's *Summa* (Sm): St Raymundus de Peniafort, *Summa de poenitentia et matrimonio [a facsimilie of the Rome edition of 1603]*, Farnborough 1967, 533–6, with one small section compared with *Bracton*, ii. 200 (Br).

1   [1] 'De triplici cognatione [2]Raymundi'

2   [3]Item [4]triplex est cognatio, scilicet carnalis, spiritualis, et legalis; et quia [5]carnalis, cognatio [6]'consanguinitas' appellatur, [7]alias duas species cognationis precedit naturaliter, ideo [8]primo videamus de ea [9]que consanguinitas [10]appellatur.

3   Quamvis [11]sint multa et varia de consanguinitate scripta a doctoribus et maioribus nostris, super expositione tam arboris quam diversorum canonum,

---

[1]   'Tertio modo secundum Philosophum ut levius intelligatur' is the rubric in W; 'De cognatione carnali' is the title in Sm.

[2]   Raymundi] H has 'R' with the leg extended horizontally and crossed by a vertical line, with a small supercript 'a' above it. This is not the usual canon law abbreviation of Raymón's name. The closest abbreviation in A. Cappelli, *Dizionario di abbreviature Latine ed Italiane*, 6th edn, Milan 1990, is 'Roma'; it might also be 'Rubrica'; however, here it is translated as 'Raymundi' for sense.

[3]   Item] Sciendum est quod W; Rertractato de impedimento voti, subsequenter dicendum est de impedimento cognationis. Ad quod sciendum est, quod Sm

[4]   triplex est cognatio] cognatio triplex est Sm

[5]   carnalis] carnalis que est H

[6]   consanguinitas] consanguinitatis H W; quae consanguinitas Sm

[7]   alias] om. H

[8]   primo ... ea] de ea primo videamus W; prius de ea videamus Sm

[9]   que consanguinitas appellatur] om. Sm

[10]   appellatur] appellatur et Sm

[11]   sint ... scripta] scripta sint multa, et varia de consanguinitate Sm

175

[12]qui [13]superficialiter videntur [14]esse contrarii, [15]tamen de multis pauca utilia, que ad presentem doctrinam faciunt, hic [16]sunt [17]compilata.

**4** Videndum ergo [18]quid sit consanguinitas, [19]et unde dicatur, [20]et [21]que linea consanguinitatis, et quot [22]sunt linee, [23]et quid sit gradus, [24]et qualiter gradus [25]computentur, et usque ad [26]quem gradum [27]matrimonium prohibeatur.

**5** [28]Est enim consanguinitas vinculum personarum ab [29]eodem stipite descendentium carnali [30]compagine contractum.

**6** Stipitem dico illam [31]primam personam [32]a qua [33]alii [34]duxerunt originem, sicut Adam fuit stipes [35]Caym et Abel et filiorum qui ab eis processerunt.

**7** Dicitur [36]enim consanguinitas a con et sanguine, quasi communem sanguinem habentes, [37]vel de uno sanguine procedentes.

**8** Linea est [38]collectio personarum ordinata consanguinitate [39]iunctarum, ab eodem stipite descendentium, diversos gradus continens.

[12] qui] que H
[13] superficialiter] super hoc W
[14] esse] om. W
[15] tamen] cum H W
[16] sunt] om. H
[17] compilata] compilater H; conpilata W
[18] quid] que H
[19] et] om. Sm
[20] et] om. Sm
[21] que] quid sit Sm
[22] sunt] sint Sm
[23] et] om. Sm
[24] et] om. Sm
[25] computentur] conputetur W; computetur Sm
[26] quem] quotum Sm
[27] matrimonium prohibeatur] prohibeatur matrimonium W Sm
[28] Est enim consanguinitas] Consanguinitas est W Sm
[29] eodem] eadem W
[30] compagine] propagine W; propagatione Sm
[31] primam] om. Sm
[32] a qua] quam W
[33] alii] aliqui W Sm
[34] duxerunt] dixerunt W
[35] Caym] Chaim W; Cain Sm
[36] enim] autem W; om. Sm
[37] vel] om. W
[38] collectio personarum ordinata] ?H (coll'o); collatio personarum ordinata W; ordinata collectio personarum Sm
[39] iunctarum] coniunctarum W Sm

**9** Linee sunt tres: [40]ascendentium, transversalium sive collateralium, sicut triplex est [41]propinquorum diversitas seu [42]etiam consanguineorum.

**10** Prima est ascendentium, a quibus originem traximus, sicut pater, mater, avus, avia, proavus, [43]proavia, pronepos, proneptis, abnepos, abneptis.

**11** Alia [44]est transversalium, [45]sive collateralium, ut ex transverso seu [46]a [47]latere venientium, a quibus non duximus originem nec [48]ipsi a nobis, ut frater [49]et soror, filii [50]enim [51]fratrum qui dicuntur [52]'fratres patrueles'; vel [53]duarum sororum filii qui dicuntur 'consobrini', et [54]eorundem filii et [55]nepotes.

**12** Et nota quod due linee descendentes unam faciunt transversalem, ut [56]in hoc exemplo apparet: filii duorum fratrum attinent sibi linea transversali, et [57]quilibet eorum recta linea descendit ab avo [58]eorum, qui [59]fuit [60]stipes communis a quo traxerunt originem, et sic de omnibus aliis [61]est intelligendum tam de [62]propinquioribus quam remotioribus.

**13** [63]Sequitur [64]videre quid sit gradus, ad quod [65]notandum quod secundum

---

[40] ascendentium] ascendentium, descendentium, et *Sm*
[41] propinquorum diversitas] propinquior diversitas *W*; diversitas propinquorum *Sm*
[42] etiam] *om. Sm*
[43] proavia] proavia, abavus, abavia. Secunda descendentium, qui duxerunt originem a nobis, sicut filius, filia, nepos, neptis, *Sm*
[44] est] *om. W*
[45] sive . . . transverso] *om. Sm*
[46] a] ex *W*
[47] latere] latere nec a nobis ipsis *H*
[48] ipsi a nobis] a nobis ipsi *W*
[49] et] *om. Sm*
[50] enim] *om. Sm*
[51] fratrum] fratrui *W*; duorum fratrum *Sm*
[52] fratres patrueles] paternales fratres *W*; patrueles *Sm*
[53] duarum sororum filii] filii duarum sororum *Sm*
[54] eorundem] eorum *Sm*
[55] nepotes] nepotes sicut expresse notatur. 35.q.5 *primo gradu* [C.35 q.5 c.6] *Sm*
[56] in . . . apparet] apparet in hoc exemplo *W Sm*
[57] quilibet] quibus *W*
[58] eorum] eorum communi *Sm*
[59] fuit] fuerint *H*
[60] stipes communis] communis stipes *W Sm*
[61] est intelligendum] intelligendum est *W Sm*
[62] propinquioribus . . . remotioribus] remotioribus quam de propinquioribus *W*; remotioribus, quam propinquioribus *Sm*
[63] Sequitur] Similiter *W*
[64] videre] videndum est *W*
[65] notandum] nota *Sm*

diversas computationes, [66]legales, [67]spirituales, et [68]canonicas, [69]diverso modo [70]describitur.

**14** Nam secundum [71]leges, quelibet persona facit gradum.

**15** Secundum canones in transversali linea, due persone faciunt gradum: ut puta [72]duo fratres sunt in primo gradu secundum canones, qui sunt in [73]secundo secundum [74]leges.

**16** Et sic de singulis, que diversitas computationum et [75]disputationum inventa est: ad expositionem quorumdam decretorum et [76]arboris doctrinam.

**17** Sed quantum ad presentem materiam, scilicet quando consanguinitas computari [77]debet matrimonio [78]coniungendo vel [79]disiungendo, quia ex utraque parte [80]sunt persone numerande, [81]sicut una processit ex altera et gradus [82]distinguendi et [83]computandi ex utroque [84]latere.

**18** Gradus est habitudo distantium personarum qua cognoscitur quota generationis [85]distantia due persone inter se [86]differunt.

---

[66] legales] legalem *Sm*
[67] spirituales] scilicet *Sm*
[68] canonicas] canonicam *Sm*
[69] diverso modo] diversi mode *H W*
[70] describitur] scribitur *W*
[71] leges] legales *W*
[72] duo] duos *H*
[73] secundo] secundo gradu *W*
[74] leges] leges filii duorum fratrum secundum canones sunt in secundo, qui secundum leges sunt in quarto. *Sm*
[75] disputationum] diffinitionum *Sm*
[76] arboris] arborum *H*
[77] debet] *om. H*; debet a *W*; debet pro *Sm*
[78] coniungendo] contrahendo, iungendo *Sm*
[79] disiungendo] dissimulando *H*
[80] sunt persone] persone sunt *W Sm*
[81] sicut ... computandi ex] *om. W*
[82] distinguendi] disiungendi *H W*
[83] computandi] computandi sunt *Sm*
[84] latere] latere. Extra de consanguinitate et affinitate *ex litteris. In fine. Et quod dilectio.* Ideo sufficiat ad præsens hæc definitio. [X 4.14.1 & 3] *Sm*
[85] distantia] *after correction* H
[86] differunt] differant *H W*

**19** Gradus ita [87]computantur in linea ascendenti: pater [88]et mater sunt in primo gradu; avus [89]et [90]avia in secundo [91]gradu; [92]proavus, proavia in tertio; [93]abavus, abavia in [94]quarto.

**20** In [95]linea [96]descendenti hoc modo [97]computantur [98]gradus: filius [99]et filia sunt in primo gradu; nepos neptis [100]sunt in secundo; pronepos [101]proneptis in tertio; abnepos abneptis in quarto.

**21** In [102]linea transversali ita [103]computantur secundum canones: duo fratres sunt in primo gradu; filii duorum fratrum [104]sunt in secundo [105]gradu; [106]nepotes eorum in tertio; [107]pronepotes in quarto.

**22** Ultra quem gradum nulla [108]est consanguinitas, [109]sic nec olim ultra septimum [110]progrederentur.

**23** Sed secundum leges: duo [111]fratres sunt in secundo gradu; [112]filii in [113]quarto; et sic [114]duplicatur in quolibet gradu.

[87]  computantur] computatur *H W*
[88]  et] *om. Sm*
[89]  et] *om. Sm*
[90]  avia] aviam *H*
[91]  gradu] *om. W Sm*
[92]  proavus] proavus et *W*
[93]  abavus] abavuus et *W*
[94]  quarto] quarto gradu *W*
[95]  linea] *om. Sm*
[96]  descendenti] descendenti vero *Sm*
[97]  computantur] computatur *H W*
[98]  gradus ... computantur] *om. W* | gradus] *om. Sm*
[99]  et] *om. Sm*; (*om. W*)
[100]  sunt] *om. Sm*; (*om. W*)
[101]  proneptis] pronepter *H*. (*H* often uses the 'er' abbreviation at the end of words for apparently any ending) (*om. W*)
[102]  linea transversali] transversali linea *Sm*; (*om. W*)
[103]  computantur] computatur *H W*
[104]  sunt] *om. Sm*
[105]  gradu] *om. Sm*
[106]  nepotes] nepos *H W*
[107]  pronepotes] pronepotes eorum *Sm*; abnepos *H*; abnepos eorum *W*
[108]  est] est hodie *Sm*
[109]  sic] sicud *W*; sicut *Sm*
[110]  progrederentur] gradum progrediebatur. 35.q.5. *ad sedem* [C.35 q.5 c.2] *Sm*
[111]  fratres sunt] sunt fratres *W*
[112]  filii] filii eorum *Sm*
[113]  quarto] tertio *W*
[114]  duplicatur] duplicato *H*; duplica *W*

**24** Pretermissis [115]istis computationibus, tam secundum leges quam secundum canones, videndum [116]est qualiter consanguinitas est [117]adinvenienda et [118]computanda inter aliquos.

**25** Cum [119]velis scire [120]consanguinitatem [121]aliquorum, quantum inter se [122]distant, recurre ad communem personam a qua [123]traxerunt originem, ut [124]Petrus generavit Seyum et [125]Ticium, qui fuerunt fratres: ecce primus gradus.

**26** Si vero [126]sciri non possit quis [127]fuit pater eorum, dicas Seyus et Ticius [128]fuerunt fratres. Hoc [129]ideo dico, [130]quia fratres [131]semper ponendi sunt in primo gradu, [132]et frater et soror, [133]deinde due sorores.

**27** Deinde [134]in [135]computatione Seius et Ticius [136]fuerunt fratres qui, [137]secundum quod dicitur, faciunt primum gradum.

**28** [138]Idem genuit A: ecce secundus gradus. A genuit B: ecce [139]tertius. B genuit C: ecce [140]quartus de quo nunc [141]ago.

---

[115] istis computationibus] computationibus istis *Sm*
[116] est] *om. Sm*
[117] adinvenienda] adnuanda *or* adimanda, *or* adnumeranda *H*
[118] computanda] computando *W*
[119] velis] vis *Sm*
[120] consanguinitatem] de consanguinitate *Sm*
[121] aliquorum] alicorum *H*
[122] distant] differant *W Sm*
[123] traxerunt] extraxerunt *W*
[124] Petrus] Patrus *W*
[125] Ticium] Menium *H*; Nenium *W*
[126] sciri non possit] non potest sciri *W Sm*
[127] fuit] fuerit *Sm*
[128] fuerunt] sunt *W*
[129] ideo] idem *Sm*
[130] quia] quoniam *Sm*
[131] semper] *om. Sm*
[132] et] ut *Sm*
[133] deinde] vel *Sm*
[134] in] procede in *Sm*
[135] computatione] computationem *H*
[136] fuerunt] sunt *W*
[137] secundum quod dicitur] sicud dictum est *W*; ut dictum est *Sm*
[138] Idem ... gradus] *om. H*; Idem Seius generavit A. ecce secundus gradus *Sm*
[139] tertius] tertius gradus *W*
[140] quartus] *after correction from* tertius *H* ; quartus gradus *W*
[141] ago] agitur *Sm*

**29** [142]Revertaris ad alium fratrem et procede sic: Ticius et Seius fuerunt fratres et [143]sunt in primo gradu, ut dictum est. [144]Ticius genuit [145]G: ecce secundus gradus. [146]G genuit [147]H de [148]qua agitur, et ita habes tertium gradum.

**30** Et sic [149]ipsi dicuntur [150]se tenere universaliter in una parte in tertio gradu, [151]alia vero [152]in quarto [153]tantum.

**31** Ultimo videndum est usque ad quem gradum aliquis [154]prohibetur ducere uxorem de consanguinitate sua, et est dicendum quod usque ad quartum gradum [155]inclusive.

**32** Ut [156]si aliquis contra prohibitionem [157]huiusmodi [158]presumpserit copulari, [159]nulla longinquitate [160]defendatur annorum; cum [161]diuturnitas temporis non [162]minuit peccatum, sed [163]auget: [164]tanto [165]enim [166]graviora sunt [167]peccata, quanto diutius infelicem animam detinent [168]alligatam.

[142] revertaris] modo revertaris *Sm*

[143] sunt] *om. Sm*

[144] Ticius] *om. W*

[145] G] *S H W*

[146] G] *S W*

[147] H] H ecce tertius gradus *Sm*

[148] qua] quo *W Sm*

[149] ipsi] isti duo, vir, et uxor *Sm*

[150] se tenere universaliter] sic tenere universaliter *W*; usualiter attinere sibi *Sm*

[151] alia] alii *W*; in alia *Sm*

[152] in quarto tantum] tantum in quarto *W*

[153] tantum] usualiter dico, quia non attinent sibi revera in tertio gradu, sed in quarto tantum *Sm*. At this point a reference and 52 lines from the *Sm* edition, the remainder of section 4, are omitted from both manuscripts.

[154] prohibetur] prohibeatur *Sm*

[155] inclusive] inclusive ita *Sm*

[156] si aliquis] superius *W*; si quis *Sm*

[157] huiusmodi] huius *W*

[158] presumpserit] presumpserunt *W*

[159] nulla] longa *Sm*

[160] defendatur] deffendatur *W*; non defendatur *Sm*

[161] diuturnitas] diurnitas *W*

[162] minuit] minuat *W Sm*

[163] auget] augeat *Sm*

[164] tanto] tantum *W*; tantoque *Sm*

[165] enim] *om. Sm*

[166] graviora sunt] sint graviora *Sm*

[167] peccata] crimina *Sm*

[168] alligatam] At this point another reference has been omitted from both manuscripts, as have the remaning 26 lines of the *Sm* edition.

**33** [169]Et qualiter gradus cognationis [170]computentur, [171]in [172]quoto gradu quis distet ab alio in linea descendente [173]vel ascendente, in figura inferius depicta [174]manifestius ad oculum [175]apparebit.

---

[169] Et qualiter] At this point the manuscripts incorporate a section from *De legibus: Bracton*, ii.200.
[170] computentur] *Br*; computetur *H*; computantur *W*
[171] in ... ascendente] et in ... ascendente written above *W* | in] et *Br*
[172] quoto] quo *W*
[173] vel] et *W*
[174] manifestius] manifestius quasi *Br*
[175] apparebit] apperebit *W*

# Bibliography

## Unpublished primary sources

The contents listed for these manuscripts are not exhaustive, but indicate their principal use in this book.

Anon., 'Arborem consanguinitatis describas hoc modo', BL, Cotton Roll XIV.12
*Bracton*, with image of an *arbor*, CUL, MS Dd.7.14
—— with Johannes de Deo's 'Arbor versificata', with treatises 'Quibus modis' and 'Triplex est' and image of an *arbor*, BL, MS Harley 653
—— with Kilwardby's 'Ad arborem', *Britton* and images of *arbores*, CUL, MS Dd.7.6
—— with treatise 'Sciendum est' and images of *arbores*, BL, MS Add. 41258
—— with treatise 'Sciendum est', Bodl. Lib., MS Rawlinson C 160
—— with treatises 'Quibus modis' and 'Triplex est', WCL, MS F 87
*Britton*, with image of mort d'ancestor schemata, BL, MS Add. 25004
—— with image of mort d'ancestor schemata, BL, MS Harley 324
—— with image of mort d'ancestor schemata, BL, MS Harley 529
—— with image of mort d'ancestor schemata, BL, MS Harley 869
—— with image of mort d'ancestor schemata, BL, MS Harley 870
—— with image of mort d'ancestor schemata, BL, MS Harley 4656
—— with image of mort d'ancestor schemata, BL, MS Harley 5274
—— with image of mort d'ancestor schemata, BL, MS Lansdowne 652
—— with image of mort d'ancestor schemata, Bodl. Lib., MS Digby 136
—— with image of mort d'ancestor schemata, Bodl. Lib., MS Douce 98
—— with image of mort d'ancestor schemata, CUL, MS Add. 3584
—— with image of mort d'ancestor schemata, CUL, MS Ff.2.39
—— with image of mort d'ancestor schemata, CUL, MS Gg.5.12
—— with image of mort d'ancestor schemata, CUL, MS Hh.4.6
—— with images of *arbores* and mort d'ancestor schemata, BL, MS Egerton 1842
—— with images of arbores and mort d'ancestor schemata, BL, MS Harley 3644
—— with images of arbores and mort d'ancestor schemata, BL, MS Lansdowne 574
—— with images of arbores and mort d'ancestor schemata, BL, MS Lansdowne 1176
—— with images of arbores and mort d'ancestor schemata, Bodl. Lib., MS Rawlinson C 898
—— with images of *arbores*, Bodl. Lib., MS Bodley 562
de Deo, Johannes de, 'Arbor versificata', Bibliotheca Apostolica Vaticana, MS Palatini Latini 629
Hostiensis, *Lectura*, BL, MS Royal 10 E VI

183

Images of *arbores consanguinitatis et affinitatis*, Bibliothèque Nationale, Paris, MS Latin 4000
Images of family pedigrees in a teaching context, BL, MS Lansdowne 467
Kilwardby, Robert, 'Ad arborem' (partial), BL, MS Royal 9 B VI
—— 'Ad arborem' (partial), BL, MS Royal Appendix 85
—— 'Ad arborem', Balliol College, Oxford, MS 3
—— 'Ad arborem', Balliol College, Oxford, MS 215
—— 'Ad arborem', Bibliotheca Apostolica Vaticana., MS Borgh. 296
—— 'Ad arborem', Bibliothèque Mazarine, Paris, MS 3642
—— 'Ad arborem', Magdalen College, Oxford, MS 114
—— 'Ad arborem', Münster Universitätsbibliothek, MS 157
—— 'Ad arborem', New College, Oxford, MS 106
Miscellany with image of *arbor*, BL, MS Harley 493a
Penyafort, Raymón de, 'Quia tractare intendimus', BL, MS Royal 6 E VI
—— 'Quia tractare intendimus', BL, MS Royal 10 D VII
Plea roll records, CP 40/69, mm. 8, 50d, 64d, 113d; CP 40/70, m. 62d; CP 40/75, m.9d
Plea roll records, JUST 1/303 (1292 Herefs eyre), m. 26.
Statutes with short 'Quia tractare intendimus' and mnemonic on divorce, BL, MS Hargrave 433
Statutes with short 'Quia tractare intendimus' and mnemonic on divorce, Bodl. Lib., MS Douce 17
Statutes, with Penyafort's 'Quia tractare intendimus', WCL, MS 18
Year books, with image of a family pedigree, BL, MS Add. 25183
Year books, with image of a family pedigree, BL, MS Add. 35094
Year books, with image of a family pedigree, BL, MS Add. 37658
Year books, with image of a family pedigree, BL, MS Harley 3639
Year books, with image of a family pedigree, CUL, MS Ff.3.12
Year books, with image of a family pedigree, CUL, MS Gg.5.20

## Published primary sources

Accursius, 'Gloss' on Institutes, from *Institutiones imperiales [with the gloss of Accursius]*, ed. J. Chappuis, Paris 1503
Andreae, Johannes, 'Declaratio arboris consanguinitatis' and 'Declaratio arboris affinitatis', in *Corpus iuris canonici*, i. 1427–36
Augustine, *The city of God against the pagans*, London 1966
*The Bible: authorized King James version with apocrypha*, intro. and notes R. Carroll and S. Prickett, Oxford 1997
*Biblia sacra: vulgatae editionis sixti v Pontificis Maximi iussu recognita et Clementis VIII auctoritate edita*, Turin 1883
Bracton, *De legibus et consuetudinibus Angliæ*, ed. G. E. Woodbine, trans. (with revisions and notes), S. E. Thorne, Cambridge, MA–London 1968–77
*Bracton's note book: a collection of cases decided in the king's courts during the reign of Henry III, annotated by a lawyer of that time, seemingly by Henry of Bratton*, ed. F. W. Maitland, London 1887
*Brevia placitata*, ed. G. J. Turner, completed with additions by T. F. T. Plucknett (Selden Society lxvi, 1951)

*Britton: the French text carefully revised with an English translation, introduction and notes*, ed. F. M. Nichols, Oxford 1865

Burchardi Wormaciensis Ecclesiæ Episcopi, 'Decretorum libri viginti', *PL* cxlff. 538

*Casus placitorum and reports of cases in the king's courts, 1272–1278*, ed. and intro. W. Huse Dunham, Jr (Selden Society lxix, 1952)

'Clementintis P. V Constitutiones', in *Corpus iuris canonici*, ii. 1125–200

*Corpus iuris canonici: editio Lipsiensis secunda post Aemilii Ludouici Richteri*, ed. A. Friedberg, Leipzig 1879–81

*Councils and synods with other documents relating to the English Church*, ed. F. M. Powicke and C. R. Cheney, Oxford 1964

*Curia regis rolls, of the reign of Henry III*, London 1957

'Decretales Gregorii P. IX', in *Corpus iuris canonici*, ii.1–928

*Die Briefe Des Petrus Damiani*, ed. K. Reindel (Monumenta Germaniae Historica, 1983–93)

*The Digest of Justinian*, Latin text ed. T. Mommsen with P. Krueger; English trans. ed. A. Watson, Philadelphia 1985

*The earliest English law reports*, ed. P. A. Brand (Selden Society cxi, cxii, cxxii, cxxiii, 1996–2007)

*English historical documents c. 500–1042*, ed. D. Whitelock, 2nd edn, London 1979

*The eyre of Northamptonshire 3–4 Edward III (1329–30)*, ed. D. W. Sutherland (Selden Society lxxxxvii, 1983)

'Fet Asaver', in Woodbine, *Four thirteenth century law tracts*, 53–115

*Fleta*, ed. and trans. H. G. Richardson and G. O. Sayles (Selden Society lxxii, lxxxix, lxxxxix, 1955–84)

'Fouke Fitz Warin', ed. T. E. Kelley, in T. H Ohlgren (ed.), *A book of medieval outlaws: ten tales in modern English*, Stroud 2000, 106–67

Geoffrey of Trani, *Summa in tit. decretalium*, Venice 1519

Gratian, 'Decretum', in *Corpus iuris canonici*, i

Hooper, W., *The law of illegitimacy: a treatise on the law affecting persons of illegitimate birth, with the rules of evidence in proof of legitimacy and illegitimacy; and an historical account of the bastard in mediæval law*, London 1911

Horace, *Satires, epistles and ars poetica*, with an English translation, by H. Ruston Fairclough, London 1966

Hostiensis, *Summa*, Lyons 1548

*The Institutes of Justinian: text, translation and commentary*, ed. J. A. C. Thomas, Amsterdam–Oxford 1975

Kilwardby, R., *On time and imagination: de tempore, de spiritu fantastico*, ed. P. Osmund Lewry, Oxford 1987

'Lectura arborum consanguinitatis et affinitatis Magistri Ioannis Egitaniensis', ed. I. da Rosa Pereira, *Studia Gratiana* xiv, Collectanea Stephan Kuttner iv (1967), 155–82

*Leges Henrici Primi*, ed. and trans. L. J. Downer, Oxford 1972

'Liber Sextus Decretalium Bonifacii P. VIII', in *Corpus iuris canonici*, ii. 929–1124

Liebermann, F., *Die Gesetze Der Angelsachsen: Heraus gegeben im Auftrage der Savigny-Stiftung*, Halle 1903

Lombard, Peter, *Sententiae in iv libris distinctae, tomus ii, liber iii et iv*, ed. Collegii S. Bonaventurae, Grottaferrata 1981

Lower ecclesiastical jurisdiction in late-medieval England: the courts of the dean and chapter of Lincoln, 1336–1349, and the deanery of Wisbech, 1458–1484, ed. L. R. Poos, Oxford 2001

Malory, Works, ed. E. Vinaver, 2nd edn, Oxford 1971

The mirror of justices, ed. W. J. Whittaker, intro. F. W. Maitland (Selden Society vii, 1895)

'Modus componendi brevia', in Woodbine, Four thirteenth century law tracts, 143–62

Ochoa, X. and A. Díez, Summula de consanguinitate et affinitate (Universa Biblio-theeca Iuris 1-C, 1978)

Papiensis, Bernardus, Summa decretalium, ed. E. A. T. Laspeyres, Regensburg 1860

Parma, Bernard of, 'Ordinary gloss to the Liber extra', in Decretales Gregory IX, Venice 1489

Pauli, 'Sententiarum', in Lex romana visigothorum: ad LXXVI librorum manu scriptorum fidem recognovit septem eius antiquis epitomis quae praeter duas adhuc ineditae sunt, titulorum explanatione auxit, annotatione, appendicibus, prolegomenis, ed. G. Haenel, repr. Aalen 1962, 338–444

Peniafort, Raymundus de, Summa de poenitentia et matrimonio [a facsimilie of the Rome edition of 1603], Farnborough 1967

'Poem of the Battle of Maldon', in English historical documents c. 500–1042, 319–24

Quinque compilatione antiquae nec non collectio canonum Lipsiensis, ed. A. Fried-berg, Leipzig 1832

The register of John Catterick, bishop of Coventry and Lichfield, 1415–19, ed. R. N. Swanson (Canterbury and York Society lxxvii, 1990)

The roll of the Shropshire eyre of 1256, ed. A. Harding (Selden Society lxxxxvi, 1981)

Rolls of the justices in eyre: being the rolls of pleas and assizes for Lincolnshire, 1218–9, and Worcestershire, 1221, ed. D. M. Stenton (Selden Society liii, 1934)

The Saxon mirror: a sachsenspiegel of the fourteenth century, trans. M. Dobozy, Philadelphia 1999

Select cases from the ecclesiastical courts of the province of Canterbury c. 1200–1301, ed. N. Adams and C. Donahue, Jr (Selden Society lxxxxv, 1981)

'Sententiarum receptarum libri quinque qui vulgo Iulio Paulo adhuc Tribuuntur', in Fontes iuris romani antejustiniani, II auctores, ed. Johannes Baviera, Florence 1940

Seville, Isidore of , 'Etymologiarum libri XX', PL lxxxii.73–728

Tancred, Summa de matrimonio, ed. A. Wunderlich, Göttingen 1841

Teutonicus, Johannes, and Bartholomew Brixiensis, 'Ordinary Gloss', in Decretum Gratiani cum glossis Domini Johannis Theutonici prepositi albertatensis et annota-tionibus Bartholomei Brixiensis etc, Basle 1512

The treatise on the laws and customs of the realm of England commonly called Glan-vill, ed., intro., notes and trans. G. D. G. Hall; guide to further reading M. T. Clanchy, Oxford 1993

Woodbine, G. E., Four thirteenth century law bracts: a thesis presented to the faculty of the Graduate School of Yale University in candidacy for the degree of doctor of philosophy, New Haven 1910

*Year books of 1 & 2 Edward II (1307–1309)*, ed. F. W. Maitland (Selden Society xvii, 1903)

*Year books of 5 Edward II (1311)*, ed. G. J. Turner, completed with an introduction by T. F. T. Plucknett (Selden Society lxiii, 1947)

*Year books of 5 Edward II (1311–1312)*, ed. W. C. Bolland (Selden Society xxxi, 1915)

*Year books of 5 Edward II (1312)*, ed. W. C. Bolland (Selden Society xxxiii, 1916)

*Year books of 10 Edward II (1316–1317)*, ed. M. D. Legge and W. Holdsworth (Selden Society liv, 1935)

*Year books of 11 Edward II (1317–1318)*, ed. J. P. Collas and W. Holdsworth (Selden Society lxi, 1942)

*Year books of 14 Edward II (michaelmas 1320)*, ed. S. J. Stoljar and L. J. Downer (Selden Society civ, 1988)

*Year books of the eyre of Kent, 6 and 7 Edward II* (1313–14), ed. W. C. Bolland, F. W. Maitland and L. W. V. Harcourt (Selden Society xxvii, 1912)

*Year books of the reign of King Edward the first: michaelmas term, year XXXIII and years XXXIV and XXXV*, ed. and trans. A. J. Horwood, London 1879

*Year books of the reign of King Edward the first: years XX and XXI*, ed. and trans. A. J. Horwood, London 1866

*Year books of the reign of King Edward the first: years XXX and XXXI*, ed. and trans. A. J. Horwood, London 1863

*Year books of the reign of King Edward the first: years XXXII–XXXIII*, ed. and trans. A. J. Horwood, London 1864

*Year books of the reign of King Edward the third: years XII and XIII*, ed. and trans. L. O. Pike, London 1885

*Year books of the reign of King Edward the third: years XIII and XIV*, ed. and trans. L. O. Pike, London 1886

*Year books of the reign of King Edward the third: year XIV*, ed. and trans. L. O. Pike, London 1888

*Year books of the reign of King Edward the Third: year XV*, ed. and trans. L. O. Pike, London 1891

*Year books of the reign of King Edward the third: year XVI (second part)*, ed. and trans. L. O. Pike, London 1900

*Year books of the reign of King Edward the third: years XVIII and XIX*, ed. and trans. L. O. Pike, London 1905

*Year books of the reign of King Edward the third: year XIX*, ed. and trans. L. O. Pike, London 1906

## Secondary sources

Baker, J. H., *A catalogue of English legal manuscripts in Cambridge University Library; with codicological descriptions of the early manuscripts by J. S. Ringrose*, Woodbridge 1996

—— 'Case-law in medieval England', repr. in his *The common law tradition: lawyers, books and the law*, London 2000, 133–64

—— *An introduction to English legal history*, 4th edn, London 2002

—— 'Roman law at the third university of England', *Current Legal Problems* lv (2002), 123–50

—— The Oxford history of the laws of England, VI: 1483–1558, Oxford 2003

Barton, J. L., 'The study of civil law before 1380', in Catto, University of Oxford, i. 519–30

—— 'The mystery of Bracton', Journal of Legal History xiv (1993), 1–142

Beckerman, J. S., 'Law-writing and law teaching: treatise evidence of the formal teaching of English law in the late thirteenth century', in Bush and Wijffels, Learning the law, 33–50

Bennett, A., 'Anthony Bek's copy of statuta angliae', in W. M. Ormrod (ed.), England in the fourteenth century: proceedings of the 1985 Harlaxton symposium, Woodbridge 1986, 1–27

Biancalana, J., 'For want of justice: legal reforms of Henry II', Columbia Law Review lxxxviii/1 (1988), 433–536

—— The fee tail and the common recovery in medieval England, 1176–1502, Cambridge 2001

Bourdieu, P., Outline of a theory of practice, trans. R. Nice, Cambridge 1977

—— The logic of practice, trans. R. Nice, Cambridge 1992

Boyle, L. E., 'Canon law before 1380', in Catto, University of Oxford, i. 531–64

Brand, P., 'Courtroom and schoolroom: the education of lawyers in England prior to 1400', in his The making of the common law, London 1992, 57–75

—— Origins of the English legal profession, Oxford 1992

—— '"Time out of mind": the knowledge and use of the eleventh- and twelfth-century past in thirteenth-century litigation', Anglo-Norman Studies xvi (1993), 37–54

—— 'Westminster hall and Europe: European aspects of the common law', in J. Boffey and P. King (eds), London and Europe in the later Middle Ages, London 1995, 55–85

—— 'The age of Bracton', in J. Hudson (ed.), The history of English law: centenary essays on 'Pollock and Maitland', Oxford 1996, 65–89

—— 'Family and inheritance, women and children', in C. Given-Wilson (ed.), An illustrated history of late medieval England, Manchester 1996, 58–81

—— 'Legal education in England before the Inns of Court', in Bush and Wijffels, Learning the law, 51–84

—— Kings, barons and justices: the making and enforcement of legislation in thirteenth-century England, Cambridge 2003

Brundage, J. A., 'Book review of 'Summa de paenitentia; Summa de matrimonio by Raymond of Peñafort: edited by Xavier Ochoa and Aloisius Diez', The Jurist xlix (1979), 514–17

—— Law, sex, and Christian society in medieval Europe, Chicago–London 1987

—— Medieval canon law, London 1995

Bush, J. A. and A. Wijffels (eds), Learning the law: teaching and the transmission of law in England, 1150–1900, London 1999

Cappelli, A., Dizionario di abbreviature Latine ed Italiane, 6th edn, Milan 1990

Carpenter, D. A., 'The English royal chancery in the thirteenth century', in K. Fianu and D. J. Guth (eds), Écrit et pouvoir dans le chancelleries médiévales: espace français, espace anglais, Louvain 1997, 25–53

Catto, J. I., History of the University of Oxford, Oxford 1984

—— 'Theology and theologians, 1220–1320', in his University of Oxford, i. 417–517

Charles-Edwards, T., 'Anglo-Saxon kinship revisited', in J. Hines (ed.), The

*Anglo-Saxons from the migration period to the eighth century: an ethnographic perspective*, Woodbridge 1997, 171–204

Clanchy, M., *From memory to written record: England, 1066–1307*, Oxford 1993

d'Avray, D. L., 'Peter Damian, consanguinity and church property', in L. Smith and B. Ward (eds), *Intellectual life in the Middle Ages: essays presented to Margaret Gibson*, London 1992, 71–80

—— 'Lay kinship solidarity and papal law', in P. Stafford, J. Nelson and J. Martindale (eds), *Law, laity and solidarities: essays in honour of Susan Reynolds*, Manchester 2001, 188–99

—— *Medieval marriage: symbolism and society*, Oxford 2005

De Zuleta, F. and P. Stein, *The teaching of Roman law in England around 1200* (Selden Society s.s. viii, 1990)

Donahue, Jr., C., 'The monastic judge: social practice, formal rule and the medieval law of incest', in P. Landau and M. Petzolt (eds), *De iure canonico medii aevi: Festschrift für Rudolf Weigand*, Rome 1996, 49–69

—— *Law, marriage, and society in the later Middle Ages: arguments about marriage in five courts*, Cambridge 2007 (*Texts and commentary* at http://www.cambridge.org/uk/catalogue/catalogue.asp?isbn=9780521877282)

Douglas, M., *Purity and danger*, New York 2002

Duby, G., *The chivalrous society*, trans. C. Postan, London 1977

Dumont, L., *Introduction to two theories of social anthropology: descent groups and marriage alliance*, ed. and trans. R. Parkin, Oxford 2006

Emden, A. B., *A biographical register of the University of Oxford to A.D. 1500*, Oxford 1959

Evans-Pritchard, E. E., *Kinship and marriage among the Nuer*, Oxford 1951

Faith, R. J., 'Peasant families and inheritance customs in medieval England', *Agricultural History Review* xiv (1966), 77–95

Farge, J. K. (ed.), *Marriage, family, and law in medieval Europe: collected studies*, Toronto 1996

Fletcher, R., *Bloodfeud: murder and revenge in Anglo-Saxon England*, London 2002

Galbraith, V. H., 'Statutes of Edward I: Huntington Library ms. H.M. 25782', in T. A. Sandquist and M. R. Powicke (eds), *Essays in medieval history presented to Bertie Wilkinson*, Toronto 1969, 176–91

García y García, A., 'La canonística Ibérica (1150–1250) en la investigación reciente', *Bulletin of Medieval Canon Law* n.s. xi (1981), 41–75

—— 'Glosas de Juan Teutónico, Vincente Hispano y Dámaso Húngaro a los arbores consanguinitatis et affinitatis', *Zeitschrift der Savigny-Stiftung für Rechtsgeschichte* xcix (Kanonistische Abteilung LXVIII, 1982), 153–85

Garnett, G. and J. Hudson (eds), *Law and government in medieval England and Normandy: essays in honour of Sir James Holt*, Cambridge 1994

Goody, J., *The development of the family and marriage in Europe*, Cambridge 1983

Gould, S. J., 'Evolution by walking', in his *Dinosaur in a haystack: reflections in natural history*, London 1996, 248–59

—— and R. Wolff Purcell, *Crossing over: where art and science meet*, New York 2000

Guerreau-Jalabert, A., 'La Désignation des relations et des groupes de parenté en Latin médiéval', *Archivium Latinitatis Medii Aevi* xlvi–xlvii (1988), 65–108

Hanawalt, B. A., *The ties that bound: peasant families in medieval England*, Oxford 1986

Heers, J., *Le Clan familial au moyen âge: étude sur les structures politiques and sociales des milieus urbanes*, Paris 1974

Helmholz, R. H., 'Bastardy litigation in medieval England', *American Journal of Legal History* xiii (1969), 360–83

—— *Marriage litigation in medieval England*, Cambridge 1974

—— *Canon law and English common law*, London 1983

——'Continental law and common law: historical strangers or companions?', *Duke Law Journal* xl/6 (1990), 1207–28

—— *The ius commune in England: four studies*, Oxford 2001

—— *The Oxford history of the laws of England*, I: *The canon law and ecclesiastical jurisdiction from 597 to the 1640s*, Oxford 2004

Holt, J. C., 'The *casus regis*: the law and politics of succession in the Plantagenet dominions, 1185–1247', in his *Colonial England*, 307–26

—— *Colonial England, 1066–1215*, London 1997

—— 'Feudal society and the family in early medieval England, I: the revolution of 1066', in his *Colonial England*, 161–78

—— 'Feudal society and the family in early medieval England, II: notions of patrimony', in his *Colonial England*, 197–221

—— 'Feudal society and the family in early medieval England, IV: the heiress and the alien', in his *Colonial England*, 245–69

—— 'Politics and property in early medieval England', in his *Colonial England*, 113–59

Holy, L., *Anthropological perspectives on kinship*, London 1996

Howell, C., *Land, family and inheritance in transition: Kibworth Harcourt, 1280–1700*, Cambridge 1983

Hudson, J., *Land, law, and lordship in Anglo-Norman England*, Oxford 1994

Hyams, P., *King, lords and peasants in medieval England: the common law of villeinage in the twelfth and thirteenth centuries*, Oxford 1980

—— *Rancor and reconciliation in medieval England*, Ithaca–London 2003

John, E., *Reassessing Anglo-Saxon England*, Manchester 1996

Joyce, G. H., *Christian marriage: an historical and doctrinal study*, 2nd edn, London 1948

Jurasinski, S., '*Reddatur parentibus*: the vengeance of the family in Cnut's homicide legislation', *Law and History Review* xx/1 (2002), 157–80

Kaeppeli, T., *Scriptores ordinis praedicatorum medii aevi*, Rome 1970–93

Ker, N. R. and A. J. Piper, *Medieval manuscripts in British libraries*, Oxford 1992

Kuttner, S., 'The Barcelona edition of St Raymond's first treatise on canon law', *Seminar* viii (1950), 52–67

—— 'On the method of editing medieval authors', *The Jurist* xxxvii (1977), 385–6

—— and E. Rathbone, 'Anglo-Norman canonists of the twelfth century: an introductory study', *Traditio* vii (1949–51), 279–358

Lancaster, L., 'Kinship in Anglo-Saxon society', *British Journal of Sociology* ix (1958), 230–50, 359–77

L'Engle, S. and R. Gibbs, *Illuminating the law: legal manuscripts in Cambridge collections*, London 2001

Loyn, H. R., 'Kinship in Anglo-Saxon England', *Anglo-Saxon England* iii (1974), 197–209

MacFarlane, A., *The origins of English individualism: the family, property and social transition*, Oxford 1978

——— *Marriage and love in England: modes of reproduction, 1300–1840*, Oxford 1986

Maitland, F. W., *Domesday book and beyond: three essays in the early history of England*, London 1969

Martínez-Torrón, J., *Anglo-American law and canon law: canonical roots of the common law tradition*, Berlin 1998

Melville, G. and M. Staub (eds), *Enzyklopädie des Mittelalters*, Darmstadt 2008

Michael, M. A., 'A manuscript wedding gift from Philippa of Hainault to Edward III', *Burlington Magazine* (Sept. 1985), 582–99

Milsom, S. F. C., 'Legal introduction', in *Novae narrationes*, ed. E. Shanks, completed with a legal introduction by S. F. C. Milsom (Selden Society lxxx, 1963)

——— *Historical foundations of the common law*, 2nd edn, London 1981

Moore, J. S., 'The Anglo-Norman family: size and structure', *Anglo-Norman Studies* xiv (1991), 153–96

Murray, A. C., *Germanic kinship structure: studies in law and society in antiquity and the early Middle Ages*, Toronto 1983

Oschinsky, D., *Walter of Henley and other treatises on estate management and accounting*, Oxford 1971

Owen, D. M., *The medieval canon law: teaching, literature and transmission*, Cambridge 1990

Pedersen, F., *Marriage disputes in medieval England*, London 2000

Pennington, K., 'Henricus de Segusio (Hostiensis)', repr. in his *Popes, canonists and texts, 1150–1550*, Aldershot 1993, XVI, 1–12

Plucknett, T. F. T., 'The Harvard manuscript of Thornton's *Summa*', *Harvard Law Review* li (1937–8), 1038–56

Pollock, F. and F. W. Maitland, *The history of English law before the time of Edward I*, 2nd edn, with new introduction and select bibliography by S. F. C. Milsom, Cambridge 1968

Razi, Z., 'Intrafamilial ties and relationships in the medieval village: a quantitative approach employing manor court rolls', in Z. Ravi and R. Smith (eds), *Medieval society and the manor court*, Oxford 1996, 369–91

Reynolds, S., 'Bookland, folkland and fiefs', *Anglo-Norman Studies* xiv (1991), 211–27

Richardson, H. G., *Bracton: the problem of his text* (Selden Society s.s. ii, 1965)

——— and G. O. Sayles, 'The early statutes', *LQR* l (1934), 201–23, 540–71

Rider, C., *Magic and impotence in the Middle Ages*, Oxford 2006

Schadt, H., *Die Darstellungen der arbores consanguinitatis und der arbores affinitatis: Bildschemata in juristischen Handschriften*, Tübingen 1982

Seipp, D. J., 'Roman legal categories in the early common law', in T. G. Watkin (ed.), *Legal record and historical reality: proceedings of the eighth British legal history conference Cardiff 1987*, London 1989, 9–36

——— 'The mirror of justices', in Bush and Wijffels, *Learning the law*, 85–112

Sheehan, M. M., 'The formation and stability of marriage in fourteenth-century England: evidence of an Ely register', in Farge, *Marriage, family, and law*, 38–76

—— 'Marriage theory and practice in the conciliar legislation and diocesan statutes of medieval England', in Farge, *Marriage, family, and law*, 118–76

Simpson, A. W. B., *A history of the land law*, 2nd edn, Oxford 1986

Skemer, D. C., 'From archives to the book trade: private statute rolls in England, 1285–1307', *Journal of the Society of Archivists* xvi/2 (1995), 193–206

—— 'Sir William Breton's book: production of *statuta Angliae* in the late thirteenth century', in P. Beal and J. Griffiths (eds), *English manuscript studies, 1100–1700*, London 1997, vi. 24–51

—— 'Reading the law: statute books and the private transmission of legal knowledge in late medieval England', in Bush and Wijffels, *Learning the law*, 113–31

Smith, R. M., 'Kin and neighbours in a thirteenth-century Suffolk community', *Journal of Family History* iv (1979), 219–56

Sommer-Seckendorff, E. M. F., *Studies in the life of Robert Kilwardby O.P.*, Rome 1937

Sparrow Simpson, W. J., *Dispensations*, London 1935

Thomson, R. M., *A descriptive catalogue of the medieval manuscripts in Worcester Cathedral Library*, Cambridge 2001

Turner, R. V., 'Who was the author of *Glanvill*? Reflections on the education of Henry II's common lawyers', *Law and History Review* viii/1 (1990), 97–127

Van Caenegem, R. C., *The birth of the English common law*, 2nd edn, Cambridge 1988

van Houts, E., *Memory and gender in medieval Europe, 900–1200*, Basingstoke 1999

von Schulte, J. F., *Die Geschichte der Quellen und Literatur des canonischen Rechts*, Stuttgart 1877

White, S. D., 'The discourse of inheritance in twelfth-century France: alternative models of the fief in *Raoul de Cambrai*', in Garnett and Hudson, *Law and government*, 173–97

—— 'Kinship and lordship in early medieval England: the story of Sigeberht, Cynewulf, and Cyneheard', *Viator* xx (1989), 1–18

Whitwell, R. J., 'The libraries of a civilian and canonist and of a common lawyer, an. 1294', *LQR* xxi (1905), 393–400

Winroth, A., *The making of Gratian's Decretum*, Cambridge 2000

Worby, S., 'Consanguinity and the common law: 'idle ingenuities' in *Bracton*?', in A. Lewis, P. Brand and P. Mitchell (eds), *Law in the city: proceedings of the seventeenth British legal history conference, London 2005*, Dublin 2007, 24–41

—— 'Kinship: the canon law and common law in thirteenth-century England', *Historical Research* lxxx (2007), 443–68

Wormald, P., 'Quadripartitus', in Garnett and Hudson, *Law and government*, 111–47

—— *The making of English law: King Alfred to the twelfth century*, I: *Legislation and its limits*, Oxford 1999

## Unpublished thesis

Worby, S., 'Kinship in thirteenth-century England: the canon law in the common law', PhD, London 2005

# Index

*Page numbers in bold type refer to illustrations.*

CPSIA information can be obtained at www.ICGtesting.com
Printed in the USA
BVOW05s0147040815

411641BV00004B/26/P

9 780861 933389